SAME SPIRiT DIFFERENT TEAM

THE POLITICISATION OF THE DEAFLYMPICS

To Grace

Best Wishes

STUART R. HARRISON

actionDEAFNESSBooks

First published in 2014 by
Action Deafness Books

A CIP Catalogue of this book is available from the British Library

ISBN: 978-0-957-08228-1

Cover designed by
Euan Carter
(www.euancarter.com)

Typeset by
www.chandlerbookdesign.co.uk

Printed in Great Britain by
Berforts Information Press,
Stevenage, Hertfordshire.

CONTENTS

SECTION 4

Why Have I Not Heard of the Deaflympics?

SECTION 5

Why are the Deaflympics not recognised and supported?

SECTION 6

A Conclusion

APPENDIX

Foreword

This book is a real addition to the literature around international sport, and fills a glaring gap in public knowledge about the challenges, which advocates and organisational leaders of sport for people with impairments or disabilities have faced, and continue to face. All activists for equity in sport, physical education and physical activity experience, daily, the frustrations and barriers, which are presented by the inherent conservatism and protectionism of so-called "mainstream" sport organisations, which, for the most part, continue to resist change, and which reproduce in their own images.

Stuart Harrison, in a characteristically honest fashion, lays bare the struggles and internal strife of a sport movement – the Deaflympics - which (along with women, people with other disabilities and impairments, social, ethnic, sexual and cultural minorities, the young and the old) has experienced all those frustrations and barriers. But Harrison offers more – he provides a cogent account of the specific, complex features of deafness, and of its contested characteristics, which illuminates the processes and politics of its relationships with the other national and international organisations responsible for sport. Inclusion, he argues, is not about being the same – it is about equality of experience and opportunity.

I have many times pointed out that sport institutions seem to exclude more people than they include and that this implies the need for those sport institutions themselves to change, rather than expecting the excluded to change their behaviour to fit into sport's established institutional norms and practices. Harrison illustrates this view on behalf of deaf people (p140): *"Society, sport and disabled sport have been built on the cultures of hearing and speaking. This culture will never be accessible to deaf people unless changes in attitude and practice occur. Deaf people want to see hearing people (both disabled and able-bodied) change their perspective about deafness so that deaf people can become full and participant members of civil society. Hearing people should not be trying to synchronise the lives of deaf people with that of their own and should instead look to respect the communication needs of deaf people, within the institutions of society."*

There is a fascinating account of the impacts, for deaf children, of the policies of integration of children with impairments and disabilities into mainstream schools. Harrison also recognises the central importance of positive experiences of school physical education and sport, and the role of talented and well-trained teachers to deliver it effectively. He points out the correlation between the amount of time a student is physically integrated into the mainstream teaching programme and the chances that they will become involved in school sport. The need for improved teacher education and parental support to ensure this progression is clear, as is the need for applied research and sport science.

He chronicles the historical development of the deaf sport movement, and its struggles to represent, advocate and provide for its complex constituency. In doing so, he argues with absolute commitment for the continued need for leadership from within that constituency, describing and providing examples of the distinctive needs of deaf players and performers, and of the specific forms of discrimination experienced by the organisations, which led to the Deaflympics.

Harrison's accounts of the movement's challenges of marginalisation and denial, and struggles to secure sustainable funding and support, show many decision-makers, politicians and bureaucrats believing that, like children, deaf sports players and performers and their organisations should be "seen and not heard". On the other hand, there are positive examples of the ways in which "good practice" for deaf athletes can be seen simply as "good practice" for all, hence contributing to improvements in logistics, organisation and procedures for other large-scale events and programmes.

Harrison's call for Deaflympics to focus less on history and more on the future, along with his reflective analysis of the weaknesses of the movement and its need to seize emerging opportunities, concludes optimistically (p196) that *"if the Deaflympic Movement is willing to change and manage that change in a way that does not become disempowering to deaf and other disabled people, then the Deaflympics will have a better chance of raising its profile and status, with the support and recognition that it deserves, for as long as there are deaf people in this world who want to play sport".*

There is a serious shortage in sports policy literature, of analysis of the real struggles for consensus, power and clarity of purpose within and between organisations and individuals. This book is an important addition to that literature. It reveals the internal dynamics and contested power struggles within the Deaflympics movement, and their influence on Deaflympics' ambivalent and problematic relationships with the International Paralympic Committee and International Olympic Committee. One of the features, which makes this book special, is the tracking of decisions and reflections, on the impact of different leaders and activists and their networks, on the development of the movement. It is my personal view that scholars and leaders of sport, from across the sport spectrum, will recognise this important addition to sport policy analysis.

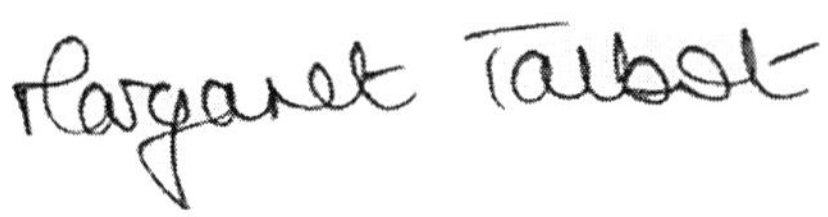

Prof Dr Margaret Talbot, PhD OBE FRSA
President, International Council of Sport Science and Physical Education
Chair, Education Committee of the International Paralympic Committee

About the Author

Stuart Harrison has over 30 years' experience in deaf sport as an athlete, administrator and leader. The work has been varied and has covered both professional and voluntary roles.

After leaving school, he worked at Friends for Young Deaf People, organising and delivering sports and outdoor activity programmes, and assisted in the development of a complementary leadership and project management programme.

Following a short spell in retail management, Stuart qualified as a PE teacher at Reading University and was Sports Representative on the Students Union. After a year teaching in a local primary school, he moved to London and built a ten-year career working at Blanche Neville School for the Deaf, culminating in senior management as a deputy head teacher.

From the mid-1990s he began to examine the state of deaf sport in the UK and the implications for the students he was teaching. Along with a group of other deaf professionals, he was instrumental in establishing the Deaf Sports Strategy Group that gave rise to the founding of UK Deaf Sport in 2003.

Stuart was employed to establish UK Deaf Sport and deliver its operational objectives, brokering relationships between national governing bodies of sport and national Deaf sports organisations and helping to prepare and support the GB team at the 2005 Deaflympics in Melbourne, Australia. He resigned from his post in 2006 when it became apparent that the UK government was not going to continue providing core funding to Deaf sport. The resignation was tactical in order to enable UK Deaf Sport to continue operating on the limited budget it had available. He was invited onto the Board of UK Deaf Sport in 2010 and currently holds the position of Vice Chair.

Stuart has written for sports coach UK's magazine "Coaching Edge" and sub- edited "Achieve" magazine for UK Deaf Sport, most recently writing a blog to cover Deaf sports related issues during the 2012 Paralympic games.

He is an experienced public speaker and is often asked to comment on TV and radio on the subject of Deaf sport.

List of Abbreviations

ISG	International Silent Games (1924 – 1967)
WGD	World Games for the Deaf (1967 – 1999)
DWG	Deaf World Games (1999 – 2001)
CISS	Comité International des Sports des Sourds (1979 – 2003)
ICSD	International Committee of Sports for the Deaf (2003 - present)
AAAD	American Athletic Association of the Deaf
BDSC	British Deaf Sports Council
BPA	British Paralympic Association
BSAD	British Sports Association for the Disabled
CP-ISRA	Cerebral Palsy International Sports and Recreation Association
CTSAD	Chinese Taipei Sports Association for the Deaf
EDSO	European Deaf Sport Organisation
EFDS	English Federation of Disability Sport
FIS	Federations of International Sports
FYD	Friends for Young Deaf People
IAAF	International Amateur Athletics Association
IBSA	International Blind Sport Association
ICC	International Coordinating Committee
IDSF	International Deaf Sports Federations
INAS-FID	International Association of Sport for Persons with Intellectual Disability

INAS-FMH	International Sports Federation for Persons with Mental Handicap
IOC	International Olympic Committee
IOSD	International Organisation of Sport for the Disabled
IPC	International Paralympic Committee
ISOD	International Sports Organisation for the Disabled
ISMGF	International Stoke Mandeville Games Federation
ISMWGF	International Stoke Mandeville Wheelchair Games Federation
ITF	International Tennis Federation
NDSF	National Deaf Sports Federation
NOC	National Olympic Committee
NPC	National Paralympic Committee
RCDS	Russian Committee of Deaf Sports
RDSU	Russian Deaf Sports Union
SDC	Slovakian Deaflympics Committee
SDSF	Swiss Deaf Sports Federation
SOI	Special Olympics International
UEFA	Union of European Football Associations
UKDS	UK Deaf Sport
UNOSDP	UN Office on Sport for Development and Peace.

Non-sports Organisations

AoHL	Action on Hearing Loss (UK)
DOC	Department of Culture (Taiwan)
NAD	National Association of the Deaf (USA)
NDCS	National Deaf Children's Society (UK)
WFD	World Federation of the Deaf

Other

CPD	Continuing Professional Development
LTAD	Long Term Athlete Development
MoU	Memorandum of Understanding
SLI	Sign Language Interpreter
TGMD	Test of Gross Motor Development

List of Tables

Introduction

6th July 2005, the day London won the bid to host the 2012 Olympics and Paralympics, I was visiting Oak Lodge School for the Deaf in London as part of my work at UK Deaf Sport. Joanne Davison our Deaflympic Javelin gold medal-list accompanied me. The whole school was assembled for our presentation and in it we announced that London had won the bid - the whole school erupted with joy – along with all the other citizens of our proud nation.

This was the start of a seven-year journey to the Opening of the 2012 Paralympics and what should have been the greatest opportunity for Deaflympic sport in the UK to benefit from its legacy. Instead, we were taken on a nightmare ride that resulted in our Deaflympic sportsmen and women becoming the forgotten casualties of an event that is very close to our hearts – we felt as though we were collateral damage.

By the time we all sat down to watch the Opening Ceremony of the 2012 Paralympics on TV (nobody from UK Deaf Sport had been invited to join in the celebrations with our counter-parts from other UK-based disability sports organisations) a groundswell of public resentment, disappointment and confusion began to emerge, as we experienced the bittersweet taste of admiring our deaf relatives, friends and colleagues performing at the ceremony (Swinbourne 2012b), knowing that we were not going to see the world's greatest Deaf athletes compete.

Almost immediately, mobile phones, emails and social media posts were raising the same repetitive questions that I have been asked countless times during my 30-odd year career in different roles as teacher, volunteer, coach, coach tutor and administrator. Over the years, whenever I have responded, I would give a different answer depending on whom I was talking to and the prevailing circumstances involved, whether it was a parent on the telephone wondering why their deaf child could not be given the same funding support as another disabled swimmer in her swimming club or whether it was Lord Coe when we met on brief occasions in the lobby of the Department of Culture Media and Sport. In all cases the answers were brief. They could never tell the whole story and provide the answers that everyone associated with sport was looking for.

As I was watching the Opening Ceremony a notion came to me that if deafness was inherently visible, people might be more understanding of the needs of deaf sport and act accordingly. What would we have to do? Amputate our ears or something else? So, I decided to start the Internet blog *TwoBigEars* and, for the duration of the 2012 Paralympics, I wore a pair of 'big ears' when out in public to raise awareness about the Deaflympics. It was during that time, that readers of the blog asked me to write this book.

With the exception of Stewart's *DEAF SPORT: The Impact of Sports Within the Deaf Community* (1991) all books on Deaf sport are either chronological records of events with facts and statistics, or autobiographical in nature. There are no challenges to the political and social argument to ensure that Deaf sport is taken seriously and supported. The plethora of literature on disability sport that has emerged from the Paralympic Movement makes scant reference to Deaf sport, in a way that suggests it is a subject of minor relevance, because it is not seen as contributing to the greater scheme.

The book is written to inform the following groups of readers:

- Sports professionals, both staff and volunteers, who need to understand and make decisions about the inclusion of deaf people in sport at local, national and international levels.
- Academics and students, who cover a variety of subjects related to sport, disability sport, sociology and the study of deafness and disability (culture, community and language).
- The Deaf world and its associated organisations and people, parents, teachers, coaches of aspiring athletes, athletes, supporters and spectators.
- Politicians and policy makers.

I have tried to appeal to an international audience by writing in a non–partisan manner so that the concepts and philosophies of the Deaflympics can be appreciated on a global scale.

Perspectives of this book.

The approach to this book is an expression of my different backgrounds as a professional in education and sport and my management experience in the voluntary sector associated with young people and sport. Before beginning a ten-year career as a teacher of the Deaf I had participated in sport at school and county level; once representing Great Britain at the European Deaf Cross-Country Championships.

I also worked in sport and physical activity development and leadership with the Friends for Young Deaf People. Although qualified as a PE teacher, I taught widely across the primary and secondary curriculum. Through my work developing extra-curricular sport, I became involved in the Board of the British Sports Association of the Disabled in London and I have served on different sports committees for the deaf since then.

In the late 1990s, working with other professionals and volunteers in Deaf and mainstream sport, we began to realise that Deaf sport in the UK and worldwide needed to reform and become a contemporary entity or risk terminal decline. In time, I became involved in the Deaf Sports Strategy Group and then worked full time as Development Manager for UK Deaf Sport when it was first established.

My views in this book should not be taken as a definitive representation of UK Deaf Sport's (UKDS) position on the Deaflympics. UKDS is a pluralistic organisation and we hold a multitude of different views in terms of how we govern and manage elite sport, so these views are primarily my own as are my interpretations of all others referred to throughout the book.

This book is an examination of the consequences of decision-making in the 90-year development of the Deaflympics to date and attempts to rationalise its current position. Decision-makers within organisations move on after serving their terms and take the experiences, rationale and the memories of the decision- making with them. The successors are unaware of the history, and make decisions which can be counterproductive to the work of forbears. This book is intended to bring everyone to the starting line with the information they need.

Terminology

If you are familiar with disability sport you may be tempted to skip this section, but I recommended that you read it in full because of specific terms related to deafness and Deaf sport. Even if you consider yourself an expert, if you do not understand my terms, the book will be read out of context.

In discussing the different aspects of the Deaf community, most commentators make a distinction in the meaning of 'Deaf' and 'deaf'. When referring to individuals who identify themselves as having a shared cultural experience of deafness and their use of sign language, they refer to them as culturally 'Deaf' (in other words, the Deaf Community). They also capitalise 'Deaf' when making references to organisations and activities directly related to the Deaf community; Deaf sport, Deaf culture, Deaf mainstream and Deaf world. When referring to individuals or groups that include people who have a significant hearing loss (or hard of hearing) then they refer to them as 'deaf'.

But we also need to make a distinction in relation to sport. People who are deaf and do not use sign language do participate in Deaf sport and thus I also refer to these individuals as 'Deaf'. The deaf, who remain in Deaf sport for any length of time, become part of the Deaf mainstream. They take the opportunity to develop their understanding of Deaf culture and sign language and benefit from the Deaf world at a level that suits them. There are Deaf and deaf people in elite sport, who may never compete in the Deaflympics or Deaf international sport. Their careers are within the sports mainstream, but they are affected by deafness and its impact on their performance in sport.

Structure of this Book.

The book is structured to answer the most prevalent questions that are asked of Deaf sport and the Deaflympics. The five questions are answered in their own sections, containing chapters to provide a multitude of answers and perspectives. Whether or not the definitive answer is given depends on your experience as the reader. It is my intention to motivate you to take action that benefits everyone in sport and enriches your lives through your future contribution to the Deaflympics.

First of all, a word about the title of this book: *Same Spirit - Different Team: The Politicisation of the Deaflympics.* The International Silent Games were created in the 1920s in the spirit of Olympism as a way of providing self-expression, self-confidence and independence. The book demonstrates how, in a very short space of time, political and social leadership, disability politics, sports politics and the media have marginalised the Deaflympics. As time progressed, the Deaflympic Movement has not been part of the Olympic and Paralympic Movement in the way that the Deaf community would expect and, as a result, it has been forced to become entrenched in social and sporting politics as it tries to maintain its status as the original and purest opportunity in elite Disability sport.

To help you understand what the Deaflympics are, I start by covering the true history of organised sport for disabled people and chart a potted history of the Deaflympics and the major landmarks of an 89-year journey from 1924 to 2013. This follows an examination of the internal politics of the Deaflympics and its general relationship with the IOC and IPC. This section ends with a contemporary look at the Deaflympics.

The second section observes the relationship between the Deaflympics and the Paralympics to understand why there are no opportunities for Deaf athletes to compete under their Deaflympic classification. The concepts of inclusion and integration are applied to this relationship, and the logistics that come with organising major multi-sport events for disability sport and whether or not it is possible to include a new disability into the Paralympics.

"How does deafness affect sports performance?" The third section answers the question in three parts. Firstly, by examining the physical, social, emotional and technical influences on high-performance sport for deaf athletes. Secondly, we look at the influences of society on decisions made by athletes and those who influence them. Finally, we examine the model of Long Term

Athlete Development and how it applies to deafness in sport.

The fourth section explains why there has been very little public knowledge of the Deaflympics and Deaf sport. It demonstrates the social and political forces at play by comparing the leadership profiles of key founders of the Olympics, Deaflympics and Paralympics. It examines how key decisions made in 1880, 1975 and 1995 are still influencing the development of the Deaflympics. The monopoly of the IPC on disability sport is discussed, to explain why the Deaflympics are still comparatively unknown.

Section five explores some of the politics of disability sport, the dominance of Paralympism, international politics and classification of athletes, to try and explain why the Deaflympics are not supported and recognised. I challenge the argument that the Deaflympics are not an elite sports event and how the ICSD is fighting for resources to finance them.

I conclude with a summative answer to each of the five questions and a look at the way forward for the Deaflympics into the 21st Century; and how you, the reader, can contribute to the five actions needed to ensure that deaf people can participate, sustain and excel at any sport of their choosing within the Spirit of the Olympic, Deaflympic and Paralympic Movements.

SECTION 1

What are the Deaflympics?

"You have now cleared the path, in all countries, for committees of your type to allow young men and women, disfavoured by fate, to get to know the joys of sport and also to learn, through sport, to tackle life better."

(IOC Citation to CISS, 1966)

1

Deaflympics 1924 – 1990

The Origins of Sport for Disabled People.

If you are reading this book, you are highly likely to have at least a passing interest in sport and it is possible that you can recall the Opening Ceremony of the 2012 Olympics in London. The theme celebrated the Industrial Revolution and the birth of modern-day Britain. If you looked carefully amid the glitz and spectacle, you would have spotted a game of cricket symbolising the emergence of sport as an organised pastime for the common man. Prior to this, and during the boom years of the Industrialised Age, people had very little leisure time and very little access to organised sport.

It was the new Factory Act of 1844 and the Ten-Hour Act of 1847 that made it possible for people to have time for education, self-improvement, pastimes and sport. Improvement in transportation and communications facilitated the growth of competitive sport, whilst mass-spectator venues were built at, or conveniently close to, major transport hubs.

As access to mass sport increased, people began to notice

that the laws and treaties on governing differing sports varied from region to region and so, as a result, and in response to spectator representation, sports began to address the assembly of formal Laws & Rules. In football, Nottingham County Football Club formally established itself in 1862 and, as such, is now the oldest football club in the world. Other clubs quickly followed, many originating in cotton towns where members of church congregations and Sunday schools took to the field after divine worship. The rules of Cricket became formalised shortly thereafter and, by 1868, the appeal of the game led to an Australian side touring England and dominating the field.

The Football Association was inaugurated in 1863. Rugby Union followed in 1871, from which evolved American Football. The All-England Lawn Tennis Championships were staged in 1877. Organised sport spread globally as people both participated in and watched their chosen pursuits; communicating in a common language and engaging with like-minded people. With the growth of global civil society and increased individual financial wealth, sport fans were able to take their interest to even higher levels, travelling nationally and internationally in support of their sporting heroes.

Researching for evidence of the origins of organised sport for disabled people is hampered by the lack of written records by disabled people themselves (Atherton et al 1999). It has only been through the development of a historical study of deafness in the 1990s that a clearer picture of Deaf sport emerges. However, the deluge of publications and research associated with Paralympic sport has buried this history. The effort and endeavour associated with its compilation has gone sadly unrecognised.

Media coverage of the 2012 London Olympics and Paralympics inaccurately celebrated the work of Dr Guttmann and the Stoke Mandeville Games of 1948 as the birthplace of disability sport. We can set the record straight by rewinding to the 19th century. The oldest Deaf football club in the world is Glasgow Deaf FC founded in 1871 at the Glasgow Deaf and Dumb Institute. Records indicate that the club is likely to have been established as an Old Boys Club for the Institute rather than for pupils at the local school for the Deaf as some commentators have suggested. According to Atherton et al in *Playing to the Flag* (1999), their earliest recorded match was against Oxford University in 1874. Innovative and progressive for its time, Glasgow Deaf FC helped to form other clubs in Scotland and England, by providing advice on the intricacies of establishing a club and offering to play matches once they were ready.

Deaf sport has always mirrored mainstream sport and in the early stages, was heavily influenced by the principles of '*Muscular Christianity*'; the faith doctrine that saw *'manly fitness'* as a means to further Christian morality and as a route to heavenly salvation (Watson et al 2005). Rugby was popular because:

> ***"it gave plenty of opportunity to 'take hard knocks without malice'***
> (Mason 1981 in Watson et al 2005)

It was a doctrine that was applied to the *"scores of young and stalwart deaf mutes"*. In 1895, *The British Deaf Mute* recorded:

> ***'Of all the healthy outdoor sports that which should be the most popular among the deaf of the United Kingdom is football.'***
> (In Atherton et al 1999)

The 1800s were a time of great oppression for many and, for disabled people, especially so. The Industrial Revolution removed unproductive disabled people and placed them in institutions and marginalised them (Howe 2008:63). Philosophical and religious notions applied to deaf people by the likes of Plato and Aristotle, the Bible and the Koran, were that deaf people were not capable of individual thinking and that they were not able to acquire language; they were lesser beings 'not in god's image' (Enerstvedt 1996). As a result they were treated with disdain, fear and suspicion. Yet despite this, by the 1870s, education became available to all; elementary schools for the masses, grammar and public schools for the privileged and special schools for the handicapped, with local mental health deficiency committees dealing with the mentally deficient.

The education of deaf people was divided by two methodologies: instruction in Sign Language or instruction using speech (in order to 'normalise' deaf children). This division in educational philosophy is one that divides still today and one that has had a profound effect on the stigmatisation of deaf people and on their participation in sport.

There was hope that the increasing availability of education for all would have led to the development of a more enlightened and tolerant society – one that embraced diversity and disability. This was, after all, a time when Deaf people held positions of public authority in education, health and law throughout Europe and elsewhere. Unfortunately, this was all to come to a cataclysmic end in 1880 when a group of Oralist[1] educators manipulated the outcome of the *2nd International Congress of Education for the Deaf* in Milan, Italy. Here, they took it upon themselves, unanimously, to stop the teaching of sign language, because they saw it as stigmatising deafness and, in comparison to spoken language, it was unequal, non-grammatical and lacking in abstract vocabulary (Kinsey et al 1880).

The greatest immediate impact on Deaf education at the time was the sacking of Deaf teachers and others who taught using sign language. This then influenced a prevailing attitude that saw sign language marginalised and the disenfranchisement of Deaf people both in the community and in the workplace.

---

[1] Oralism is the method of teaching deaf children using spoken language

The consequences of *Milan 1880* still reverberate today, with continuing negative notions of deafness, an ongoing belief that spoken language is superior to sign language and that hearing people are intellectually superior to deaf people. Regrettably, the *Milan 1880* pronouncements impacted upon Deaf sport too.

Yet despite the changes, Deaf people continued to develop their own identity, culture and community. Sport played a major part in progressing matters as evidenced by the number of Deaf clubs and associations that emerged in the late 1800s and which began to grow in prominence into the early 1900s.

Yet misconceptions abounded and some took a view that in developing a Deaf identity and representational community, Deaf people were isolating themselves further from society. But Lars Havstad, the first Norwegian Deaf person to go to university, observed that:

> ***"Deaf people are getting together not to isolate themselves, but to gather power and information for life in a society where sounds and spoken language are prevalent.'***
>
> (In Fosshaug 2004)

The Origins of the Deaflympics

From the time when the first schools for the Deaf were established in Paris in 1755, Deaf people began to meet in organised formal situations. Deaf sports clubs in European countries began to compete against each other in friendly competitions. Their pioneering leaders began to push the movement forward. The first sports club for the Deaf opened in Berlin in 1888. In Paris, Eugene Rubens-Alcais helped to establish the Fdération Sportive des Sourds Muëts de France and became its first President. Sport for the Deaf in London was governed by the Federation of London Deaf Clubs which was founded in July 1918 by Arthur James Wilson as Chairman and William

Baird as Secretary (Whalley 2010). Hundreds of people took the opportunity to compete in tournaments and competitions, watched and supported by spectators.

Throughout the 1920s, Eugene Rubens-Alcais and Antoine Dresse of Belgium, met frequently. As representatives of their respective national associations, they would have discussed and debated the impact of the Milan 1880 congress on the development of Deaf sport, culture and identity. Inspired by the concept of Olympism, advocated by Baron de Coubertin, Rubens-Alcais and Dresse formulated an approach to address the oppression of deafness with an "Olympic" event for Deaf sport. They saw young Deaf people as the means to realise their dreams and so set about contacting their international counterparts in a move to federate the sports clubs and organisations of their various nations into an international sports body. Their industrious efforts culminated in the 1924 International Silent Games (ISG). Held in Paris, these Games saw them put forward the need for an international organisation to oversee the development of structures and bylaws, with which to govern the new event and the sporting activities within it. In addition, the Games gave a further opportunity for Deaf leaders to meet internationally and to debate national politics together.

The Deaflympics has its critics, both in and outside the Deaf community. Some claim that it is a participation-level event that has become more of a social gathering than an arena for competitive sport. This book discusses that perception in Sections 2 and 3. In order to illustrate the elite ethos of the Deaflympics, this chapter and the next gives a brief chronology of the events that have occurred in the ISG over the past 90 years, with eyewitness records from athletes and others. Salient information about each games is also taken from the Deaflympics website whose address you can find on page 7. I have tried not to make this book parochial by dwelling on Westernised viewpoints, but this is unavoidable, because most of the existing published material is in English. I also want to make an early mark of reinforcing that the Deaflympics and its predecessors have always been regarded as an elite sporting event by its participants and have therefore drawn heavily from Whalley's *The History of Deaf Tennis* to illustrate this. This suggests ever more, the need for readers in every nation of the Deaflympic Movement to discover and relate their own experiences.

Since 1924, the ISG has evolved to become the Deaflympics with its accompanying global brand. The event mirrors the Olympics and consequently has been heavily influenced by global sports and politics. Readers searching for an almanac of detailed times and distances for their sport will not find them in this volume. Such detailed information can be found in *CISS 2001 A Review* and on the Deaflympics website at www.deaflympics.com. In Chapter 13, I will discuss the notion that Deaf sport is in decline and suggest that the situation is not hopeless and that, with public support, matters can change.

Paris, France. 10 – 17 August 1924

1st International Silent Games

- **148 athletes**
- **7 sports**
- **9 nations**

The Deaf version of the Olympics opened on the 10th August at the Pershing Stadium in Paris, 14 days after the closing ceremony of the 1924 Olympics. Rubens-Alcais and Dresse had persuaded nine nations to compete in athletics, cycling, diving, football, shooting, swimming and tennis. Italy, Romania and Hungary sent one athlete each, since they had not yet formed national federations. The only woman to take part was Hendrika Nicoline Van der Heyden (NED) who competed alone in the 100m backstroke. Her event is probably, the first and only 'walkover' in the history of the Deaflympics.

The Reverend Vernon Jones assembled a British team of 36 men who were:

> ***"all keen as knives, to do their best for the old country."***
> (In Whalley 2010:229)

I can only imagine what it must have felt like for young Deaf people, who had the opportunity to show their national allegiance and pride through international sport. The novelty of the event drew large crowds. The British later reported that they were surprised by the athletic ability of the French who were:

> ***'Splendidly trained' showing a 'fine sporting spirit and never got flurried"***
> (in Whalley 2010:229)

Immediately following the Closing Ceremony, the respective national contingent leaders met with Rubens-Alcais and Dresse in a Paris café. After much discussion, they agreed to create a governing body for the event and established the Comité *International des Sports Silencieux (CISS).*

Amsterdam, Netherlands. 18 – 26 August 1928

2nd International Silent Games

- **212 athletes**
- **6 sports**
- **10 nations**

The Silent Games followed the Olympics for the second time to Amsterdam, where the opening ceremony was held one week after the Olympics closed. A Dutch newspaper reported that the following Games in 1931 were unable to follow the Olympics to America and so Germany was chosen as a venue instead. (in Whalley 2010:230) The governing Congress was inaugurated and it adopted the CISS statutes with Rubens-Alcais elected as founder President and Dresse as its first Secretary General.

Nuremburg, Germany. 19 – 23 August 1931

3rd International Silent Games

- **316 athletes**
- **7 sports**
- **14 nations**

The 1932 Summer Olympics were held in Los Angeles, but this occurred during the *Great Depression* when many nations and athletes were unable to pay for the travel and subsistence involved. Not surprisingly, CISS had to break with tradition and find a European host. Los Angeles saw fewer than half the number of the previous Olympics in Amsterdam and President Hoover chose not to attend either the opening or closing ceremonies. In contrast, by staying in Europe, the ISG enjoyed a 33% increase in competitors attending.

Furthermore, and despite the economic situation, a number of governments gave considerable grants to their teams to assist with their expenses. However, members of the British team had to fundraise to cover their costs. (in Whalley 2010:231)

London, England. 17 – 24 August 1935

4th International Games for the Deaf

- **221 athletes**
- **6 sports**
- **12 nations**

At the 5th Congress of CISS, in Copenhagen in 1933, a Commission was established to monitor and list world records in athletics and swimming. Congress admitted Japan as the first Asian member of CISS and the USA as the first from the Americas. Noel Curtis-Bennett, a member of the IOC for Great Britain (1933-1950), was Chairman of the 1935 event and he wrote a letter to the Editor of 'The Times' appealing to the British public for more understanding and compassion for Deaf people. You can read the letter in Chapter 15: *Marketing the Deaflympics*.

Stockholm, Sweden. 24 – 27 August 1939

5th International Silent Games

- **250 athletes**
- **7 sports**
- **13 nations**

A Technical Commission was established by Congress to govern each sport. At the opening ceremony the flag of CISS was inaugurated as designed by Mr. Chante, featuring blue and green colours upon which the CISS symbol was emblazoned. The guest of honour was Prince Gustaf Adolf of Sweden.

Throughout the summer of 1939, Nazi aggression moved Europe to the brink of war. Betty Shrine[2] (in Whalley 2010:

---

[2] Betty Shrine (1918-2006) Tennis player and Captain, Team Official for Great Britain.

235-236) noted her own account of the declaration of war and the effect this had on competitors and officials who had their post-Games touring holiday cut short. Not being fully aware of world events, the Deaf party innocently returned to Gothenburg to join their boat home. They noticed that the boat was late departing and it was only around 10pm that they began to realise the seriousness of the situation, when the boat began to fill with more British people and cars. In the evenings, at sea, they had to face sparsely lit lamps because the windows were blackened - making it very difficult for Deaf people to communicate with each other. In the middle of the North Sea the party was eventually told of the declaration of war and that the ship was being diverted to another port. On arrival at Aberdeen, all signposts had been removed; a small group decided to stay on for the day sightseeing and to catch the night train home, playing cards on the long journey. But once again, the train was lit by tiny blue lights, with hardly light enough to see around them let alone play cards or communicate with each other. All they could do was go to sleep.

The Second World War created the first and only interruption to the Summer Olympics and the International Silent Games.

Copenhagen, Denmark. 12 – 16 August 1949

6th International Silent Games

- **391 athletes**
- **9 sports**
- **14 nations**

The 1948 Olympics in London became known as the *Austerity Games*, so-called because of the economic climate and post-war rationing. Germany and Japan were not invited to participate because of their roles as aggressors in WW2. Russia was invited but chose not to send any athletes. Germany did not compete in the ISG and Russia and Japan did not enter until 1957 and 1965 respectively. Also absent were countries that had become absorbed into the Soviet Union.

The 1949 event set the precedence for CISS and later the International Committee of Sport for the Deaf (ICSD) to stage the Deaflympics in the year after the Olympics. With hindsight, the implications of this decision were far reaching as it removed Deaf sport from public association with the Olympics and the Olympic ethos. However, standards of organisation and delivery were certainly improving:

> *"The whole thing was based on Olympic standards and we certainly have never seen the like before. The Danish government officials, the officials of the various Danish sports associations and the Teachers of the Deaf can be justly proud of their work. This was no CISS-job and we do not intend to be derogatory, we just mean that there isn't a sports association or any group of sports associations for the Deaf which could have made such superlative arrangements."*

And on the rising standards of athletes competing:

> *"Our players and ourselves, were disappointed it had not been possible to finance some of the British Women players...We did spot a very up and coming youngster only 16 years of age, Anderson of Sweden. This boy is tall and maybe there is more to come! He's a very nice player and when he gets more experience and developed physically he is going to be quite a handful for Smith or for anyone else in the Deaf tennis world."*
>
> (in Whalley 2010:237)

Seefeld, Austria 26-30 Jan 1949

1st International Winter Games for the Deaf

- **33 athletes**
- **2 sports**
- **5 nations**

Heinz Prochazka, President of the Austrian Deaf Sports Association was instrumental in establishing this competition.

Brussels, Belgium, 15 – 19 August 1953

7th International Silent Games

- **473 athletes**
- **8 sports**
- **16 nations**

At the 12th Congress, Rubens-Alcais retired as President after serving for 29 years and was succeeded by Oscar Ryden (SWE). Australia became the first southern hemisphere nation to compete in the ISG, having won the bid to host the 1956 Summer Olympics in Melbourne. The economic environment still made it difficult for the ISG to be held outside of Europe, and it was not until 2005 that the games arrived in Melbourne, to compete in the same stadium used for the 1956 Olympics. Saarland (a short-lived post WW2 protectorate partitioned from defeated Nazi Germany) represented post-war Germany at the 1952 Summer Olympics. Like their Olympic counterparts, the Russians decided not to send a team to the ISG. The Opening Ceremony was held in the Stade du Hysel led by the Colonel in Chief of the Belgian army, Rombrants, who represented King Bauduin. The Leopold Club, a Davis Cup venue, was the host for the Tennis competition. The Games finished with the flourish of a military band marching around the ground, *"something for us to see but not hear"*. (Baird in Whalley 2010:239-240.)

Oslo, Norway 20 – 24 Feb1953

2nd International Winter Games for the Deaf

- **44 athletes**
- **9 events**
- **6 nations**

Paris, 9-19th June 1955

International Olympic Committee 50th session

CISS was admitted into the Olympic movement under the auspices of the International Olympic Committee (IOC) as an International Federation with Olympic Standing.

Oberammergau, Germany. 10-13 Feb 1955

3rd International Winter Silent Games.

- **59 athletes**
- **4 sports**
- **8 nations**

Congress elected a new President, Jens Peter Nielsen (DEN). Australia and New Zealand became the first Oceania members.

Milan, Italy 25 – 30 August 1957

8th International Silent Games

- **635 athletes**
- **13 sports**
- **25 nations**

As a gesture towards the Suez crisis of 1956, the closing ceremony of the Olympics was arranged to allow the athletes to mingle in a show of global unity. Britain and France continued to occupy the Suez region militarily until March 1957, but by the late summer, relations had improved sufficiently enough for Russia to compete in the ISG for the first time ever (perhaps due to having been a major broker over the Suez affair with the USA).

China, Korea, Chile and 10 others sent representatives in anticipation of future participation. Dimmock reported that an Italian athlete stood on the rostrum and gave the 'athlete prayer' in sign language; *'it is not important to win but to struggle well".* A helicopter dropped a scroll that was then handed to the Mayor of Milan who then officially declared the Games open. Hundreds of balloons with the words *"Deaf Olympics"* were released in all directions. A British cyclist, Lewis, was involved in some *'nasty spills'* and was taken to hospital, where he declined the offer of a bed and competed in the massed race *'swathed in bandages'*. He finished tenth. Most Italian newspapers gave prominence to news of the Games and the results. Giuseppe Riva, President of the Italian Olympic Organising Committee, closed the Games. Volleyball was introduced as a demonstration sport. At Congress, Finland beat Yugoslavia to host the next Games. Argentina, Chile and Uruguay become the first South American members of CISS (in Whalley 2010:241-242).

Montana-Vermala, Switzerland. 27-31 January 1959

4th International Winter Games for the Deaf

- **53 athletes**
- **3 sports**
- **9 nations**

Helsinki, Finland 6 – 10 August 1961

9th International Games for the Deaf

- **613 athletes**
- **13 sports**
- **24 nations**

The 1960 Rome Paralympics saw the emergence of a force that would eventually dominate disability sport and create the International Paralympic Committee (IPC) with its strong ties to the IOC. Organised by the International Stoke Mandeville Games Federation for spinal cord injuries, all participant athletes were guaranteed a medal.

CISS Congress elected Pierre Bernhard (FRA) as President. Although all the venues and facilities were close at hand for the spectators, the admission prices were found to be prohibitive. The Prime Minister, Mr Martti Miettunen, opened the Games. Russia won most of the medals despite sending just 34 athletes. France was able to send a team of only 13, because they did not receive their usual government grant. (Dimmock in Whalley 2010:243 – 244)

Are, Sweden. 12-16 March 1963

5th International Winter Games for the Deaf

- **60 athletes**
- **2 sports**
- **9 nations**

Sweden stepped in at the last minute to host the event as no other country could be found. Bibbo Nordenskold, a famous winter sports coach, was the Games Secretary General and Prince Bertil was Patron.

Washington DC, USA 27 Jun – 3 July 1965

10th International Games for the Deaf

- **687 athletes**
- **11 sports**
- **27 nations**

Whilst the 1964 Tokyo Olympics were the first to be held in Asia, the 10th ISG was the first to be held outside Europe. Crowds of 8,000 deaf people were present for the opening ceremony. Interior Secretary, Stewart Udall, the trusted lieutenant of Lyndon B Johnson, opened the Games. One of the privileges of international sport is the experience of international travel. The British contingent, 187 strong, hired 5 Greyhound buses for a road trip to Niagara Falls and Toronto, which ended in New York *"covering 1,150 miles"* (Dimmock in Whalley 2010:246 – 247).

1966, IOC awarded the Coubertin Cup to CISS

The award was in recognition of the CISS's strict adherence to the Olympic ideal and its service to international sport. The citation letter declared:

> ***"You have now cleared the path, in all countries, for committees of your type to allow young men and women, disfavoured by fate, to get to know the joys of sport and also to learn, through sport, to tackle life better."***

Berchtesgaden, Germany. 20-23 February 1967

6th International Winter Games for the Deaf

- **77 athletes**
- **2 sports**
- **12 nations**

After 43 years of enduring service, Antoine Dresse decided not to run for re-election and was succeeded by Osvald Dahlgren as 2nd Secretary General. Congress also decided to replace the name 'International Silent Games' with the 'World Games for the Deaf' (WGD) so as to recognise its global nature.

Belgrade, Serbia 9 – 16 August 1969

11th World Games for the Deaf

- **1889 athletes**
- **14 sports**
- **34 nations**

Whilst the Olympics and the Paralympics continued to be hosted on different continents, the WGD returned to Europe. There were complaints that the inadequate allocation of training times led to limited opportunities for practice. Marshall Tito's representative oversaw the opening and closing ceremonies. During the evenings:

> ***"...a fine and massive club for the deaf given by the Government was packed with people."***
> (Edwards in Whalley 2010: 248 – 249).

Adelboden, Switzerland. 25-29 January 1971

7th World Winter Games for the Deaf

- **92 athletes**
- **2 sports**
- **13 nations**

Congress elected Jerald M. Jordan (USA) as President.

Malmo, Sweden 21 – 28 July 1973

12th World Games for the Deaf

- **1116 athletes**
- **12 sports**
- **31 nations**

The 1972 Olympics were overshadowed by the Palestinian massacre of Israeli athletes and officials in Munich. The Summer Paralympics demonstrated Goalball, allowing Visually Impaired athletes to compete for the first time. The priorities for Deaf athletes competing in Malmo was clear:

> *"They were all looking forward to the journey to Malmo where all the months of training for the 'great week' would reveal whether it was to be a 'gold', 'silver', 'bronze' or just all that one could give in the name of sport for one's country"*
> (Crellin & Keech in Whalley 210:250 – 251).

CISS Congress elected Knud Sondergaard (DEN) as its third Secretary-General.

50th anniversary of CISS 1974

A celebratory event was held in Paris and the CISS museum opened in Rome.

Lake Placid, USA. 2-8 February 1975

8th World Winter Games for the Deaf

- **139 athletes**
- **4 sports**
- **13 nations**

South Africa joined CISS as its first African member. Ice Hockey and Speed Skating were demonstration sports.

Bucharest, Romania. 17 – 27 July 1977

13th World Games for the Deaf

- **1150 athletes**
- **13 sports**
- **32 nations**

The Games were held for the first time in Eastern Europe.

Great Britain sent its smallest ever team to a WGD with just four swimmers and their accompanying officials:

> ***"They set off to the earthquake battered city of Bucharest… After several days en route, they finally arrived at the hotel in the late evening of 16th July. There was to be one day for the parade plus training, followed by five days of competition, then an early return home for the swimmers!"***
> (Whalley 2010:252)

Congress recognised the need to strictly control the hearing eligibility of competitors. In the previous year, African nations had boycotted the Montreal Olympics in protest at the New Zealand rugby tour of South Africa. This had little impact on the WGD, because, although South Africa joined CISS in 1975, they did not make their Deaflympic debut until 1993, along with Algeria.

Meribel, France. 21-27 January 1979

9th World Winter Games for the Deaf

- **113 athletes**
- **2 sports**
- **14 nations**

Congress voted to change the CISS title to 'Comité International des Sports des Sourds' (CISS). The classification for eligibility to compete internationally was introduced as a minimum hearing loss of 55dB in the better ear.

Köln, West Germany 23 July- 1 August 1981

14th World Games for the Deaf

- **1198 athletes**
- **13 sports**
- **32 nations**

The original host, Iran, was experiencing political and social upheaval. Thus, CISS decided to award the event to Köln in West Germany. With only two years notice, the Federal government, the City of Köln and the German Sports Association for the Deaf drew together to make the WGD possible. CISS President J Jordan reported in the Olympic Review:

> *"Our confidence regarding the ability of the 'Deutscher Gehörlosen-Sportverband' (German Sport Federation for the Deaf) to take charge of the organisation of the Games at short notice has proved well-founded. All the preparations have been completed and the number of minor problems remaining to be solved is minimal. It seems that the Games will take place without any hitches, which is typical of German efficiency..."*
>
> (in Olympic Review 1981)

Eyewitnesses described the mass of Deaf people from all over the world. A thunderstorm interrupted the opening ceremony:

> *'We stood our ground for about ten minutes and then realised that we were there for the sports, not to get pneumonia. We all ran for cover under the*

> ***stands, all except Godfrey Harvey who obtained a wet suit and stood firm in the storm to keep the Union Jack flying."***
>
> (D.T. Harris in Whalley 2010:253.)

The standard of play continued to improve:

> ***"I feel we have the best team available to us, but we must now try to find new players and endeavour to arrange coaching. This is obviously the strong point of the American players, who, like the American hearing players, are given constant coaching, but can we afford this in our true amateur status?"***
>
> (Paddy Corcoran GB Tennis Team Manager in Whalley 2010:254.)

CISS became the first international sports organisation to elect a woman to its senior echelons when Mrs. Maria de Bendeguz of Venezuela joined its Executive Committee. Juan Antonio Samaranch was the first IOC President to attend the Games. English was adopted as the language of correspondence but the title *Comité International des Sports des Sourds* was retained in respect of its origins. Doping tests were also introduced.

Sixty-five countries boycotted the Moscow Olympics over the Russian invasion of Afghanistan. When the International Stoke Mandeville Games Federation requested USSR to host the Paralympics, they claimed not to have citizens with disabilities (Legg et al 2004). Hence, the 1980 Paralympics were held in Arnhem, the Netherlands, and included Cerebral Palsy athletes for the first time.

Madonna di Campiglio, Italy. 16-23 January 1983

10th World Winter Games for the Deaf

- **147 athletes**
- **3 sports**
- **15 nations**

True adherence to the CISS motto "Equal through Sports" was ensured when Congress voted to forbid competitors from wearing hearing aids during competition.

Los Angeles, USA 10 – 20 July 1985

15th World Games for the Deaf

- **995 athletes**
- **12 sports**
- **29 nations**

Since 1985 the flag of the IOC has flown next to that of the CISS and ICSD at both the Summer and Winter World Games and Deaflympics. The WGD followed the Olympics to Los Angeles after the Soviet Bloc (except Hungary) boycotted the 1984 Olympics in retaliation for the 1980 Moscow boycott, which had been led by the USA. Accordingly, USSR and the GDR did not send teams, whereas Romania and Yugoslavia followed their Olympic counterparts and sent teams to compete. Iran did not compete, because of continuing internal social and political unrest.

Whalley (2010) ends his report for 1985 with a summative account of the development of British Deaf tennis up to that point.

> ***"Thirty years ago the British team collected many medals in World Games for the Deaf, but with more countries and tennis players participating and coaching raising the standard of the game***

> ***to a higher level, our team is being praised for sportsmanship, but not for winning medals. British Deaf tennis needs more dedicated players at competitive level and coaches who can communicate effectively to give us the chance to challenge for medals at the next Games. It may take years to rebuild our team and I look forward to the day, seeing a British player standing on the rostrum to receive a medal."***
>
> (Whalley 2010:256)

It wasn't just Deaf sport that was struggling to maintain funds and ensure competitive standards. In 1984 the "Last minute Games" of the Paralympics were held in Long Island (USA) and Stoke Mandeville (UK) because the original sponsor, the University of Illinois, pulled out three months before the opening, owing to a lack of funds.

CISS Congress recognised all regional confederations.

Oslo, Norway. 7 -14 February 1987

11th World Winter Games for the Deaf

- **129 athletes**
- **3 sports**
- **15 nations**

Oslo was the first city to host the WGD for a second time.

Christchurch, New Zealand 7 – 17 Jan 1989

16th World Games for the Deaf

- **955 athletes**
- **13 sports**
- **30 nations**

These were the first Games to be held in the Southern hemisphere and the last time that the sports powers of the Soviet Union and East Germany dominated the competition results.

Restricted grants and funds forced the British team to select only medal prospects to travel to Christchurch. The tennis squad stayed behind to concentrate on re-building. Whilst a benefactor came forward at the very last minute, Whalley decided to use the funds for the development of a new squad and the young players within. GB had its most successful WGD ever; with 27 medals, twelve gold, nine silver and six bronzes in athletics, badminton, swimming and football. The British noted that Ronald Kreig (GER) and Barbara Oddone (ITA) performed exceptionally well, winning their tennis singles, doubles and mixed doubles, raising standards to even higher levels.

The 1988 Paralympics was held concurrently with the Seoul Olympics and the term "Paralympic" was used for first time. The global profile of the Paralympics was now beginning to overshadow the Deaflympics.

The International Disability Sports organisations were finding it more difficult to control the administration and management of the Paralympics and they had come together as the International Coordinating Committee (ICC). One of the main influencers was Dr Bob Steadward, a sports scientist, who wanted to integrate disabled events into the Olympics. The IOC were uneasy about this but wanted to ease the burden of supporting different disability sports and thus encouraged the CISS to join with the ICC, which subsequently formed the International Paralympic Committee in 1989.

2

Deaflympics 1990 – 2012

Banff, Canada. 2-9 March 1991

12th World Winter Games for the Deaf

- **181 athletes**
- **4 sports**
- **16 nations**

This event lacked publicity, as there was no coverage outside the small town of Banff. Stewart and Ammons (1994) suggested that Deaf sport was 'satisfied' in managing its own events without external support.

Ice hockey was recognised as a new winter discipline and curling was a demonstration sport.

Sofia, Bulgaria, 24 Jul – 2 Aug 1993

17th World Games for the Deaf

- **1679 athletes**
- **14 sports**

- **51 nations**

The Barcelona Olympics saw South Africa compete for the first time and Germany entered as a single team following reunification. The Soviet Union dissolved in 1991, enabling the Baltic states of Estonia, Latvia and Lithuania to enter as individual nation states. The other Soviet republics entered as a "Unified Team". The breakup of SFR Yugoslavia gave debuts to Croatia, Slovenia and Bosnia & Herzegovina. Due to UN sanctions, the FR Yugoslavians were not allowed to compete under their own flag but rather as independents under the Olympic flag and as Independent Olympic participants. The 1992 Barcelona Paralympics saw two events; Barcelona for the main Games, which was followed by the Madrid Games for people with intellectual disabilities.

There were concerns about Bulgaria's ability to host the 1993 WGD in the wake of the international political upheavals. In the end, the event was managed by a Bulgarian advertising agency KRES and 5,000 spectators turned up to watch the games; this was also partly due to the games being held in Europe and therefore accessible to more spectators (Stewart & Ammons 1993). Stewart also remarked on the higher 'calibre' of athlete being drawn from mainstream schools.

The British tennis team began to see the efforts of consolidation pay off when Vaterlaws & Schofield won a bronze in the Ladies Doubles. The team also engaged a hearing coach for the first time, Aled Hughes who reported that:

> ***"all matches were very competitive but never after a game of tennis have I seen so much affection towards each other. The friendship was astonishing to watch and the players would spend all day together, making friends for life."***
>
> (In Whalley 2010:258-259)

"The Deaf culture is one where the Deaf people make the most of the time they have together, because in the hearing world they are the ones who are sometimes segregated due to their inhibitions. Hughes left Bulgaria with the feeling that he had gained a lot of new friends and companions for life. The Deaf culture has warmth that he couldn't put on paper but was easy to feel when in their company. For Aled, the WGD was an experience that will never leave him."

(Mark Perry in Whalley 2010:258 – 259.)

Yllas, Finland. 13-19 March 1995

13th World Winter Games for the Deaf

- **258 athletes**
- **3 sports**
- **18 nations**

In 1995, CISS abandoned its attempts to incorporate the World Games for the Deaf into the Paralympics, with Congress voting to withdraw from the IPC and remain independent, but with IOC support. John M. Lovett (AUS) was elected as the sixth President. The "Fair Play' award was inaugurated and awarded to its first recipient, Paul Malaney of the USA.

Stewart and Ojalas (1995) reported on the event which was hosted by the Finnish Athletics Association of the Deaf, established in 1904 and one of the oldest members of the CISS. Finland had to compete hard to win the rights to host the games because competition was strong and because the Deaf population in Finland was small, representing just 1:1,000 of the population. In addition, geographical conditions made it challenging for members of the Deaf community to congregate and plan for such events. The Games were held across two sites, 120 km apart and this created issues when trying to raise the profile of the games, with small numbers congregated across two locations. The organisers had to compete with others for the rental of ski slopes, Nordic tracks and ice time as well as for commercial sponsorship. Severe weather conditions forced the postponement of several alpine events and this led to difficulties in completing the planned programme with the time allowed.

Copenhagen, Denmark 13 – 26 July 1997

18th World Games for the Deaf

- **2028 athletes**
- **16 sports**
- **65 nations**

These Games were hosted by the Danish Deaf Sports Association on the occasion of their 75th anniversary year. Congress elected Donalda Ammons (USA) as its first woman Secretary General. Lisa Kauppinen, President of the World Federation of the Deaf (WFD) delivered a keynote speech to Congress where she highlighted a global deaf population of 70 million and advocated the need for deaf people to work together, with an emphasis on those in the northern hemisphere supporting deaf people in the south. Congress passed Germany's motion to enable Regional Confederations to be wholly responsible for authorising all international events held in their respective regions.

Bowling and Orienteering were added to the programme and Congress agreed to a Beach Volleyball demonstration event at the 2005 Summer Deaflympics. Furthermore, Congress agreed to follow Olympic and Federations of International Sports regulations governing the number of men and women entries into alpine skiing events. Interestingly, Congress refused Switzerland's request to field a female to play in an all-male Ice

Hockey team despite the International Ice Hockey Foundation's agreement to such.

The Italian representative for the 2001 Rome Deaflympics reassured Congress that there would be no problems with transportation for the Games as the Italian armed forces would be providing the requisite transport.

The British tennis team now had three hearing coaches - Aled Hughes, Roger Smith and Julie Jones. All the British players were better placed than in previous Games but lost out on medals:

> ***"It was a very exciting time with each GB player recording at least one win in an event and it is clear that the GB team is very strong overall. Hopefully this will give us a platform for winning medals in the next World Games."***
>
> (Perry in Whalley 2010:260)

The 1996 Atlanta Paralympics admitted 'intellectually disabled' athletes and the IPC announced that it had secured mass media sponsorship to the value of US$81m.

Davos, Switzerland. 8-14 March 1999

14th World Winter Games for the Deaf

- **265 athletes**
- **4 sports**
- **18 nations**

Congress celebrated the 75th Anniversary of the CISS. Knud Sondergaard (DEN) was made Honorary CISS Life Member after 24 years as Secretary General. A name change was undertaken from 'World Games for the Deaf' to 'Deaf World Games' (DWG) as a number of East Europeans felt the word 'for' suggested paternalism.

The proposal for raising the participation fee from US$15 to US$50 was met by protest as a number of the participant countries said it would prevent them from bringing larger teams. Congress moved to state that DWG would not be more than 10 days in duration from opening to conclusion. Associate membership of CISS was made available to International Deaf Sports Federations (IDSFs) whose sport was not on the DWG programme. Difficult discussions ensued on the practice of Regional Confederations using their team sports championships as qualifying events for the Deaflympics. Criteria varied in different regions and it was difficult to move to a consensus as ICSD tried to align matters with 'hearing' International Sports Federations.

CISS also became the controlling body of World Championships ensuring that sets of conditions were met in order to recognise a world championship event and programming that did not conflict with regional championships. Australia requested the publication of World rankings and Melbourne was voted host for the 2005 Summer DWG.

16 May 2001

The IOC granted permission to replace the 'Deaf World Games' with 'Deaflympics'.

Rome, Italy. 22nd July- 1 Aug 2001

19th Summer Deaflympics

- **2208 athletes**
- **16 sports**
- **67 nations**

The IPC and IOC signed a Treaty confirming that IOC/IPC would jointly host the Paralympics. In June 2001, CISS launched its new website to provide updated information on the Rome Deaflympics.

With its new title of 'Deaflympics', the Deaf sports community had high aspirations and hoped for change for the better. Unfortunately, athletes and spectators remember the Rome Deaflympics for its chaos and confusion. The opening ceremony was not accessible as no sign language provision was accorded. When an interpreter eventually appeared on a large monitor, they were found to be using International Sign Language. Frustrated at the lack of access to communication in the mode of choice, Donalda Ammons (CISS Secretary General at the time) allegedly disconnected the main feed to the PA system so that hearing spectators would not be able to follow proceedings and would thus empathise with the deaf (Wheatley, in Whalley 2010:262).

According to Wheatley, Italians consider the Oral method of communication to be superior to Sign Language and this was reflected in the lack of information available to sign language users. People found it difficult to secure tickets for events, obtain information about scheduled times among other things. The situation was compounded by most of the organisers and volunteers being non-signers.

The following year, CISS became a member of Sport Accord.

Sundsvall, Sweden. 28 Feb - 8 March 2003

15th Winter Deaflympics

- **247 athletes**
- **4 sports**
- **21 nations**

Ammons had stepped in as Acting President, because Lovett had been taken ill on arrival in Sweden and was hospitalised.

Congress passed several key motions:

- To rename CISS as the 'International Deaflympics Committee' (IDC) This was later disallowed by the IOC for breaching the Olympic Charter and changed to the International Committee of Sports for the Deaf (ICSD)
- The Secretary General position to be directly appointed by the Executive Committee and to be a salaried position.
- Athletes at Deaflympics to be allowed to wear advertising on competition kit. The sizes to be no larger than $400cm^2$ on front and back.

The Congress sought clarification on the authority of the Deaf World Championships under the auspices of the International Sport Federations of the Deaf. A Legal Commission was tasked to define clearer terms of reference so that the CISS's overall power was clarified.

Patricia Tracey was announced as CEO of the Melbourne Deaflympics. The Organising Committee had been awarded AUS$8m and was certain of reaching its goal of AUS$10m. Owing to the nature of funding agreements between the Games Organising Committee and the Victoria State Government, most sports were to be located in Melbourne. The Marathon, Cycling, Orienteering and some football matches would be held in Ballarat some 90km away.

Taiwan was selected as host for the 2009 Summer Deaflympics.

Melbourne, Australia. 5 – 16 January 2005

20th Summer Deaflympics

- **2038 athletes**
- **17 sports**
- **74 nations**

Melbourne, which had previously hosted the 1956 Olympics, was also preparing to host the Commonwealth Games in 2006. The IOC lodged a trademark challenge against the Organising Committee. Kevan Gospar an Australian IOC member intervened to allow the use of 'Deaflympic Games' in Australia. Congress elected Ammons (who had been standing in after the death of John Lovett in 2004) as President and, as a result, she became the first woman President of the Executive of an International Sports Organisation with Olympic Standing. The following year ICSD was in compliance with WADA Signatory Code.

- AUS$10m investment with a return of AUS$16.5m to the local economy
- 3,488 athletes / team officials from 74 countries attended
- 21 international media groups were present
- Web streaming was provided to over 4 million subscribers
- 14,000+ attended opening ceremony
- 65 interpreters serviced the Deaflympics (19 international sign, 35 Auslan[3], 10 Deaf relay interpreters)
- 1783 volunteers (266 Deaf / hard of hearing)
- Beach Volleyball added to the programme

[3] Australian Sign Language

The emergence of the Internet as a tool for instantaneous on-line coverage of world events was now available, though Internet coverage of the Athens Olympics had been severely restricted by the IOC. However, the Deaf community began to take advantage of this new technology, with collaborations between broadcasters and corresponding home nation team organisers.

All eight of the GB tennis players were playing for medals on the final day of competition at Boroondara Tennis Centre. Kreig (GER) beat Sinclair (GBR) in the Men's Singles, Wilcox (GBR) lost to Yang (CHN) for the bronze. GB took bronze in the Men's, Ladies and Mixed Doubles.

Salt Lake, USA. 3-10 February 2007

16th Winter Deaflympics

- **298 athletes**
- **5 sports**
- **23 nations**

During Congress, Ammons tendered her resignation as President in protest at Congress opposition to Proposal 65, which she interpreted as a lack of respect for her leadership of ICSD. She expressed her gratitude for having served on the ICSD board since 1995. Lanesman took over as President and shortly afterwards Wilmerdinger, ICSD Sports Director, and Fosshaug, ICSD Member at Large, also resigned.

The discussions that followed led to a realisation that members had misunderstood the voting procedures and a remedial vote of confidence in Ammons occurred. All three came back onto the Executive Committee.

Congress passed the following:

- Approved Athens, Greece, as host city for the 2013 Summer Deaflympics.

- The Greek Deputy Sports Minister and the President of the Organising Committee Athens signed a Memorandum of Agreement.
- Congress accepted greetings from the World Federation of the Deaf and mentioned the adoption of the new UN Convention on the Rights of Persons with Disabilities and the possibility of using this protocol as a means to keep Deaf sports independent.

The 2007 Winter Deaflympics Chair, Dwight Benedict, gave a summative presentation that featured a number of notable points; namely:

- The importance of sponsorship
- The need for a supportive board and volunteers
- The success of the Salt Lake City 2007 Organising Committee who generated a profit of US$84,000 which was shared 50% between ICSD and the USA Deaf Sports Federation

Taipei, Taiwan. 5 – 15 September 2009

21st Summer Deaflympics

- **2553 athletes**
- **21 sports**
- **77 nations**

The previous year, the world watched as South African, Natalie Du Toit, who had had her leg amputated after a motorbike accident, qualified for the Beijing Olympics as the first amputee swimmer since Oliver Halassy in 1936. Polish table tennis athlete Natalia Partyka, born without a right forearm, competed in both the Olympics and Paralympics. Meanwhile, and in complete contrast, Terence Parkin and other deaf athletes competed without a mention.

In preparation for the 2009 Deaflympics and to attract other global sporting events, the Taipei City Government redeveloped its forty-year-old stadium and other sports stadia to provide the best possible standards of facilities. Unfortunately, the swimming pool was found to be too small and all swimming events had to be held outside the city. Judo, Karate and Taekwondo were added to the summer programme. All things considered, the City of Taipei exceeded all expectations:

The first Deaflympics to be held in Asia

- US$200m investment with a return of approx US$25m to the local economy
- 2553 Athletes, 1341 team officials from 77 countries attended
- 21 sports; 20 disciplines; 177 events
- 278,884 spectators attended
- 6193 volunteers (including interpreters)
- WIDEX Fair Play Awarded to Gabor Mathe of Hungary
- Judo, Karate and Taekwondo added to the programme

Congress had to choose between three candidates for President. Ammons requested her name to be withdrawn as it was 'time to move forwards now that ICSD was in good shape". Congress elected its eighth President, Craig Crowley (GBR), who narrowly beat Valery Rukhledev (RUS) with a margin of just one vote. Other elections were Vice President of World Deaf Sport, Josef Wilmerdinger (GER), and Vice President of Deaf Youth Sports, David Lanesman (ISR). Congress noted that there were now 104 nation states as ICSD members.

With the backing of the British Tennis Foundation, the GB tennis squad was able to acclimatise at the Bankok Pantana School in Thailand en route to Taiwan. This acclimatisation training and pre-match practice paid dividends with Sinclair and Graham winning GB's first Deaflympics, Mixed Doubles, gold since 1953 and the first GB tennis gold since 1961.

It was at about this time that weaknesses within the ICSD and Congress began to be exposed. The Deaflympics in Taipei had been an incredible success, the Organising Committee demonstrating huge commitment and passion to the task in hand. However, this success lulled the ICSD into a sense of false security. The monitoring of processes and procedures for awarding host nation status for the Summer and Winter Deaflympics were flawed and, at best, not fit for purpose. This was demonstrated as the Executive Committee failed to grasp the complexities of the economic crisis in Greece and its likely impacts on the Athens Deaflympics. In addition, the ICSD failed to monitor effectively the implementation of the specification for the Deaflympics: venue infrastructures, logistic requirements, media needs and more. When, at the closing ceremony of the Taipei Deaflympics, the ICSD flag was handed over to the Athens OC representative; it was Ammon's body language that startled this observer. Her face was seen to be one of ambiguity and instead of signing the expected 'THUMBS UP" for Athens, she signed "FINGERS CROSSED". Seemingly oblivious, ICSD was heading into a storm largely of its own making.

Extraordinary Congress, Bratislava, Slovakia 12-13 September 2008

Congress was presented with updates on the progress of the forthcoming Winter Deaflympics 2011, in High Tatras in Slovakia. Mr. Ruda, representing the Organising Committee, noted that preparations for the Winter Deaflympics were well advanced. Mr. Mokos, Mayor of High Tatras, read greetings from the President of Slovakia. There had been initial difficulties in obtaining government and National Olympic Committee (NOC) support for these Games, because the government expected to be dealing with a National Deaflympic Committee. Accordingly, it issued an ultimatum to Ruda to form a Slovakian Deaflympic Committee (SDC) or face the threat of the event being organised and managed by the Slovakian Paralympic Committee. After further negotiations, the government and NOC mandated the SDC to oversee the National Deaflympic programme and the 2011 Deaflympic games. This situation clearly indicated a lack of due diligence by the ICSD before allowing bids to be presented to Congress and then awarding contracts to the hosts

The 2013 Athens Summer Deaflympics Organising Committee reported that work was progressing well and that it was expecting to provide an excellent event. A number of high-class venues had been readied to satisfy the requirements of ICSD and national federations.

2010

Since withdrawing from the IPC in 1995, National Deaf Sports Federations (NDSFs) were under threat of assimilation by National Paralympic Committees (NPCs). In March 2010, Craig Crowley and Josef Wilmerdinger met with the FFH (Federation France Handisports) President, Gerard Maison, because the FFH was now the governing Deaf sport under Paralympic auspices, but ICSD statutes required its Federations to be Deaf-lead. This first meeting ended acrimoniously but a resolution was later reached in 2011 with the appointment of a Deaf representative to the FFH Committee. (See further discussion in Chapter 6)

Other problems occurred in Africa, the United Arab Emirates and Botswana, which resulted in countries refusing to give permission for their athletes to enter the Deaflympics. In her 2008 annual report to the IOC, ICSD President Ammons indicated that there were 'five or six' nations who had been mandated to establish National Deaflympic Committees in order to receive full support from their national governments and NOC. Such an estimate by the President in a written document suggests three things: (a) that the ICSD lacked empirical intelligence information; or (b) an indication of NPCs not co-operating with ICSD in the spirit of the ICSD/IPC MoU; or was it (c) a problem brought on by lack of resources available to ICSD, in a way that would have enabled Deaf representatives to provide accurate information?

May 2010: ICSD announced the cancellation of the 2011 Winter Deaflympics, given that the Slovakian Deaflympic Committee was deemed unable to deliver the Winter Deaflympics. ICSD believed that the SDC was not able to provide evidence of adequate funding for the event or give detailed information on the final venue arrangements. Comprehensive quarterly progress reports were late and this, combined with a lack of information about pre-event marketing, informed the ICSD decision.

Months of attrition followed between ICSD and a small number of countries that were expected to compete in Slovakia. ICSD President Craig Crowley was accused by some of making premature decisions and that he lacked the ability to assess properly the ability of organising committees. There was an ensuing campaign of 'no confidence' in the Executive Board, which was carried out amidst a storm of emails, blogs and social media activity. A bid to gain consensus for an Extraordinary Congress to remove the Executive was not supported. However, pressure from both the Slovakians and the Winter Deaflympics participating NDSFs persuaded the Executive to overrule Crowley's decision.

December 2010: ICSD announced that the 2011 Winter Deaflympics were to proceed with the full approval of the ICSD Executive Board and that participant nations were urged to complete their preparations to attend. Tiffany Granfors, the Executive Officer of ICSD stated with confidence:

> *"My recent trip to Slovakia showed me that the organising committee has made great strides in ensuring that all sports venues, lodging facilities, and transportation services will be available during the Winter Deaflympics."*
>
> *"While some financial issues remain for the organising committee,"*

Granfors added,

> *"the average athlete or fan should not notice any difference in the Winter Deaflympics experience. ICSD has developed a reputation of putting on stellar Winter and Summer Deaflympics over the past decade and we wanted to ensure that this tradition continues. I am looking forward to a successful 17th Winter Deaflympics in Slovakia this coming February!"*
>
> (ICSD Press release Dec 2010)

February 2011: ICSD declared the Winter Deaflympics officially cancelled for the second time with less than a week to the opening ceremony and postponed the 43rd Congress to a later date.

May 2011: The serious economic conditions in Greece meant that ICSD had no confidence in the Athens Organising Committee being able to secure confirmation for the 2013 Summer Deaflympics. It therefore sought alternative host cities, anticipating that Athens would withdraw. They also confirmed the withdrawal of Vancouver as hosts for the 2015 Winter Deaflympics.

Barcelona and Buenos Aires announced they were tendering bids for the 2017 Summer Deaflympics to be presented at the next Congress.

> *"ICSD fully understands the concerns of deaf athletes around the world, when it comes to the future of the Deaflympics."*
>
> *"Deaf sport is now faced with some immense challenges, due to decisions made as long as four years ago. The future is uncertain, but one thing is clear: ICSD will need the support of partners throughout the sports world. And we'll need the continued efforts of every ICSD member country in order to overcome these challenges."*
>
> (Crowley)

5 July 2011: The Greek government confirmed its lack of support for 2013 Summer Deaflympics.

> *"Today's decision is deeply disappointing,"*
>
> (Crowley)
>
> *"But the decision is also not a complete surprise, especially given the economic crisis in Greece at the moment. On becoming President, I was deeply concerned about the hosting arrangements for Slovakia, Athens and Vancouver. Our athletes deserve to be able to train with certainty about their future competitions. ICSD is already working on possible alternatives to Athens 2013. ICSD expects to make a formal announcement about alternatives before the end of July."*
>
> (Crowley)

ICSD Congress Rome, Italy. 13-15 September 2011

The delegates from New Zealand reported back via their website on reasons for the cancellations of the Winter Deaflympics and the lessons learnt:

- Mistakes made – no written government support for the Deaflympics; no MoU signed; ICSD inspectors failed to carry our infrastructure checks or to check infrastructural details.
- Ruda in custody awaiting trial on 11 charges.
- Monies could not be reimbursed because legal authorities had frozen bank accounts belonging to Ruda and containing 1.8 million Euros.
- Lessons learnt - any Deaflympics event must have confirmed government support and financial guarantees in place. Thorough inspections are mandatory.

President Ma-Ying-Jeou was a guest at the Congress and announced that Taipei would be bidding for the 2024 Olympics, citing its successful hosting of the 2009 Deaflympics, 2009 World Games and the 2017 Summer Universiade.

2012 - Turkey withdrew its bid for 2013 Deaflympics and instead opted for the 2017 event. The reason given was because it was hosting the 2013 Mediterranean Games and it was felt these would distract from the Deaflympics.

London 2012 – Massive Coverage of the Paralympics, which generated debate on the involvement of deaf people.

26 September 2012 – Bulgarian and Sofia authorities signed a contract with the ICSD to host the 22nd Summer Deaflympics between 26 July – 4 August 2013.

3

Inside CISS – ICSD

Structure of ICSD

At the time of writing, the International Committee of Sports for the Deaf (ICSD) (also known as the *Comité International des Sports des Sourds [CISS]*) is the supreme organisation for the governing of Deaf sports globally. Recognised by the International Olympic Committee (IOC) and a member of SportAccord, it works to develop a range of training and international competition opportunities, which culminate in the Summer and Winter Deaflympics.

An Executive Committee leads the ICSD and comprises a President, Vice President - World Sports, Vice-President- World Youth Sports and two Members at Large, who are elected by the Congress of Full Members (National Deaf Sports Federations) during the Summer and Winter Deaflympics. The Executive also has four non-voting Presidents of the Regional Confederations (Asia/Pacific, Africa, Europe and Pan-America). Its salaried officers report to its Chief Executive.

ICSD liaises and co-ordinates activities with the IOC,

International Paralympic Committee (IPC), SportAccord and other governments and sports organisations to extend opportunities for deaf people to participate in sport. The organisation is currently planning to restructure in order to move in line with The Olympic Charter. These changes are also discussed elsewhere.

The ICSD motto: PER LUDOS AEQUALITAS (Equality through Sport), celebrates the *Spirit of Deaf Sports* where Deaf athletes come together as members of a cultural and linguistic minority to strive to reach the pinnacle of competition. Its mission is in accordance with the United Nations Convention on the Rights of persons with Disabilities, specifically:

> *Article 5 (Equality and non-discrimination) where specific measures, which are necessary to accelerate or achieve de facto equality of persons with disabilities, shall not be considered discrimination under the terms of the present convention*

And

> *Article 30 (Participation in cultural life, recreation, leisure and sport) where persons with disabilities shall be entitled and empowered, on equal basis with others, to recognition and support of their specific cultural and linguistic identity, including sign language and Deaf culture. In addition, countries should take appropriate measures to ensure that persons with disabilities have opportunity to organise, develop and participate in disability-specific sporting and recreational activities and, to this end, encourage the provision, on an equal basis with others, of appropriate instruction, training and resources.*

What sets ICSD apart from other international disability sports organisations of Olympic-status are that, at all levels, it is Deaf-led. The concept of empowerment is central to the ICSD ethos. As an international organisation it also has to address challenges that are unique and specific to the Deaf community: identifying a deaf person by their preferred mode of communication; deliberating as to whether or not Deaf people are a linguistic and cultural minority; or whether they are disabled. In order to maintain the profile of international Deaf sport, ICSD has, from the outset of the CISS, engineered a working relationship with the IOC and latterly, in the past two decades, with the IPC. Before we proceed further with that, we must examine three fundamental concepts concerning the unique position of the ICSD to date: Empowerment; Sign Language; and the concept of Disability.

Empowerment (Self-Determination)

The IOC has never been comfortable with the concept of segregated sport. In the 1980s they had challenged the Special Olympics on the 'segregated nature of its program delivery' (Orelove & Wood 1984; Orelove & Moon 1984) and the IOC has suggested to the ICSD that, by advocating self-determination for Deaf people and constitutionally insisting upon Deaf sport being Deaf-led, that the organisation is discriminating against able-bodied people and that this is counter-productive to the inclusion of disabled people in society (IOC 2009). In contrast, many international and national development organisations (Handicap International, Sport for Development and Peace) recognise that sport is one of the best ways to empower disabled people. In my opinion, Eugene Rubens-Alcais should be credited with this concept, instead of Guttmann as accredited by Espagnac (1986:134-135). It was Rubens-Alcais's initiative and drive, as a disabled person along with Antoine Dresse, that saw the federation of national Deaf sports organisations emerge and which served as a catalyst to unite young deaf people internationally; so that, through sport, they were able to develop their self-esteem and self-confidence, which in turn gave them the power, authority and strength to advocate for themselves and others, both within and outside of sport in wider society.

At the end of the 19th and on the cusp of the 20th century, when Rubens-Alcais formulated his vision, disabled people faced huge obstacles to integration. Sport was seen as a means to reduce stigma and tackle discrimination (UN 2011). Fosshaug (2004) argues that empowerment for Deaf people still requires a fusion of both the Deaf sport and majority sport experience; a collaborative experience, where there is a level of integration that enables Deaf individuals to function without losing control of their own destiny. Thus they must have the freedom of choice to decide how much integration or segregation they personally need. This point is illustrated from the perspective of Paralympians in Chapter 7.

Stewart (1991a) explains how social systems and civil society, since the 1800s, have gradually taken over and dominated all the major decision aspects of Deaf people's lives. The majority of deaf children are born into hearing families and therefore parents make decisions about their child's education in collaboration with education professionals who are non-deaf. Medical decisions and all other social welfare, employment, and government policy decisions are made with no reference to the deaf perspective. Stewart argued that Deaf people advocate self-determination and Deaf leadership for Deaf sport, because it is one of the last Deaf social institutions where they have true control. The opportunities to be an international-level coach, administrator and leader are attainable to Deaf individuals within Deaf sport and thus provide them with the opportunity to reach and maximise their potentials (Stewart 1991a: 4). Handicap International advocates the view that, if potential is not achieved, it may lead to further loss of motivation, self-esteem and increase the poverty and isolation of the disabled person concerned (Right to Play 2008).

Over time, non-deaf people in positions of power in international sport and government – both local and national – have misunderstood self-determination. Likewise, politics advocating the Deaf community as a linguistic minority in society have permeated into Deaf sport in such a way as to hinder the Deaflympic Movement. The concept of self-determination in relation to inclusion and collaborative leadership is covered later in this book.

The Oral V Sign Language Debate

Chapter 1 described how the philosophy of educating deaf children has centred around the debate that either speaking and listening (Oralism) or Sign Language are the best methods of teaching, thus developing the skills required to make an effective contribution to society. This is made complex because Deafness covers a wide spectrum: from those who have a mild deafness, usually the inability to hear high frequency sounds, but are still able to hear normal speech and to communicate orally; to those who are profoundly deaf and are not able to hear speech or sound and for whom sign language is the most effective form of communication.

It is only in the last 20 years that educationalists around the world have come to accept that the decision in 1880 to outlaw sign language was fundamentally wrong, and there is now a growing acceptance that sign language should be made widely available.

The CISS was created in the aftermath of Milan 1880 (the abolishment of Sign Language in education) and the International Silent Games (ISG) were seen as a platform for self-determination and self-preservation against the stigmatisation of sign language, in such a way that Deaf Sport became synonymous as a societal construct for people who used sign language and, therefore, predominantly those who are severely/ profoundly deaf.

The 1970s saw further changes and developments in educational policy for disabled children and continued advancement in paediatric medicine and hearing aid technology. All of this resulted in an ever greater number of deaf young people, who are eligible to be Deaflympic athletes, yet who are not sign language users or described as culturally Deaf.

In a global society where speech is the dominant means of communication, it is obvious that those who are profoundly deaf, and who use sign language as their first language, are likely to have fewer opportunities in education and employment. Consequently, leaders of Deaf sport have struggled to strike a balance to ensure sport remains accessible to those in greatest need, whilst accepting that increasing numbers of oral-deaf could naturally outnumber and thus marginalise sign language users. In 1979, the eligibility classification for Deaflympic athletes was introduced, which specified that, in order to compete within international Deaf sport, a hearing loss of 55dB or greater in the better ear is required. Later, the rule to prohibit the wearing of hearing aids and cochlear implants during competitions was introduced in 1983 – to ensure a level playing field for Deaf athletes.

Stewart and Ammons (2001) observed that they foresaw society changing further with the impact of mainstreaming in schools and that Deaf sport would need to adapt too, so that it reflected the language profile of the Deaf community with its unique mix of sign language and oral modes.

Deafness as a disability v Deafness as a linguistic minority

In order to govern Deaf sport effectively, the CISS/ICSD had to address the challenge of identifying Deaf sport as either part of disability sport or as a stand-alone cultural and linguistic entity. Later, Chapters 9, 10 and 14 examine deafness in detail and in terms of how it can impact upon an athlete's performance in sport and how deafness itself is socially and culturally different from other disabilities.

In Chapter 1, it was mentioned how the study of Deaf sport history has been limited by the scarcity of written records kept by Deaf people. Indeed, it has only been since the mid 1990s that the study of deafness as a cultural concept has been properly studied as an academic concern. Paddy Ladd (2003) has been a leading researcher in this field, developing the concept and entity of 'Deafhood'. The definition of 'Deafhood' is centred upon the notion of Deaf people as a linguistic and cultural minority who should be classed with, and administered by, political and other agencies concerned with minority languages. It is therefore believed that Deaf people do not consider themselves to be disabled.

Breivik et al (2002) discussed how the concept of the social and medical models of deafness played their role in relation to the classification mark of 55dB, as cultural Deaf people would consider this method of identifying an individual as being one that is 'oppressing' outside the realms of sport (Breivik et al 2002:33-34). During CISS deliberations, the suggestions of defining a person as being socially deaf were ambiguous and therefore it was necessary to use the audiometer as it was more objective (Stewart 1991a: 23). It is argued later that this is where CISS/ICSD has struggled with its case when trying to raise the profile of Deaf sport in the face of IPC dominance.

Working with IOC

The CISS/ICSD relationship with the IOC began when it was identified that the International Silent Games (ISG) were not a one-off event and that there was a Deaf-led movement that would gather increasing momentum and importance. According to the CISS (2001) the first formal contact was a reception arranged by the IOC to honour CISS during the CISS Congress in May 1951 and this was followed up by the IOC recognising the CISS as an 'International Federation with Olympic standing' in 1955. for this to have happened, there needs to have been some deeper form of relationships between IOC members and the CISS. According to Bailey (2008) the IOC recognition of CISS was down to the 'lengthy and regular communication' between Robey Burns (CISS) and Avery Brundage (IOC). For his research, Bailey had full access to IOC documentation and correspondence in IOC and IPC archives, but his work only offers the cursory acknowledgement. My own search elaborates further in Chapter 12.

It seems the CISS leadership had untoward expectations of IOC. Gold & Gold (2007:109) regarded the Deaflympics as a vehicle for the 'possibilities' of working closely with the IOC, but the CISS decided to remain independent, with its Deaf autonomy retained, rather than merge into the Paralympic Movement.

This book chronicles the struggle CISS/ICSD faced as it sought to be recognised as a movement of equal standing to the IPC. It has been only as recently as 2007, under the leadership of Ammons (USA), that the ICSD established an internal commission to bring ICSD up to date on the IOC principles. Titled *Deaf Sport Reform* (ICSD 2008), this included a proposal for a Youth programme to deal with the declining numbers of young people taking part in Deaf sport and the Deaflympics – a problem highlighted by Stewart almost a decade earlier as an important factor in the future sustainability of the World Games for the Deaf (WGD). A change of ICSD Presidency in 2009 saw Craig Crowley (GBR) take over the stewardship of driving the *Deaf Sport Reform* initiative forward and to continue the enhancement of the ICSD relationship with the IOC. At the ICSD 2011 Congress in Rome, Crowley outlined five important points to drive ICSD forwards:

- Sport FIRST
- STRONGER Deaflympics
- MORE Opportunities
- MORE Visibility and Partnerships
- BETTER member of the Olympic Movement.

Working with the IPC

Since 2009, there has been concern from some quarters of the Deaflympic Movement that Crowley has been forcing Deaf Sport towards a closer relationship with the IPC and to an eventual merger into the Paralympics. However, there are also a number of commentators, who hold the view that this is the inevitable way forward and that the CISS should never have resigned from the IPC in the first instance. It should be noted that under the leadership of Ammons, the ICSD and the IPC had already signed up to a 'final agreement' in 1990 (see p93), updated in a 2004 Memorandum of Understanding (see p109).

This book demonstrates, with references, how this MoU has worked in practice and will suggest that subsequent decision-making and public comments by both parties have not been helpful to the Deaflympic Movement. Section 3 will also tackle the public debate about whether or not deaf people should be allowed to compete in the Paralympics. Some people have perceived the ICSD and its athletes of having an argument with no foundation and that there is a deliberate unwillingness to work collaboratively with the IPC (AoHL Forum 2012).

4

The Deaflympics Today

The Deaflympics are the original and purest form of Disabled Sport and the highest form of multi-sport event, of Olympic standing, for Disabled people. Those already familiar with the Deaflympics and those new to the subject will now be aware from reading previous chapters, that the Deaflympics are wholly governed, managed and delivered by an organisation and committees that are Deaf-led. In other words, they provide and deliver the ultimate empowerment role model for disabled people. There are those within the Paralympic Movement who have attempted to attain such power but have found that their ideals and their concerns are overlooked by the non-disabled, within a hierarchy of importance which governs the priorities of the Paralympic Movement, a movement which itself claims to represent the best interest of disabled people (Howe 2008:52-55).

The International Committee of Sports for the Deaf (ICSD) gives the highest level of opportunity for disabled people to govern sport according to the principles of Olympism. However, decisions made by the International Olympic Committee

(IOC) have frustrated the ICSD in furthering these ideals and providing the 'possibilities' so required. The ICSD's recent public announcement to change its vision of *Athletes first, Deaf second*, is in fact nothing new; and, historically, forces outside Deaf Sport have dominated and diverted attention away from the elite Deaf athlete.

The classification of Deaflympic athletes and the concept of a level playing field are discussed in Section 3, where I also explore beyond the notion that Deaf people require very little modification to respective Rules and Laws of sport. I will be demonstrating how the development of classifications and regulations governing technology have also established the Deaflympics as the event that provides the purest test of the ability of a disabled person to compete in sport.

Each edition of the Deaflympics is organised by a host National Deaf Sport Federation (NDSF) after their successful bid for the event. The respective NDSF then forms a Company/Board specifically to organise and manage the Deaflympics on the NDSF's behalf. The Company/Board is responsible for raising funds and seeking sponsorship support to ensure the Deaflympics are held at an elite level as required by ICSD regulations. In some instances governments, in partnership with the NDSF, play a key role in both the operation and delivery of the Deaflympics. Mainstream national and local sporting organisations are enlisted to assist with the running of the composite Deaflympic events. The involvement of hearing government and hearing sports officials necessitates a high level of sign language interpreting to assist them in effectively communicating with Deaf officials and athletes.

Visual presentation of information for both athletes and visitors is a critical part of the Deaflympics infrastructure and ordinarily includes the use of video screens, captioning and information boards. A visual environment is clearly and very obviously critical for communication with Deaf athletes, officials and spectators. (Ammons 2008)

Critics suggest that the Deaflympics and its athletes do not deserve to be given equal status to that of the Paralympics, because the social and economic potential of the Deaflympics can never match that of the Paralympics. I can now challenge this by demonstrating how the 2009 Taiwan Deaflympics enabled the Taiwanese political authorities to further their own social, economic and political agendas. The ICSD has further interests beyond the hosting of events, with its notable success being the empowerment and integration of deaf and hearing women in sport. Being a Deaf-led concern has allowed the Deaflympics to evolve a participation framework that presents an optimum model of inclusion and one that positively encompasses women.

Taiwan 2009 – "Power In Me"

Professor Tsung-Min Hung of the National Taiwan Normal University gave a post-Deaflympics presentation on the Impact of the Deaflympics on Taiwan. The following information is taken from the PowerPoint he used (Hung n.d.). Professor Hung's connections to the Olympics began in 1991 when he was a delegate to the International Olympic Authority and in 1992 when he was a coach at the 1992 Paralympics. He is also a sports psychology consultant for Taiwanese Olympic athletes and a member of the International Affairs Commission of the Chinese Taipei Sports Association (CTOC).

Having failed to obtain the hosting rights for any major World-Class sports events, the Taiwanese government decided that they would work with the Chinese Taipei Sports Association for the Deaf (CTSAD) to bid for the 21st Summer Deaflympics. All of this was aimed at revitalising the morale and confidence of the people of Taiwan. CTSAD had successfully hosted the Deaf Asia-Pacific Games in 2000 and members warmly encouraged the bid for the 21st Deaflympics. By hosting the event, CTSAD wanted to show the world the capability of Taiwan to host a major event and to create a new image for the deaf with resultant increased public respect and acceptance of deafness.

The first part of the bid process was to secure the support of the National Sport Authorities: The Sports Affairs Council, The Chinese Taipei Olympic Committee and the host city's government, Taipei. They took advice and encouragement from ICSD President John Lovett[4], who visited Taipei on a fact-finding tour and prepared a bid for the 38th ICSD Congress in Sundsvall, Sweden. With 84 votes available, Taipei won with 52 votes; against 32 for Athens. The design of the 2009 Deaflympics emblem was a combination of the Chinese character for north, representing the host city Taipei, an ear representing the Deaflympics and a figure representing the athletes. The 2009 mascot was a Taipei green tree frog, the tiniest of Taiwan's indigenous species of frog with a remarkable ability to jump long distances.

In order to become a more friendly and welcoming city for visitors, the Taipei City Government implemented a campaign titled *'5 no, 3 ok'* to encourage drivers to respect pedestrians. The 5 'no's' (being) no honking, no speeding, no passing, no illegal parking and no hurry. The 3 'ok's' were zero casualties, zero accidents and zero injuries. The public transport system received a number of environmental enhancements and sign language provision was made available via video link on the MRT train system. Bus drivers received training in using sign language. The Taipei City government also worked with regional government departments to improve the standards of hotels and to ensure reception arrangements were as inclusive as possible.

Links were forged between 81 of the city's elementary and junior schools and 80 of the visiting nations as a way of building relationships between the younger generations of hosts and

---

[4] John Lovett (d. 30.10.03) Australian, ICSD President 1995 - 2003

visitors alike. Prior to the event, the Department of Culture also held arts performances and events to market the Deaflympics. This culminated in an International Deaf Festival that lasted for the whole duration of the Games and was aimed at helping people understand the intricacies of Deaf culture.

Professor Hung's own assessment was that the Taiwan Deaflympics were a huge success; with 80 participant nations in attendance with 2553 athletes, 1341 team officials, 20 sports in 177 events and 6193 volunteers in support. Hosting the event not only enabled all deaf people to enjoy the diverse sporting excitement on offer, but also enabled the Deaf community to bask under one communal spotlight. By demonstrating their coordinating and organising ability to the world at large, Deaf people were able to enjoy increased recognition and status as never before, as more and more hearing people began to understand and enjoy the uniqueness of Deaf culture.

The success of the home team added further value to the Taiwanese experience as they won 11 gold medals, 11 silver and 11 bronzes, retaining 5th place on the rankings table. In 2005, they had won 9 Gold medals, 4 silver and 3 bronzes taking fifth place on the medals table.

The Department of Culture (DOC) reported event attendances and visitor numbers that exceeded all expectations. Some 12,000 spectators attended the Deaflympics in 2005; whereas in Taiwan, over 250,000 witnessed the full spectacle. Emile Sheng, CEO of the DOC, pointed out that the real 'gold' in staging the event was not connected to medals or to even the generation of a financial profit; but rather it was about raising Taiwan's international profile, initiating a regeneration of Taipei City and, for the country's leading businesses, showcasing their products and services. The DOC estimated the cost of staging the best Summer Deaflympics to date to be approximately US$200m, with most of the money coming from local and central government funding. Support was received from 40 partners and the fourteen sponsors contributed over US$4.34m. The Taipei City government estimated that the Deaflympics generated US$25m for the local economy.

During the event, the DOC and the Bureau of Foreign Trade, under the Ministry of Economic Affairs, worked together to showcase 21 of Taiwan's top brands at the Deaf Culture – Taiwan Excellence exhibition. These included Aiptek, Giant, Penpower Technology, SportsArt Fitness and Transcend. As Tony Phoo, an economist with Standard Chartered Bank Taiwan PLC, observed;

> ***"Taiwan has long been seen primarily as a supplier of electronics components. This will change after the nation's socioeconomic development is displayed for all to see."***
>
> (In Brisebois 2009)

Building on the success of the Deaflympics, the City of Taipei has since gone on to win the bid to host the 2017 Universiade and is now preparing a bid to host the 2024 Olympics.

Deaf Gain

Writing in 1991, Stewart (1991a) explained that Deaf Sport does not threaten mainstream sport and that both can work together, but it is inevitable that Deaf sport would struggle to compete for money, space, research, sponsors and spectators (Stewart1991a: 96). I recommend that the ICSD examine what the Deaflympics and Deaf sport in general have to offer in return for the support it needs. It is my belief that the offer is the concept of *Deaf Gain*.

Deaf Gain was originally a concept tabled by Aaron Williamson who described his experiences when he found himself losing his hearing. When he went to consult with doctors they all told him that he was *losing his hearing*. Yet he wondered why not one of them told him that he was *gaining his deafness*. To Bauman & Murray (2009) *Deaf Gain* is about re-presenting deafness as a form of sensory and cognitive diversity that has the potential to contribute to the greater good of humanity. Using sign language, there are three signs for *Deaf Gain*, the first being DEAF INCREASE, which expresses the opposite of hearing loss. The second is DEAF BENEFIT, indicating that deafness is not just a loss but a benefit as well. The third is DEAF CONTRIBUTE, which considers all the ways that deaf people contribute to mankind.

Deaf people have a visual based language; a well developed peripheral vision; a greater ability to form quick mental images; and better facial recognition skills. Deaf people are visually orientated to the world around them (Bahan 2008). We all have our own unique ways of understanding the world around us and we all have different learning styles. One example to illustrate this is Bauman & Murray's (2009:6) description of how the Swiss national snowboarding team hired a Deaf coach to teach the junior national team. The coach realised that the snowboarders were listening to the sound of the board cutting into the snow to tell whether or not they were making the quickest stops and the sharpest turns possible. Not satisfied with their reliance on auditory cues, the coach had all his athletes practice with earplugs. Depriving them of their usual sensory feedback, they were forced to depend upon the feel of the snow beneath their boards. This progressive approach saw a dramatic improvement in the snowboarders' performance.

The Deaflympics demonstrates the cultural diversity of Transnationalism (Bauman & Murray 2009:6), where culture is not a fixed referent to one locality but rather a fluid process, shaped by multiple human interactions. For example, when Deaf people assemble for the Deaflympics they are able to strike up instant and complex conversations using improvised international sign language. *Deaf Gain* helps people establish these bonds with each other. For instance, when two Deaf people engage in conversation whilst walking down a street, the first person who is signing also looks ahead for obstacles in order for the second person to concentrate on the signing, with complete trust in the signer, who is looking out for their safety. If Deaf people took over the field of architecture there would be a revolution in building design. All rooms would be open to light with a proliferation of round tables so that everyone can see and follow conversation.

Returning to the snowboarding example, coaches could consider the perception of how we coach in sport and whether, in fact, we can improve our performances by being less reliant on listening and better at using our senses or non-verbal communication. Would starting lights for Olympic sprinters produce faster times?

Breivik, Haualand and Solvang (2002), researchers from Bergen University, carried out a fieldwork exercise during the 2001 Deaflympics in Rome. Their work, entitled *Rome - A Temporary Deaf City!*, provides some interesting observations. One in particular was that waiters without any formal training became adept at interacting with Deaf customers and taking their restaurant orders. Initially, they were observed to be confused and puzzled when dealing with Deaf customers and tended to shout out numbers or questions. Yet within a few days, their non-verbal skills had improved dramatically; they showed gesticulated prices with their fingers, and used pen and paper when gestures failed (Breivik et al 2002:20-21).

The Mayor of Rome suggested in his welcome pack that the presence of the 'physically disadvantaged' in Rome was an 'occasion for all of us to enrich our moral luggage' (Breivik et al 2002:20). For two weeks, the city was transformed into a 'Deaf Village' leading to much discussion about deafness and the issues of Deaf culture and sign language, all of which prompted incisive moral debate on how best to change oneself for the better and how minorities, such as the deaf, could be both understood and helped. Indeed, this impact manifested in 2009 when all the preparations put in place by the Taipei City government before the Deaflympics - the promotion of Sign Language, Deaf awareness training for municipal services staff, bus drivers and other service support workers - led to many deaf people describing Taipei as a city that felt 'safe'.

With Salt Lake City 2007, the Chief Operating Officer described the Deaflympics as a valuable learning experience for the City authorities and the Park City Mountain Resort (Gorrell 2007). Interestingly, whilst the ICSD is constitutionally a Deaf-led organisation and, as far as possible, all the participant sport Technical Directors are Deaf, the last four Deaflympics have been headed up by non-deaf Chief Operating Officers.

In Russia, the nation that dominates the Deaflympics medals table, the President of the Centre for Paralympics Sports stated that victory in the Deaflympics brings attention and visibility to disability sport in Russia and that the athletes are unquestionably the 'pride' of Russia (RCDS 2009).

Dean Barton-Smith, (AUS) credits his first experience at the 1985 Deaflympics as life changing. It set him on course to the 1992 Olympics and the 1990 and 1994 Commonwealth Games (Paxinos 2005c). John Lovett, ICSD President 1995-2003, always sought to remind administrators and decision makers of the value of the Deaflympics and that they were a vital pathway along which deaf competitors could access the Olympics.[5]

---

[5] CISS, Meeting Notes with the IOC- 26th June 1995 page 2

SECTION 2

Why are the Deaf Not in the Paralympics?

"At the Olympics, I experienced the beauty of color of many nations flags, TV camera, flashing lights, huge street and stadiums turnouts, spectator's screams and their hand and facial expressions while I competed as a lone deaf walker, and at the World games I was always the happiest man because I could freely converse and socalize with any foreign deaf athlete"

(Gerhard Sperling, in Ammons and Eikman 2011:1155)

5

Dusseldorf 1989 – key decisions – were CISS right?

Dusseldorf 1989

A major landmark in disability sport took place on 21st September 1989, when a meeting, brokered by the International Olympic Committee (IOC), brought together the Comité International des Sports des Sourds (CISS) and the International Co-ordinating Committee (ICC) for Wheelchair, Amputee, Blind and Cerebral Palsy sport. Everyone present agreed to work through a set of conditions that would form the International Paralympic Committee (IPC). But after a few years, the CISS, with the support of the IOC, withdrew. Consequently, there is no classification for deaf athletes in the Paralympics. In this Section of four chapters, I answer the question *'Why are the Deaf not in the Paralympics?'* And in this chapter I start by discussing whether or not the CISS took the right decision to withdraw from the IPC.

Why was the meeting called, and what were the motives of the IOC?

By the late 1970s, it was becoming difficult for the International Stoke Mandeville Games Federation (ISMGF) to control the development of international sport for their disabled athletes, with their four main disability-specific sport groups all vying to get IOC recognition that had already been given to the CISS in 1955.

After the Arnhem ISMGF Games in 1982, the International Organisations of Sports for the Disabled (IOSDs), namely the Cerebral Palsy CP-ISRA; Blind IBSA; Disabled ISOD and Stoke Mandeville Wheelchair Games Federation ISMWGF, established the International Co-ordinating Committee of the World Sports Organisation (ICC). The ICC had two aims; firstly, to effectively organise and co-ordinate international sport for the disabled and, secondly, to form a united voice in negotiations with the IOC. Its main purpose was to organise the Paralympics in the same host city as the Olympics. The ICC Chairman, Robert Steadward, also lobbied for the IOC to include the disabled in the Olympics and set up the CIAD (Commission for the Inclusion of Athletes with a Disability). The IOC President, Antonio Samaranch, who had established a very good working relationship with the CISS and its President, Jerald Jordan, now found himself dealing with the newly emergent ICC and increasing demands for support from both the CISS and the ICC. Some members of the ICC, including Steadward and Merklinger, were insistent that the CISS was 'wooed' to join ICC so that it could be truly representative of all disabled sports federations (Bailey 2008: 50). John Grant of the ISMGF believed that the ICC would greatly increase its chances of obtaining IOC membership if it could persuade CISS to join (Bailey 2008: 71)

On the 14th March 1987, at Arnhem in the Netherlands, the IOC tabled the proposal that a new inclusive organisation be formed. This organisation would include representatives from all nations that ran sport for the disabled as well as the IOSDs. It also wanted to give athletes a voice in issues such as governance. This all worked very much in Samaranch's favour as he wished to see the IOC dealing with one, all embracing, international organisation.

After a successful Paralympics in Seoul, the ICC and national and IF representatives met in Dusseldorf in September 1989; and it was here that the IPC was established. Samaranch had persuaded Jordan to bring in the CISS as a founder member, because he wished to see a united body; and the CISS, in turn, was convinced that an umbrella body would be of benefit to disabled and Deaf sport.

Why did the CISS withdraw?

The CISS joined the ICC on condition that it would continue to organise the World Games for the Deaf, until at some point a new way forward could be found. According to Ammons (1990) it was the CISS who were was instrumental in getting the name of the collective organisations changed to the IPC. All this was aimed at positioning Deaf sport to remain self-governing. Unease occurred immediately and in 1990, Ammons went to lobby at the IPC Executive Congress in Holland, to ensure that it did not assume jurisdiction over international sport for the Deaf (Ammons 1990). On the 16th July 1990, the IPC Executive Congress approved a 'final agreement' between CISS and IPC in which:

1. IPC grants full recognition to CISS as supreme authority for sports for and of deaf people.
2. IPC accepts and acknowledges the CISS World Games for the Deaf (both Summer and Winter) as international events of status equal to the Paralympic Games.
3. The IPC shall direct the affiliated national federations to recognise and respect the autonomy and independence

of national deaf sports federations. The IPC shall also encourage governments to recognise and respect the autonomy and independence of national deaf sports federations.

4. The IPC shall not accept membership in the IPC of a national federation purporting to represent deaf people unless such federation has been recognised by the CISS.
5. Because of the unique nature and relationship of CISS with the IPC, any negotiations with representatives of international bodies, such as IOC, UN, IFSD, GAISF (SportAccord), etc., shall include a member nominated by CISS.
6. In the event of establishing a permanent secretariat, the IPC shall set aside adequate space for CISS to relocate its secretariat. The annual fee will be mutually agreed upon. CISS secretariat shall have access to necessary services available to the IPC.
7. Disbursement of funds in the name of sports for the disabled shall be shared with CISS on a proportionate basis. The proportion or formula shall be negotiated between CISS and the IPC Executive Committee.

After four years, and frustrated by the difficulties of building relationships with other members of the IPC, the CISS began to question the validity of its membership. In August 1993, the 33rd Congress of the CISS established an investigation team and directed them to (a) ask the IPC six questions in relation to possible participation in the Paralympics and (b) to meet with the IOC and review the CISS's membership of the IPC.

In November 1993, Jordan and Sondergaard met with Samaranch and Troger of the IOC, who requested a deferral on the decision to withdraw until after the CISS 34th Congress, which would enable matters to be discussed by its national association members. Meanwhile, according to the CISS, the IPC never replied to the six questions. The CISS Executive met in 1994 and prepared a proposal to the 34th Congress to discontinue membership of the IPC.

During the weekend of 12th/13th March 1995, a Congress workshop debated membership of the IPC and Hans Lindstrom of the IPC and Walther Troger of the IOC gave presentations. The final decision to withdraw went to a vote of 96 delegates. The result was 71 to discontinue membership and 25 abstentions. This decision was related to CISS membership of the IPC and not the NDSFs membership of NPCs, which could remain, as they so desired. It was agreed that the CISS and IPC Presidents would meet from time to time and would also invite each other to Congress.

Ammons and Eickman (2011) reflected on the decision to withdraw:

- That accepting a reduction from 19 summer disciplines to perhaps only three or five Deaf events as part of the Paralympic programme was *not a sacrifice worth taking (p1156)*
- The IPC would not be able to afford the bill of providing sign language interpreters, which was approximated to be US$3m (p1156)
- The ethos of self-determination was paramount and many wanted the ICSD and the Deaflympics to remain self-governed *by its constituents as a opposed to being managed by an outside group on their behalf* (p1157)

It was Jordan's final Congress as President, and so it fell to his successor, the Australian John Lovett, to write formally to the IOC and IPC to tender withdrawal and explain the reasons why.

On 26th June 1995, Lovett met with Samaranch and outlined the reasons for withdrawing, making a number of proposals for moving forward:

- Resignation from the IPC occurred because it was 'difficult/impossible' to get understanding/co-operation from the other organisations and their executive committee members.
- That the IOC and CISS continue to work together to deliver a WGD event that would be a pathway for individuals wishing to compete at the Olympics.
- The pathway would also develop national sports leadership and skills development.
- That CISS sought the support of the IOC to promote Deaf sport globally - "Equality Through Sport".

The ICSD pushed for the 1990 'final agreement', as a means of influencing the NOCs and the NPCs to accept the autonomy of the IPC and ICSD and resolve conflicts at national level, and also to ensure that IPC negotiations with the IOC included a representative of CISS. However, during the next Olympic quadrennium, the IOC/IPC relationship grew stronger and the Organising Committee of the Sydney Olympics 2000 took a lead in organising the Paralympics, in partnership with the IPC. In 2001, the IOC and IPC signed a new Treaty that included shared IOC/IPC responsibility for the marketing, media, licensing and sponsorship of the Olympic and Paralympics.

Had the CISS made the right decision to leave the IPC? Should it have remained within the fold and tried to work things out? This discussion continues here by encompassing public comment and critique.

Was it the right decision to withdraw from the IPC?

No, it was wrong to put Deaf culture before Sport

"There was such an opportunity lost when the Deaf refused to drop the Deaflympics for participation in the Paralympics, which as we saw yesterday (London 2012 Opening Ceremony) is a prime platform to promote disability and Deaf sport, and the Deaflympics as per the UK is a dead duck now, since UK Sport withdrew funding so they could train properly. We saw some Deaf sports people going to Japan to train, and in the USA some being given food parcels. Venue-wise they have hit real issues and getting funds, so the standard is dropping even further too. It's great to have a culture; it is not great when that culture prevents you from pursuing sport at the highest level. But for the dogmatic view of Deaf sport hierarchy, we could have been watching Deaf sporting participants today, not a few signing singers and a kid's integrated choir, and younger deaf would see more point in doing sport. The Olympics embraces all cultures and all languages, but the Deaf seem determined they are not going to be one of them and want to go it alone. It is a shame really for those deaf dedicated to sport. Deaf participation is virtually token that's all."

(Action on Hearing Loss [AoHL] Forum)

"I have been critical, not of Deaf sports people but certainly their sporting body, who have just played cultural politics to the exclusion of participation. There is doubt Deaflympians could even qualify alongside disabled now, as the access excuses are being openly challenged. They have had 15 years to challenge Sport UK (sic) to put up and haven't."

(AoHL Forum)

No, it was the wrong decision. Not trusting others, was not a good decision

"Well at the time I remember that there was a lot of distrust of hearing people. That is what was behind an apparently irrational decision. As you know, when deaf and hearing people mix on a project the deaf ones often do not get listened to and generally get left out. So at the time there was such a high level of distrust that the decision was made to go it alone. I think it was the wrong one.

They should have got into the Paralympic movement and kept making a fuss until someone took notice. But then again at the time the Paralympics were poorly funded and not really well supported. Suddenly, due to the power of the Great God TV it's a major thing, starting at Beijing and going exponential this week."

(AoHL Forum)

No, because withdrawing is not necessarily protecting the Deaf community

'The international Deaf community has not been growing 'she dies a little'. Most of the deaf in the developed world now have cochlea implants, do they need interpreters?'

(in Bernd 2012)

"Tradition is worthy. On the other hand, nothing is constant as change. The connection to the Paralympics would create a degree of "PR" for the deaf, as the Paralympics are broadcast on major networks. There are still many misconceptions about deafness' (in Bernd 2012), suggesting that the PR of deaf within the Paralympics will do more to deal with misconceptions of deafness.

It was a decision made in 1989 when the world was different; we now have a new generation of deaf people

"Deaf people are sometimes stuck between a rock and a hard place. Sometimes not of their own doing. Regarding the lack of Paralympic funding or lack of deaf participants - the younger deaf sports generation needs to be told why this is so in the first place as the decision to separate from the Paralympics and have their own Games, did not involve them. Let them have their choice. They do not need to start protesting etc. The older generation, just needs to be reminded that their decision to separate caused their funding to cease. It would be fantastic to participate in the Paralympics AND have their own Deaflympics Games. What's wrong with that? One would be a better sportsperson, in all senses."

(AoHL Forum)

We cannot say it is a wrong decision because times have changed and things could have been different

"Had the IPC been established before the CISS, I suspect they'd have already categorised Deaf / HI and not only under the current additional disabilities - as for those who competed within the CP classifications. Methinks main issue is communication within, and wanting to organise under the same facility and not as an afterthought (using speech-to-sign interpreters). Personally I think the deaf should lobby to become a part of the Paras but with Deaf organisers as in a slightly separate arm of the umbrella organisation. Majority of the Deaf around the world have experienced negative discrimination indirectly or otherwise, so understandable is the desire to perform as a collective on an equal footing, recognition by peers is that powerful."

(AoHL Forum)

Yes, it is the right decision; otherwise you create an unequal competition.

> *It would have been unfair for the blind and deaf to race with athletes wearing prosthetics. The wheelchair athletes have to have their own events to make it fair.*
>
> (German Deaf sports website)

Yes, it is the right decision to protect Deaf culture

> *"Deaf people are now living in a world as full time listeners. It is only with each other that they do not feel hindered. It is not that different from some other disabilities but in the Paralympics the obstruction would be there. The Deaflympics is its own little world where no one is virtually disabled."*
>
> (Bernd 2012)

Yes, it was correct, because of the relationships within the IPC at the time (1989 - 1995)

In his meetings with Samaranch, Lovett explained that Jerald Jordan had found it 'impossible/ very difficult" to build relationships with other members of the IPC. (CISS, 1995). Howe (2008) verified the difficulties that faced the CISS, as the IOSDs, all of which were led by able-bodied volunteers, had already ordered themselves into a hierarchy of importance according to disabilities. When the IPC was formed, officials within the ISMGF manoeuvred themselves into the most influential posts and these machinations continued before and during the Seoul Paralympics in 1988. Howe describes how in 1989, a major political shift occurred as the IOSDs, (of which the CISS was one) became disempowered and disenfranchised.

Rebecca Hussain, writing in June 2012, described the confusion around the withdrawal, some believing that the ICSD wanted to leave and others saying that actually they were pushed out. Her article also states that the deaf were able to participate in the Paralympics at that time (Hussain 2012). The truth is, however, that nothing was ever discussed or drawn up and discussions never ever got to that point. It is quite conceivable that able-bodied people in positions of power may have politically marginalised the Deaf representatives in the IPC. Sherrill & Williams (in Howe 2008:31) and others suggest that there is a pecking order for the different disability groups, in terms of who has the right to be involved in disability sport. At the time (1980s-90s), marginalisation of the 'less able' was ubiquitous within the Paralympic movement itself, and this hierarchical attitude of who is worthy – and who is not - manifested itself when there was resentment about the inclusion of INAS-FID Intellectual Disabilities athletes at the Atlanta 1996 Paralympics (in Howe 2008:31). Today, some non-deaf disabled people still harbour negative opinions of deaf people and vice versa.

It is my opinion, based on Bailey (2008: 75) that the voting arrangements within the ICC meant that the CISS had very little to gain from its membership because the real agenda of the ICC was the creation of the Paralympic Games or which CISS did not want a part. Furthermore, when joining the ICC, the CISS did so from the perspective that it regarded the ICC as an umbrella body representing the different disabilities and not as a body solely representing the Paralympic Games. Jordan wrote *'the mouths kept saying ICC and the world kept meaning Paralympics'* (in Bailey 2008: 82) This subject has to be dealt with if there is to be a movement towards bringing the deaf athletes back into the Paralympics. In 2012, Craig Spence, Director of Communications for the IPC, was asked for his opinions. He claimed that the reasons for the CISS withdrawal were unclear and if the ICSD wanted to, they would have to re-apply for membership. According to Hussein, Spence claims that the IPC were often made out to be the 'bad guys' in this situation. (Hussein 2012)

Yes, it was correct, there was no real effort to empower disabled people at the time

Deaf people experience a weakened sense of empowerment when they meet with little understanding from hearing people in disabled sport (Fosshaug 2004). Hearing people misunderstand what is needed in order to integrate deaf people. The ICC would not cover the costs of sign language interpreters at its meetings (Bailey 2008:71) and the CISS was expected to meet its own cost for this, The IPC still does not provide communication support for its deaf athletes.

At the outset, the IPC went to great lengths to stress that it was an athlete-centred organisation, with their best interests at heart. However, there was no provision for proactive appointment of ex-Paralympians to positions of influence. Liaising with the IOC gave the IPC President considerable power of influence. (Howe 2008:44)

If the IPC was intent on being an athlete- and performance-orientated organisation, why did it not appoint Jordan as its first President? After all, was he not a successful disabled leader of an IOSD that had achieved recognition by the IOC; and had the World Games for the Deaf not already been performance-oriented for decades? As Howe argued: if the IPC was an organisation established to provide opportunities for women, it would have ensured that it was actively recruiting them into positions of power (Howe 2008:44). Indeed, during a rotation of presidencies in 1987, the ICC decided that it would not make Jordan a Vice president because it wanted ICC representatives at the Olympic Games to be those who participated in the Paralympics (Bailey 2008: 82). When explaining to Bromann the value of remaining a member, Jordan asked *'what can we contribute to the ICC other than our name and an illusion of unity?'* (in Bailey 2008 : 82)

Yes, it was the right decision to withdraw because there were unresolved issues with logistics

President Crowley explained that logistics were another reason for withdrawing from the IPC. At the time, the IOC advised the IPC to start with seven sport disciplines but the CISS already had 17 and could not commit itself to reducing participation opportunities for deaf athletes (Hussain 2012). The CISS would already have been aware of the discord within the ICC in respect of the decision to cancel 156 events for the 'severely disabled', because there were less than three athletes in each field. The IOC also influenced the IPC to ensure that each event had six athletes from at least four different countries meeting the minimum entry standard. This was a much lower standard of entry in comparison to the CISS where competitions had to have entries from at least three global regions.

Can we move forwards from here?

At the time of writing, the events and relationships of 1989 – 1995 occurred some 18 – 24 years ago. In Olympic terms that is six quadrennial cycles. Rightly or wrongly, matters have been forgotten, collective memories and experience no longer exist and, as Craig Spence at the IPC commented, the reasons for withdrawal are unclear and the IPC are often made out to be the 'bad guys'. Could all this be suggesting that a prevalence of mind-set has been inherited? Deaf sport could now do with a bit less history and a bit more future.

There is currently a difference of opinion as to whether the ICSD should re-apply for membership of the IPC or remain separate. Some inside Deaf sport have criticised Crowley for being pro-Paralympic; but, because of the duties bestowed upon the office of President in 1995 by ICSD Congress, he was obliged to maintain a strong relationship with the IPC for mutual benefits for all in disabled sport. This is also what the

IOC desired - a closer working relationship between the ICSD and IPC.

Commentators within the Deaf community have said that, whatever reasons the CISS had in 1995 for 'going it alone', it is almost certain that these issues have now been addressed by non-discrimination legislation and that now is the time for the ICSD to go back to the IPC and re-present matters; especially as the current relationship is good, based upon the 2004 Memorandum of Understanding, which looks to foster mutual respect and understanding.

The distinct reasons for this are:

- Deafness is more disabling than it first appears.
- Deaf people typically do not get a fair deal in disability sport.
- Deaf people are under-represented in sport.
- Statistically, there has to be a well of untapped deaf talent going to waste.

In its meetings with the IOC, the ICSD has been advised to consider applying for membership of the IPC and Crowley's perception was that re-admission could be sought on the basis of a self-contained Deaflympics being delivered alongside the existing Paralympics. This would ensure that the specialised expertise within Deaf sport is retained and resourced appropriately, mitigating the Deaf community's fear that a 'tandem' association with the Paralympics would mean the Deaflympics ceasing.

These aspirations will not easily be achieved; they call for compromise, diplomacy and genuine mutual understanding. Crowley believes that the ICSD should be talking with the IPC to discuss the possibilities and options for ICSD re-joining the IPC, whilst also maintaining the Deaflympics as an event that benefits from that privilege (Swinbourne 2012a). Crowley has made it clear to me personally, that advice from the IOC was about re-joining the IPC as an associate member to open up floodgates of infrastructure support, recognition, visibility, and sponsorship among other things. Thus, he was working on the mandate that empowered him to seek out the IPC's interest in welcoming back the ICSD.

If National Deaf Sports Federations experience difficulty in trying to form MoUs with their respective National Olympic and Paralympic Committees, they should remind them of IOC Clause 39 that was mandated in 2009 under *The Structure of the Olympic Movement:*

> ***2009 Clause 39 – 'The relationship between the IOC and the International Paralympic Committee (IPC) should be pursued to the benefit of all areas of mutual interests. Furthermore, cooperation with the International Committee of Sports for the Deaf and Special Olympics is encouraged."***
>
> (from IOC 2009b)

6

CISS – ICSD and its relationships with IOC and IPC

One of the key deciders in the decision to withdraw from the International Paralympic Committee (IPC) was the complex relationships that the Comité International des Sports des Sourds (CISS) had with the International Olympic Committee (IOC) and IPC. Strategic, political and diplomatic discussions occur at the highest level and the outcomes are entirely dependent on how the respective Presidents and their representatives conduct their deliberations. Presidents are mandated by their respective organisations, but they are also elected for their personal qualities and their stated aspirations. There is, therefore, an expectation that these leaders bring both their mandates and their personal visions to the negotiating table.

Analysing the relationships that the CISS and, later, International Committee of Sports for the Deaf (ICSD) have had with the IOC and IPC is convoluted and requires observation from a number of different perspectives. Therefore, in order to answer the question "Why are the Deaf not in the Paralympics?", I am going to illustrate the relationships over two stages: firstly 1989 – 2002 and then 2003 – 2013.

The first stage takes us from the moment that the CISS agreed to join the ICC and form the IPC. The CISS relied on the IOC to act as its advocate in the uneasy relationship it had with the IPC. This period was a time when the cultural and linguistic politics of deafness dominated the discourse of the CISS. It concludes just after the IOC/IPC Treaty of 2001, when the two organisations had a near simultaneous change of Presidencies and they jointly consolidated their efforts to organise the Olympics and Paralympics in unison. All of this forced the ICSD to re-think its strategy and ask the IOC for a cooperative agreement.

The second stage begins in 2003 when the city of Taipei won the bid to host the 2009 Deaflympics. The untimely death of ICSD President John Lovett marred the ascendency of Donalda Ammons. She then had the difficult task of reforming the ICSD and embracing the support and resources of external organisations, whilst seeking not to compromise the autonomy of the ICSD Congress. The meeting notes of the IOC/ICSD in January 2009 indicate that Ammons' willingness to appease the IOC was making inroads as the discussion centred on the future creation of an MoU that was to be *'the tool to define how to work together'* (p1). The second stage concludes with the Presidency of Craig Crowley that brings us to the present day, as the IOC prepare to elect a new President as Jacques Rogge's tenure reaches its conclusion.

1989 – 2002

After the CISS formalised its governance and constitution in line with that of the IOC, and then won IOC recognition in 1955 and 1966, it could be said that a good relationship existed between the CISS and IOC. But did the CISS/ICSD fail to nurture its relationship with the IOC and is this why the profile of the Deaflympics declined?

The IOC's relationship with disability sport has been described as developing through four stages (Mason 2002). Stage One: 1950s-1980s - was the monitoring of events. Stage Two: 1980s-1990s - was the personal support given by the IOC President Samaranch. Stage Three: 1990s – a direct relationship between the IOC and the Paralympics. Stage Four: since 2001 – close co-operation between the IOC and IPC. According to the writings of Mason and others, the IOC's relationship with disability sport began back in the 1950s. However, Deaf sport extends Stage One further back to the mid 1930s, when individual members of the IOC were already personally involved in the International Silent Games.

Juan Antonio Samaranch (IOC) and Gerald Jordan (CISS) both served 21 and 24 years respectively as Presidents. During their overlapping terms in office (1980-1995) they developed a very close and respectful relationship as evidenced by the mutual awards and letters of support they shared. Mason suggests that the IOC only started to take disability sport seriously during the 1970s when the International Stoke Mandeville Games began its rise to prominence and notables such as Ludwig Guttmann began commenting on developments in the *Olympic Review.* As disability sport grew, Samaranch persuaded all the governing bodies to come together in Dusseldorf and form the IPC. When the CISS insisted on the name IPC being used so that others could not assert control over Deaf sport (Ammons 1990) it is not impossible to judge that this demonstration of self-determination would have been regarded as defiance and would probably have sat uneasily with other members of the ICC, who were battling for their own positions within this new alliance; as described by Howe (2008). Similarly, in later years, Howe felt that his role on the IPC Athletes Commission as an advocate of marginalised athletes, within the remit of the IPCAC, made him unpopular (Howe 2008:56).

Further research has unearthed Bailey's (2008) perspectives of the relationship between CISS and ICC in the build up to the establishment of the IPC. It is interesting to note something that is not mentioned in deaf writings. When CISS agreed to join the ICC and maintain its own Games, other members of the ICC insisted that the CISS and the other new member INAS-FMH (Intellectual Disabilities) would not be allowed to vote on matters pertaining to the organisation and management of the Paralympics. This in effect meant that the CISS had no engagement at all in the creating of the Paralympic Games, and the inclusion of deaf athletes was never tabled on the agendas. It was only when Jordan announced that he was considering withdrawing from the ICC that any form of discussions were initiated regarding the inclusion of Deaf athletes in the Paralympic games. To Jordan, the ICC should have been an organisation that democratically represented the interest of all disabilities and not a forum for the establishment of the Paralympics, which in reality is what the ICC was intending all along.

Immediately after the Dusseldorf announcements, it became apparent that National Olympic and Paralympic Committees were making life difficult for their respective National Deaf Sports Federations. Some were being told to participate in the Paralympics, despite no classifications having been created and others were being denied permission to compete in the World Games for the Deaf. This was in defiance of the conditions under which the CISS had agreed to help establish the IPC and where it was agreed that funds coming into the IPC would be shared proportionally with the CISS. According to the CISS, this sharing of funds never materialised. The Christchurch World Games for the Deaf had been an expensive exercise for CISS and Jordan criticised the ICC for not spreading financial support more equitably amongst member organisations instead of favouring those who participated in the Paralympics. When Jordan announced that he was going to meet the IOC alone and seek financial support, according to Bailey (2008), he was dissuaded from doing so by the ICC who passed a motion to 'respect the WGD as having the same sports level as the Paralympics' (Bailey 2008: 95)

The CISS lobbied the IPC at the 1990 meeting in Assen (Ammons 1990) to be sure that it was not assuming jurisdiction over the International Games for the Deaf. Despite this move for self-determination, the CISS was willing to co-operate with the IPC and work towards solving mutual problems and achieving common goals. However, there was unease that IPC national representatives might try to drive integration with other disabled events by offering financial assistance to their national Deaf counterparts. Ammons reiterated the strong emotions the Deaf were feeling:

> ***"We, the deaf, maintain our right to self-determination and the full control of our sports organisations. This right will not be compromised, not relinquished in the interest of funding support for our various levels of sports. As demonstrated in the past, the volunteer efforts of many deaf individuals will assure our integrity in the face of efforts of assimilation by larger coalitions of disabled sports organisations"***
>
> (in Ammons 1990)

The 'final agreement' approved by the IPC Executive in 1990 appears not to have held much gravitas with the IPC; the issue was likely that non-deaf people like the IPC President, Robert Steadward, found it very difficult to understand Deaf sport as Ammons (1990) believed that he, for one, saw Deaf sport in the same manner as disability sport. At the time, the IPC declared that it had the athletes' best interests to the fore. But this was not happening; as according to the observations of Howe[6],

[6] (in Howe 2008 : 37, 44,58, 79-80, 140-145 and 152)

those who were in positions of power at the IPC and IOC were not disabled, and therefore it is possible that their decision making might have had little empathy with the stakeholders concerned. When discussing the possibility of the IOC and IPC co-ordinating efforts to co-host their Games, IOC member Vitaly Smirnov suggested that "Games for the disabled should not obligatorily be part of the Olympic Games" and "athletes with a disability were not interested in top level competitions, but wanted instead to prove that they could compete." And another member, Zhenliang, felt that "the aim of the disabled was one more of rehabilitation than of seeking top performances." (Bailey 2008 : 99).

Howe has chronicled his own struggles for athlete empowerment during his tenure of the IPC Athletes Commission (IPCAC), where he was labelled with others as 'difficult and not aware of how to run a good track and field meeting' (Howe 2008:56). Agendas were created to limit opportunities for the 'trouble makers' and in the seven years that he was on the IPCAC, the chairperson had to take him aside several times to lobby for his vote (Howe 2008:56). There were some people within the ICC and the new IPC who continually pushed to have the Paralympics integrated into the Olympics. Fortunately, they did not have their way and this is vindicated by Paralympians today, who are very clear that they do not wish to see the Paralympics integrated into the Olympics. Their view is that *Inclusion* is not about being the same; it is about having equality of experience (Young 2012). National Olympic and Paralympic Committees need to understand this and accept that trying to include the deaf in the Paralympics cannot work without investment, changes and overhauls.

Howe's (2008) observations of the IPC were that it was not interested in the development of grassroots disability sport, as it saw this is as the role of the International Sports Organisations for the Disabled (IOSDs). At the 1990 Canadian Deaf Sports

Conference (Dummer & Stewart 1991), the Americans and Canadians wanted the CISS to maintain its independence so that opportunities for Deaf sport in the Americas could be increased and brought up to the levels experienced in Europe. They cited the main obstacles as being the lack of funding for programmes, especially in South America, and the distance to travel for competitions.

In the build up to the CISS's withdrawal from the IPC, Stewart (1991a), who had worked very closely with Ammons, illustrated the different political agendas and approaches to sport taken by the IOC, IPC and CISS. Deaf sport had already been seen as a progressive movement that had helped shape the traditions of international competitions and the culture of organisations such as the IOC (Stewart 1991a: 5). Jordan's focus was that Deaf sport was different from disabled sport and that there were very necessary concerns with the developing power of the IPC. (Jordan 1996.)

The 1995 CISS Congress proceedings illustrate that the vote to withdraw from the IPC was not entirely unanimous; there were 25 abstentions, indicating that some nation states were uneasy about the collective decision. Perhaps most of them were those referred to by Ammons & Eikman (2011:1155), as those who believed that joining the IPC would help to deal with the increasing costs of hosting the Deaflympics and provide a higher public profile.

Mr Troger of the IOC advised the delegates that, whilst the IOC fully recognised the reasons for the withdrawal, it was suggested that the CISS continue to communicate closely with IPC, in order to continue to advocate the unique communication needs of Deaf athletes. Lindstrom announced that the IPC was undergoing constitutional changes and that it wished to ensure a good working relationship with the CISS.

In their joint article *Storm and Ice*, co-written after the CISS Congress had voted to withdraw from the IPC, Stewart and Ojalas felt the decision to withdraw would have serious consequences. The article discussed the financial difficulties nation states were having in preparing for the Winter and Summer World Games for the Deaf and tabled that the solution would be for Deaf organisations to affiliate themselves with umbrella organisations for disabled sport in their own countries. This was suggesting that the World Games for the Deaf (WGD) might benefit from being held in the same location as the Paralympics and that the financial burden on countries hosting the WGD might be mitigated. Their concern was that the CISS's resistance to move in that direction was not in its best interest (Stewart & Ojalas 1995).

John Lovett of Australia succeeded Jordan as President at the 1995 Congress and it fell upon him to write to the IOC and all the IPC members to break the news of the withdrawal. Mr Sanz, President of the International Blind Sports Association replied to Lovett pledging continued co-operation. Lovett's reply is indicative of the political legacy inherited from Jordan as he wrote:

> ***"In fact, CISS supports all sports for all people with disability as long as these people have full and total control of their sports!"***
>
> (CISS Correspondence 3rd June 1995.)

Despite signing the 'final agreement' (see page 55) ICSD member nations were still experiencing great difficulties by the time of Congress in 1997; Belgium and Cuba wanted the CISS to help them negotiate with their NPCs regarding control and/or the forcing of Deaf sports to join the Paralympics. Meanwhile Australia proposed that the CISS should consider holding future WGD on the same sites as the Olympics and Paralympics (a proposal also mooted by Stewart & Ojalas; 1995). With John Lovett being Australian, it suggests that the Australian proposal indicated that the policies of Jordan held less sway with him no longer at the helm.

It is not beyond conjecture to recognise that Jordan is likely to have been wary of the attitude of other members of the ICC when he attended the IPC meetings. It would appear that the interests of Deaf people were very low on the ICC's list of priorities. The incapacity of the ICC and then the IPC to reflect the values of Olympism by virtue of being an event offering rehabilitative benefits instead of Coubertin's development of youth (Howe 2008:34-35) was also likely to be at odds with a traditionalist like Jordan. The ICC/IPC wanted to empower Paralympic athletes to achieve sporting excellence and 'inspire and excite the world' (in Howe 2008:35) but Jordan's adherence to the social model of disability would have seen this as patronising and demeaning to disabled people. But, maybe, it was Jordan himself who was out of touch with the IOC's adherence to its own stated values of Olympism which many saw as lip-service, as the IOC strode ever onwards in its search for corporate sponsors.[7] I would suggest that the ICC was acutely aware of the commerciality of sport and played to this strategy by looking for 'model' Paralympic athletes (Olympic Review 1988) who would help to achieve the IPC vision to 'inspire and excite the world'. This move to make the Paralympics attractive by organising events and developing classification systems (Howe 2008:83-85) that were spectator and sponsor-friendly, and which effectively eliminated events for athletes who failed to conform to the 'aesthetics' of an ideal athlete, is discussed in detail by Peers (2012)

Meanwhile, the CISS continued its strategy of resisting assimilation by NOCs and NPCs. By the time of the Davos Congress in 1999, De Roose (BEL) asked for assistance from

[7] In the minutes of CISS Congress 1997, IOC G Felli explained that because of TV, the IOC was in a healthy position. & Howe (2008), page 4 writes of IOC lip-service to Olympism.

the CISS to prepare a position paper detailing how Deaf sports organisations could operate independently of disabled sport organisations. At the same time, Frenkl (RUS) explained that, whilst the Ministry of Sport and NPC in Russia were working in collaboration, they were excluding Deaf sports organisations. Staroyiannis (GRE) sought answers as to whether the CISS had actually been accorded official recognition and bona-fide status as an Olympic status event by the IOC.

President Lovett answered that the WGD was an Olympic equivalent event. In reply to De Roose and others, Lovett replied that he was to meet Steadward in Sydney in April 1999 and advised that Jerald Jordan's paper (1995) – *"World Deaf Games and Paralympics Games"* should be translated by the National Deaf Sports Federations and circulated as widely as possible. Such requests from delegates suggest that the CISS did not have an effective communications plan in place with which to assist and educate its national representatives as to the validity of IOC sanctioning.

The above suggests that the CISS was not providing its national deaf sports federations with enough direction on how to maximise the resolutions, agreed in 1990 with the IPC, in a way that would have allowed national representatives to deal with domestic issues more effectively.

Meanwhile, Steadward and the IPC continued with their mission to build a more businesslike relationship with the IOC, focusing less on the needs of disabled athletes and more on the successful running of the administration of the IPC (Howe 2008:44). In 2001, the presidencies of the IOC and IPC changed, with the appointments of Rogge and Craven respectively. This also culminated in the signing of the IOC/IPC Treaty committing both organisations to a shared responsibility for the planning and delivery of the Olympics and Paralympics. Just before his retirement as IOC President, Samaranch had authorised one final agreement with the CISS that recognised the new name for the World Games for the Deaf. In order to try and maintain peoples understanding of the event brand, it was now officially to be known as the 'Deaflympics'.

Stewart and Ammons wrote (2001) of the strong partisan feelings held by Deaf sport, stating, for example, that Deaf people did not want the Deaflympics to follow the Olympics and Paralympics to the same host city, because they wanted decisions to be Deaf-led; they did not want to be hearing-led. The article continued on to suggest that Deaf sport needed to think seriously about changing its ideas, because change was inevitable due to the increasing number of deaf children being educated in mainstream schools. Stewart and Ammons' article acknowledged that some aspects of the Deaflympics would be configured into a new cultural event for the Deaf and that, as with all Games in the past, sign language would continue to be the linguistic champion of the Deaf participants. *Yearning* to be with other Deaf people would still be a factor in motivating many of the athletes to participate in the Games regardless of where the event was held (Stewart & Ammons 2001). By this time, Ammons had been CISS Secretary General for four years and, on the basis of the articles she has co-authored with Stewart, it is likely that when she had accompanied Lovett to meetings or read notes and minutes, she would have seen that the CISS was holding back inevitable major decisions that it needed to address; and she was, eventually, able to do this by instigating the *Deaf Sport Reform*.

CISS Expectations of the IOC

The CISS set great store by its IOC status as a 'Recognised Organisation", but in such a way that it relied on this as one of the main justifications for support and that it regarded the IOC as its advocate. For example, when Samaranch authorised the name 'Deaflympics', the CISS declared this to be further recognition at the highest levels. However, as much as the IOC may have liked to support the concerns of the CISS, it is, in reality, quite powerless to interfere in national disability sports politics. The CISS could have taken heed of one of its own appeals in 1969 asking the IOC to encourage its Latin American members to support Deaf athletes entering the 1969 WGD. This was passed on via the Olympic newsletter:

> ***"Mr P Bernhard would like their National Olympic Committees to give them some kind of help and assistance. Would such appeal meet with the favourable reply it deserves?"***
> (IOC Newsletter 1969:116)

This is an indication that the IOC itself has no authorisation to enforce its own sentiments on NOCs and therefore creates a weak link in the chain of political influencing. Is it possible that the CISS leadership was too enraptured by plaudits when awarded the Coubertin Cup in 1966 and that it rested too much on its laurels? In hindsight, the award was a message to motivate the CISS to work harder and do much more on its own, and not to rely solely on the patronage of the IOC.

Following the IOC sanctioning of the name 'Deaflympics' in 2001, there were immediate difficulties for the CISS, which was challenged repeatedly by the IOC for infringing rights agreements, because its members were using derivatives of the word 'Deaflympics'. The IPC had reformed its governance and removed all IOSD representatives from its executive and replaced them with those from NPCs. Frustrated by the increasing problems of sanctions on CISS, whist appearing to favour the IPC, Lovett met with Rogge and Felli at IOC in 2002 and appealed for them to sign an IOC/CISS agreement. The IOC declined, because it had had fifty other International Federations and had no such agreements with them. The IOC had also been challenging the IPC over the earlier versions of its logo. Mason reports that the IOC threatened to break ties with the IPC if the logo was not changed (in Howe 2008:31). It would appear that historically, the IOC is not averse to heavy-handedness in order to protect what it regards as its supremacy over all others.

In his report on the meeting with Rogge, Lovett explained that Rogge would write formally to show IOC recognition for the CISS and its patronage of the Deaflympics. Lovett had lobbied as hard as possible:

> ***"I explained to Dr. Rogge and Mr. Felli that we need a strong statement from the IOC to the community at large, especially the national Paralympic Committees/Government Departments of Sport to support and respect independence and autonomy of the CISS and its members."***
>
> (Lovett 2002)

The relationship between the IOC and both the CISS/IPC was precarious to say the least. Lovett reported by email on his meeting with Felli in July 2002, when once again he broached the subject of using derivatives of 'Deaflympics', such as 'National Deaflympic Committees'. According to Lovett, Felli explained that the timing was not right, as there were a 'number on the IOC Executive' who would not be in favour as they were also 'unhappy' with the Paralympics. As far as the IOC Executive were concerned, it was the CISS who had decided to withdraw from the IPC and it was only due to the persuasive powers of Samaranch that the term 'Deaflympics' was approved (Lovett 2002b). Felli, however, offered guidance to Lovett suggesting that the CISS should:

> ***"focus on 'educating' National Governments, National Olympic Committees, IPC and the National Paralympic Committees on autonomy and independence of the CISS and its Deaf sports."***
>
> (Lovett 2002b)

Felli also advised CISS to put *emphasis* on the difference of disability, for example, communication versus mobility needs. Felli said that Samaranch had used this argument to persuade the IOC Executive to support the CISS withdrawal from the IPC. Lovett suggested to the CISS Board that Jordan's article *Deaf World Games and Paralympic Games* should be updated to promote the wording 'Deaflympics'. With hindsight, the CISS should have written its own position statement to emphasise the fact that deafness is a disability, because Jordan's article is self-contradictory.

In his follow-up letter to Lovett, Felli reiterated that the IOC could not impose any rulings on NOCs, which are free to take decisions whether or not to recognise IPC or CISS and that sovereign positions on disability sport 'may vary considerably' (Felli 2002; IOC 2009a). To finish off on an important note about using interpreters at meetings to enable deaf and hearing people to establish relationships, as well as provide communication support – it was fed back to Lovett that "Felli's voice was 'very warm and sincere'" (Lovett 2002b).

In my opinion, this all seems like the IOC is still in 'denial', because the IOC cannot 'see' the disability of deafness as clearly as it can with the Special Olympics. IOC patronage was given to the Special Olympics in 1988 and they have been using derivatives of 'Olympics' ever since – one cannot help wonder what Shriver and her team did right to appease the IOC. Perhaps the IOC learnt a lesson about protecting their rights after giving their name away in 1988?

Lovett went on to meet with the new IPC President, Phil Craven, who wrote to Lovett in October 2002, summarising their main points of agreement (Craven 2002):

1. The IPC will send a letter to all its member organisations recognising the CISS as the sole international organisation responsible for deaf sport.

2. The IPC and CISS will develop a new agreement of co-operation.
3. The IPC and CISS will explore the creation of an annual forum to discuss issues and share information. This forum may include other similar organisations such as Special Olympics International and the IOC. In this context, the IPC is not supportive of the proposal of an IOC Disability in Sport Commission.
4. The IPC and CISS will work together in clarifying the individual national situation related to CISS membership.

2003 – 2013

Despite a memo, sent out to NOCs by Felli, and Craven's letter to NPCs reminding NOCs, NPCs, governments and IFs that, on an international level, CISS is independent of the IPC; there were other issues that Ammons and Eikman (2011:1158) felt were creating confusion after the 2001 IPC/IOC pact:

- IOC restructuring saw the IOC games department split into the IOC Sports and IOC Games departments. The Games department oversees the management of the Olympic and Paralympic Games; whilst the Deaflympics comes under the Sports department, with all other recognised federations, thus marginalising the Deaflympics further.
- The high turnover of staff at National Paralympic Committees impacted upon the continuity of relationships with Deaf sport, resulting in the need to continuously re-educate new staffing intakes about 'Deaf sport, deaf people, signed languages and Deaflympics-related issues'.

- Disability organisations claiming to 'speak for and represent deaf sport or national governments undermining Deaf sport autonomy'.

I might also add a fourth issue – the CISS wrote to all its national members on 31st October 2002 with copies of the IOC memo and IPC letter for their use when meeting NOCs, NPCs or other governing bodies. Perhaps, those organisations given the express responsibility for upholding the Deaflympic Movement at national level were not carrying out their obligations as effectively as they should have?

Over a number of years, in the UK, Deaf sports leaders were frustrated by the lack of action from its CISS member, the British Deaf Sports Council, to engage in a dialogue with government and sports departments. As a result, UK Deaf Sport was established in 2003 and, with Craig Crowley as its Chairperson, it set about networking with key decision makers including Philip Craven of the IPC. Similar concerns were being raised elsewhere. American Glenn Lockhart (2003) recognised that agreements being made at IOC/IPC/ICSD level and the MoU with the IPC, were difficult to replicate at national level. National representatives of CISS were either reporting to two bodies - ICSD and their national IOC committee - or they were reporting directly to their related IPC body.

In 2003, Philip Craven, who had been IPC President for less than two years, was appointed onto the IOC and the British Olympic Committee (BOC). This could be seen as putting too much power into one person's hands. It gave the IPC the opportunity - should it wish to use it - to influence national government policies towards disability sport that were, in any event, becoming increasingly pro-Paralympic.

Meanwhile, nobody within the ICSD and Deaflympic Movement was taking much notice of, or heavily promoting, the significance of the support given by the Taiwanese government, its National Olympic Committee and the City of Taipei in their successful bid to host the 2009 Summer Deaflympics. As it will be discussed in Chapter 15, marketing by the CISS/ICSD and its members had simply not been effective.

CISS attempts to create an effective voice

By 2004, Tiffany Granfors had joined the CISS as the new Executive Officer, a new salaried role replacing the CISS Administrator position. By the end of the year, Ammons and Granfors had negotiated a new Memorandum of Understanding with the IPC (ICSD 2004b):

- Deaf athletes with additional disabilities to be allowed to participate in various IPC events. Conversely, multi-disabled Paralympic athletes with at least 55 dB hearing loss in the better ear will be able to compete in the Deaflympics and the Deaf World Championships.
- Providing NOCs and NPCs with better awareness and understanding of Deaflympics and Paralympics as two separate organisations that manage their own quadrennial events.
- To mutually recognise and respect the autonomy of their organisations.
- To cooperate in informing sports authorities of the international structures of both organisations.
- To cooperate in addressing conflicts between the affiliated organisations.

In 2006, Ammons met with Japanese Olympic and Paralympic representatives who pledged to support the Deaflympics. To demonstrate their support, Japan later hosted the 2011 World Deaf Championships in Table Tennis and Golf. (ICSD 2006)

Sports and human rights are interconnected: in 1961 the IOC produced the *Olympic Solidarity* programme to assist low-income countries in developing sports activities and the Council of Europe formulated its Sport for All policy in 1966. In 1981, in the UN International Year for Disabled People, the Sport for All charter was enhanced to include the rights of disabled people in sport – Disabled People Charter 1987:

> ***"What matters most for the Council of Europe as reflected in the words of Sir L Guttmann is that 'sport should be a driving force for the disabled to seek or restore his contact with the world around him and thus his recognition as an equal and respected citizen' "***

This is the same vision that inspired Eugene Rubens-Alcais and Antoine Dresse in the 1920s. Such a pity that their work and philosophies, if written down, have not been given prominence.

In 2007, Ammons represented the CISS on the International Disability in Sport Working Group, a partnership with the UN. In its publication, it addressed the significance of Article 30.5 of the United Nations Convention on the Rights of Persons with Disabilities (IDISWG 2007).

> ***"The ICSD will continue to work closely with the International Paralympic Committee in informing the competent sports authorities of the international structures of both organisations and addressing the inequalities or discrepancies that may arise at national levels between the affiliated organisations"***

> ***"The adoption of Article 30.5 shall ensure that these athletes with disabilities have a global stage to display their sporting spirit and dedication by participating in the Deaflympics. More and better athletes will now be allowed to reach the pinnacle of disability-specific competition, and establish higher benchmarks.***

> ***Even better, the adoption specifically of Article 30.5 will ensure more significant levels of respect and recognition for deaf and hard of hearing athletes, who want to compete in the Deaflympics. We welcome the challenge to work with national governments, NGOs, international and national sports organisations in understanding that deaf and hard of hearing athletes shall be treated with the same respect and dignity accorded to athletes with other disabilities."***
>
> (p34)

Despite ICSD's efforts to make the 2004 IPC/ICSD MoU work, the South African Sports Confederation and Olympic Committee (SASCOC) had a *complete change of heart* towards supporting Deaflympic athletes in 2008 and were accused of hiding behind constitutional matters, as reasons for not lending their support, by stating that they were not members of the ICSD, which was a body only for Deaf-led organisations (SADSF 2012).

Recognising that ICSD was due for a radical change, Ammons, in consultation with ICSD members at a symposium in Zagreb in July 2007, set out plans to restructure the governance and operations of the organisation. The final draft was presented to an Extraordinary Congress in Bratislava in September 2008. Titled *Deaf Sports Reform*, the plans set out the main goals for the creation of a new International Deaflympic Committee (IDC) to be recognised by the IOC as an equal organisation to the IPC. It mirrors the Olympic Charter and creates three branches of the Deaflympic Movement; Deaflympic, World Sport and World Youth Sport with the publication of three main documents; the Deaflympic Charter, IDC Organisational Regulations and IDC Competition Rules. Ammons (2009) later reported that IOC President Rogge re-affirmed his support for Deaflympics and Deaf Sports Reform.

In September 2009, the ICSD Congress appointed Crowley (GBR) as their new President and marked a couple of firsts.

He was the first Deaflympic medallist to hold the post and, secondly, he was not an ICSD Executive beforehand. His ability to evaluate and make difficult decisions came early. Before his first year was completed, he had cancelled the 2011 Winter Deaflympics as there was little evidence that there was an organising committee in situ with governmental and civic backing and there were no secured funds in place. He also met with Federation France Handisports (ICSD 2010a) and resolved an ongoing dispute, which saw France quickly reinstated as an ICSD member.

Crowley long believed that the importance of establishing effective relationships with the IOC and IPC were paramount to the future survival of the Deaflympics and he has been internally criticised for this. Is it feasible to suggest that the historical grievance within the ICSD towards the IOC has been its stumbling block and has not endeared it well with the IOC? On one occasion during the research for this book, Crowley gave me an indication of the relationship he had inherited, by describing his first meeting with IOC President Rogge in 2010; it is illuminating. When Crowley arrived at the offices of the IOC with his Chief Executive Officer, Tiffany Granfors, he was granted the customary 5-minute audience with the IOC President, but this ran on for some 25 minutes. Crowley and Granfors then went to meet with Jean-Laurent Bourquin, the IOC Sport Manager, and he was surprised to find that two other managerial colleagues and three lawyers accompanied Bourquin. Crowley recalled the discussion around the main subject of contention:

> *"Bourquin asked me when were we going to stop using the word 'Deaflympics". Everyone was giving me a very hard stare and the lawyers were poised for my response. I asked him if that was indeed the case then would he also be asking*

> ***the IPC to stop using "Paralympics"? Bourquin looked astounded and the lawyers shifted their eyes towards him in anticipation. Bourquin's answer was that the Paralympics had been established before we were. My reply was "I am sorry but with due respect I have to remind you gently, that we have actually been around since 1924 and they only came along in 1948. So, I think you will find that we got there first. However, we at ICSD are willing to discuss issues that would hopefully reach reasonable accommodation for all concerned including the Paralympics."***

After a short recess, the Managers returned without the lawyers and continued their deliberations with Crowley. After the meeting had concluded, Bourquin made a point of informing Crowley that President Rogge wanted to pass on his best wishes and he was looking forward to working with him.

Granfors explained to Crowley that such a comment was unheard of. It was later fed back to Crowley that Rogge immediately warmed to him and his staff were surprised to find that their anticipated conflict-resolution measures were quite unnecessary: 'This is a man we can work with'.

During Crowley's tenure, there were wholesale changes to the ICSD Executive and, for the first time, it appointed a non-deaf CEO, Mark Cooper, who originated from the IOC. Despite the cancellations of the 2011 Winter Deaflympics and the withdrawals of Athens 2013 and Canada 2015, the ICSD secured a last minute replacement for the 2013 Summer Deaflympics in Sofia. In addition to this, a record 15 World championships have taken place without any cancellations. The postponed 2011 Congress was re-convened in Rome and the minutes (ICSD Sept 2011) showed the main items:

- Not many NOCs have heard of the Deaflympics and therefore more work needs to be done.

ICSD wants to see National Deaf Sports Federations building stronger relationships with their National Olympic Committees, but they need educating and training to do this and they also require guidance documents on how to present the status of the Deaflympics and how to handle objections, using IOC agreements, UN Conventions, case studies etc.

- Deaf-Culture politics has crept into Deaf Sport....

....meaning that the 'culture-linguistic minority' bandwagon had taken over the reins and they need to return to the delivery of elite sports competitions. Congress delegates departed knowing that the future focus was *Athletes First -Deaf Second.* This is a reflection of public feeling, which like those of Kaufman writing in *History of British Deaf Tennis* suggested that Deaf sports should not allow their Deaf pride to interfere with their ideology. (Whalley 2010:412)

A good example of IPC rhetoric with regards to the *'Deaf pride'* deaf in the Paralympics can be challenged. For example, at one time, on the ParalympicsGB website the British Paralympic Association's answer to the following question *"Why are deaf athletes excluded?'* stated:

> ***'ParalympicsGB is non-discriminatory and applauds all disabled sportsmen and women who achieve on the world stage. Sportsmen and women who are deaf and their representative federations were part of the Paralympic movement originally but decided to move away and form their own associations and create their own Games. That is why they are not members of the BPA and are not funded in the same way as other NGBs. Athletes with a hearing impairment do compete in the Paralympic Games when the hearing loss is one of their impairments."***

The above statement was misleading on two points. Firstly, the CISS did not move away to form their own associations and establish their own Games – they were already in existence. ParalympicsGB justifying their argument by claiming that they (IPC) *got there first* is misleading. Secondly, the final sentence implies that hearing loss is an IPC classification when there is no such provision in place. UK Deaf Sport challenged this directly with the BPA and the statement has now been changed to:

> ***"ParalympicsGB is non-discriminatory and applauds all disabled sportsmen and women who achieve on the world stage. Deaf sportsmen and women have taken part in their own Games ever since the International Silent Games (now the Deaflympics) of 1924. As a result, Deaf sports are not members of the BPA and are not funded in the same way as other NGBs. Athletes with a hearing impairment do compete in the Paralympic Games when the hearing loss is one of their impairments and when they have another impairment which is classifiable at the Paralympic Games."***

Crowley's critics are concerned that he wants to work closer with the IPC. On the contrary, they need to understand that the relationship was always important to the ICSD, the difference to consider here is how each successive ICSD President has handled this relationship in public. History suggests that the ICSD position is moving from one of unease of hearing people to one of increased confidence, in that it is able to negotiate for the greater benefit of disability sport and safeguard the interests of Deaf competitions. This confidence can be illustrated in the way Crowley resolved the deadlock between the ICSD and the French Federation Handisports (FFH).

France had been suspended from the ICSD and was unable to send athletes to any ICSD-sanctioned events because FFH, the French Paralympic organisation did not have Deaf representation that fell in line with the ICSD constitution to enable it to recognise FFH as a representative of Deaf sport in France. The ICSD met the FFH in Paris early in 2010, in attendance were Crowley and Wilmerdinger (ICSD), President Maison (FFH) and Isabelle Malaurie (EDSO) as observer. Unfortunately, this meeting ended acrimoniously but Maison and Crowley met alone at the end to try and resolve things.

A second meeting was held in London in October 2010 between Maison and Crowley, with Martin Bogard (ICSD) as observer. Crowley explained to me that FFH presented its plan but did not follow ICSD advice for a Deaf sports committee to be created under FFH, which would have resolved the ICSD membership statute. A third meeting was held in Paris, early in 2011 with Mark Cooper representing ICSD (he is bilingual in both English and French) with the same mandate as October 2010. An agreement was reached with Maison so that Jeff Labes a FFH Vice President was made chair of CCSSF (French Deaf Sports Committee). Bjorne Roine (EDSO President) was observing and was satisfied that the FFH had made reasonable adjustment. This suited the ICSD in terms of its constitution and self-determination, whilst encouraging collaborative leadership between the Deaf and non-deaf.

ICSD Presidents are often asked if the Deaflympics should be part of the Paralympics. In Crowley's case, his replies have been published by journalists, whose writings insinuate that he is pro-Paralympic, when he actually shows positive caution on the concept. Crowley exercises restraint because the IPC is now governed by NPC representatives and not by IOSDs like ICSD. Therefore Crowley foresees that any inclusion of Deaf competitors in the Paralympics requires a far greater working relationship with the IPC than that which currently exists. The relationship is important as it serves to increase the profile of the Deaflympics and allows it to grow. Crowley's discussions with Craven have covered many topics but *'Deaf Sport in the*

Paralympics' is still something for the future and it cannot be completely ruled out (Degun 2011). Crowley's leadership style is one of understanding the needs and aspirations of potential partners. Only then can you make decisions that can provide mutual benefits.

Crowley and Ammons are not the only Deaf leaders to realise the benefits of collaborating with the Paralympic movement; the USA Deaf Sports Federation joined 'American Athletes with Disabilities' in 2001 to search for and prepare athletes in the sports of shooting, badminton and table tennis (USADSF 2001). There is no direct evidence to determine if this strategy has been successful, but at least the option was explored. For those who have concerns about the decline of Deaf sport under the Paralympics, they should examine the developments in Portugal where the Paralympic Committee is responsible for the Portuguese Deaflympics Mission that sent athletes to the 2009 Deaflympics in eight sports.

The ICSD Board met in London during the 2012 Paralympics in order to establish IPC collaboration and also engage with the Deaf athletes, volunteers and officials who were taking part in the event. During the Board meeting, IOC Sports Director Christophe Dubi began a discussion about International Deaf Sports, including the Deaflympics 2013 and 2015 (ICSD 2012a). Dubi:

- Spoke of the importance of making the Deaflympics and ICSD more visible to the outside world, so as to raise awareness.
- Stated that Athletes and their experience are the IOC's first priority.
- Suggested the need for best practice examples to showcase and educate less developed countries.
- Invited ICSD to continue negotiations towards a stronger relationship with the IOC through a new

MoU, which would result in greater resources for ICSD.

It is Crowley's understanding that the IOC and the IPC both see the existing ICSD Constitution as a major block to further developments, because it discriminates against non-deaf people by insisting that the organisation must be Deaf-led. Would the ICSD and its National Federations gain more headway in finding a more meaningful resolution if they made more use of anti-discrimination legislation by referring to the UN Article 30.5 and the IOC's own Charter? Handicap International, a German organisation working in developing countries, advocates that, if the potentials of a disabled person cannot be achieved, this may lead to a further loss of motivation, self-esteem and increased risk of poverty and isolation (Ikelberg et al) As long as the ICSD has competent, politically experienced Deaf leaders, then its constitutional position could be justified. But this remains to be seen.

Conclusion

The greatest challenge for ICSD in the IPC era has been the attitude of NOCs and NPCs, despite written agreements between ICSD and the IOC and IPC. The ICSD can do more to educate and lead its NDSFs, for example, by working with the IPC and adopting documents like the IPC Disability Rights Toolkit to effect change at regional and national level (IPC 2004). The toolkit advises on raising awareness of, and the implementation of, the UN Convention Article 30.5: "As a legally binding document, this convention will empower persons with a disability and will guarantee their right all across the world, no matter their socio-economic level" (p7).

The Deaflympic Movement faces an uphill challenge to demonstrate to most national governments that their policies on disability sport are unfairly biased towards Paralympism and, until that situation is resolved either way, national governments should recognise and respect the status of the Deaflympics and recognise its athletes accordingly. The ICSD also needs to keep a vigil on the statements made by IPC representatives and NPCs in relation to deaf athletes.

Whilst Ammons made a head start with Deaf Sport Reform (ICSD 2008) and in encouraging collaborative leadership with hearing people, her ideology - 'being deaf is not a disability' - still remains entrenched and this creates regrettable deadlock. Deaf Sport Reform needs to accept deafness as a disability, in the context of sport, and put sport first and move forwards on the IOC recommendations outlined in the 2009 changes to its Charter and on the outlines it presented to the ICSD at their 2012 meeting in London (ICSD 2012a).

In 2013, Jacques Rogge comes to the end of his second term as IOC President so the relationship that the role has established with Presidents Lovett, Ammons and Crowley will change. As a safeguard, for continuity, key IOC staff will remain in place to support the incoming President. The rapport between the ICSD and IOC that has been built by Craig Crowley and Christophe Dubi will therefore be even more crucial. It will be interesting to see how the ICSD maintains its relationship with the IOC, because the 22nd Congress in Sofia voted against giving Crowley a second term and elected Valery Rukhledev of Russia in his place.

7

The Inclusion of Deaf People into the Paralympics

The act of merging deaf athletes into the Paralympics would mean inclusion/integration into a hearing and speaking environment where Deaf people perceive disabled people as hearing first and disabled second. Stewart (1991a) mentions that Deaf athletes often want to know why the Deaflympics and Deaf sport is just seen as another type of disabled sport? He offered a quote from Fine and Asch (1988) to give one example of how people are classified:

> ***Why should a limb-deficient girl, a teenager with mental retardation, or a blind girl have anything in common with each other, or with a woman with breast cancer or another woman who is recovering from a stroke? What they share is similar treatment by a sexist and disability-phobic society.***
>
> (p 6 in Stewart 1991a:96)

The guardians of the Deaflympics need to consider the wider global changes that are impacting on Deaf sport, so it is only right to have this discussion. The general public is naïve about the inclusion of deaf competitors into the Paralympics.

Their solutions are too simplistic and this requires an explanation. Stewart (1991a; 126) warns us against *imposing mainstream logic on any minority people* and to *accept that participation in hearing sport does not offer the same benefits to Deaf people as it does to others*. Rubens-Alcais's original concept was about inclusion into society, but hearing people do not understand how this works. There are dangers of integration that need to be considered and this chapter refers to the long-standing idea of including the Paralympics in the Olympics to illustrate and justify why segregated events for elite sport could not be fully integrated. The International Committee of Sports for the Deaf (ICSD) is not averse to a review of the situation, but some of the potential problems of including deaf athletes in a multi-disability event need to be examined; and, if inclusion were to take place, what would it require and how would it evolve?

President Samaranch, of the International Olympic Committee (IOC), in consultation with international disability sport, engineered the evolution of the International Paralympic Committee (IPC) in order to provide a structure for disability sport within the IOC. The idea was well intentioned, but it has caused problems in disability sport that may be irreversible. Although the IOC is a supreme authority on global sport, it is still reliant on governments, which are tempted to embrace the Olympics to promote their political activities through policies that reflect the world we all live in.

With these global influences in mind, Baines (in Whalley 2010:421-427) examined the issue of merging the Deaflympics into the Paralympics. Like others in Deaf sport, he suggests that a merger could be the solution to stem the disintegration of Deaf sport. Others (Kaufman in Whalley 2010 and Crowley) share his concerns that the ICSD is not doing enough to demonstrate its relevance to global ideals and, in becoming increasingly isolated, could cause more damage and make the Deaflympics unsustainable.

Ammons was complimentary about Article 30.5 of the UN Convention for People with disabilities, but Baines (in Whalley 2010) also suggests that this could be a threat to the Deaflympics, because the ICSD constitution does not promote mainstreaming.

At the beginning of his term as ICSD President, Crowley reinforced Ammons' description of Deaf sport standing at a crossroads with choices available. He came into office because Deaf sport wanted to see change, to enhance the visibility of the Deaflympics and end its isolation. For that to work, Crowley needed the ICSD to change, stating that it could no longer continue with the same people and methods, and expect change. His predecessor, Ammons, had already recognised the inevitability of change through the impact the mainstreaming of Deaf education was having – producing Deaflympic competitors whose characteristics were now different. Two other influences of change were and continue to be medical: the prevention of deafness (gene therapies); and improving the ability to hear (Cochlear Implants, Stem Cell regeneration).

Some suggest that the risks of not being inclusive and not merging with the Paralympics in one form or another will 'ghettoise' Deaf sport and athletes may miss out on the sharing of victory parades (Kaufman in Whalley 2010); so the Deaflympics needs the media exposure of the Paralympics or it will become unsustainable. The majority of young deaf people in mainstream education know nothing about the event and it will become harder to recruit athletes into Deaf sport (Baines in Whalley 2010). There are many outside Deaf sport who have suggested the advantages of being in the Paralympics - deaf athletes would be able to integrate with Olympic and Paralympic athletes in the Village and a new Deaf classification could easily be added - but it is naïve to think that these changes could be applied instantly or effectively.

The ICSD has found it difficult to move forwards, because its own members and others in the Deaf community are continuing the argument against inclusion on the basis that: non-deaf people do not understand deafness; the Deaflympics is primarily about Deaf culture and not the ability to participate in sport; and Deaf people want to be among each other, because they are a cultural and linguistic minority who want to hold on to autonomy. It is very hard for the non-deaf to understand these issues without living or working in the Deaf community for any extended period of time – time is not something we have the luxury of.

Inclusion/Integration, if not managed and controlled carefully, can be damaging

One of the fundamental problems with society, and the IOC wanting to create inclusive sport, is that the concept is not understood from the deaf and disabled person's perspective. When the IOC brought the ICC and CISS together, it was done naïvely and without the benefit of a monitoring system that would have helped to foster understanding, knowledge and communication on how to adapt properly a multi-sport event for disabilities. As a result, there was intolerance and divisiveness that led to the withdrawal of the ICSD. This situation is not uncommon (Right to Play 2008). If not handled correctly, sport can ostracise people.

For deaf people, a sports environment that has not been designed for inclusion does not enable them to engage in spontaneous interaction with their hearing peers (able-bodied or disabled). There would always be a separation between the deaf and hearing (Ammons & Eikman 2001:1156). Whilst it is important that spectators might learn something new about disabled people in society, it has to be pointed out that the athletes themselves, particularly at the elite end of the spectrum, need to have the optimum environment possible in and out of the competition arena in order to deliver their optimum performances. One of the overwhelming experiences and memories that Olympic–type events provide for the competitors is the fun of meeting and interacting with other athletes in the Olympic and Paralympic villages. Much of this experience would simply be denied to deaf athletes (Kurtz 2009; Jordan 1991). This is why, for example, Olympic-class athletes like Terence Parkin have a preference to be at the Deaflympics. Fosshaug explains that integration can work and be beneficial, but it must not be assimilation, because it must empower the individual and give them the freedom of choice to decide on their own degree of integration or segregation (Fosshaug 2004; Ammons & Eikman 2011)

Furthermore, there is a concern shared by Howe (2008:135) that the abilities and achievements of competitors in the Paralympics may suggest to society that it does not need to change. But the event is not a normal reflection of everyday society and, for athletes with a learning disability, the physical manifestations of their disability are only evident in a societal environment. In reverse, the non-deaf persons are handicapped in Deaf sport until they learn its language and cultures (Stewart & Nulf 1996; Ammons & Eikman 2011).

Arguments in favour of segregated sports events

The Deaflympics, Paralympics and Special Olympics have a common denominator offering opportunities in a segregated setting that cannot be met by the sports system generally (Legg et al 2003). There are public discussions around the idea that the Paralympics should be integrated into the Olympics, but Paralympians disagree with this and believe that both events should be run consecutively as they are at present.

The reasons for not wanting to merge are similar to those of Deaf people, who do not wish to merge into the Paralympics. Paralympian Heath Francis explained, *"The Paralympics are all about us; we would be lost in the background of the Olympics".* Stella Young, a disabled reporter who interviewed Francis, personified the experience of 'seeing is believing'. Young (2012) described her feeling of release, *"the feeling of being among your people".* This is the same reason that Terence Parkin gave for choosing to attend the Deaflympics instead of a mainstream World Class event. Young continued; *"The Paralympics is a stand-alone event and we don't need to be part of another event to make us valuable or watchable. Not to mention the logistics of holding both events at once. It would be impossible."* Kurt Fearnley tweeted *"Paralympic Dining Hall; Disabilities as far as the eye can see and not a staring face in the joint."* For Young, the feeling she experienced inside the athletes village at the Paralympics inspired her to take up a sport or at least participate in the Paralympics in a different way. Breivik et al (2002) described the phenomenon of Rome turning into a *Deaf Village* for two weeks, inspiring the athletes, their Deaf supporters and the citizens of Rome.

In Young's opinion, people fall into the 'trap' of thinking that equality means to have or be the same as other people and equality is only achieved when everyone is treated identically. "What counts is the Paralympic spirit and the chance to compete at an elite level and to celebrate who they are, both as people with disabilities and as athletes."(Young 2012) Fosshaug (WFD News Vol 17) noted that true integration occurs when individuals are able to make the right choices that best suit them.

Governments and National Olympic Committees support the IPC commitment to 'increasing the integration of sports for athletes with disabilities into the international sports movement for the able bodied athletes, *whilst safeguarding and preserving the identity of sports for disabled athletes*" (Thomas & Smith 2009). The IPC is respected for standing its ground, the ICSD is ostracised for holding its own.

To place this into context with language barriers for other

communities in sport, let us consider the development of sports for migrant workers from Poland who have moved to the UK. A large migrant community of Polish and other nationalities has developed in the agricultural region of the Fens. As a consequence of language and cultural barriers, the Polish community has established its own sports teams and clubs instead of integrating into established local activities.

Just for a few moments, I would like to ask you to imagine a hypothetical situation where you have been sent by your employer to work in a foreign country where you are not fluent in the indigenous language and culture. You want to play a sport, but your sport is not available and you have to try and manage with the locals. Then one day you find out that in the next town there is a sports club run by people who speak your native language. What would you do? Where would you go? To where would you naturally gravitate?

Problems with multi-sports events

The reason that the Deaflympics exist as a segregated event is that society is built on the cultures of hearing and speaking and the deaf cannot talk or communicate readily and effectively to other disabled persons and non-disabled persons (SDSF 2013; Ammons & Eikman 2011). Critics argue that the ICSD should be making more of an effort to include its athletes in the Paralympics, but its hesitancy is based on experience. It knows that there are no provisions in place to safeguard against marginalisation. For example, Howe (2008) observed how the lack of independence in some Cerebral Palsy (CP) athletes meant that they were not invited to socialise and so were, 'de facto' excluded from the social environments of Wheelchair athletes. He suggests that this may be because some CP athletes find it difficult to communicate orally and therefore it was difficult for both sides to strike up a spontaneous conversation. He wonders if this was because the CP athletes lacked experience and opportunities for conversation or because they were not perceived as serious athletes. His conclusion was that a lack of understanding of impairments makes people feel marginalised by lack of understanding and awareness (Howe 2008:41).

The German Race Walking specialist Gerhard Sperling gave an account of his experiences of competing in both the Olympics and the Deaflympics:

> ***"At the Olympics I experienced the beauty of color of many nation's flags, TV cameras, flashing lights, huge street and stadiums turnouts, spectators' screams and their hand and facial expressions while I competed as a lone deaf walker, and at the World games I was always the happiest man because I could freely converse and socialize with any foreign deaf athlete."***
>
> (in Ammons and Eikman 2011:1155)

The Olympic status events of the Deaflympics and the Paralympics are not places to hold sociological experiments designed to foster integration between different disabilities; they are serious, high-level, performance events. The priority for the athlete is to prepare for the competitions and perform at the highest standards. Howe (2008:41) has observed the impact of the evolution of designing the Paralympics to meet the needs of elite athletes. He saw that each group of athletes, by excluding, teasing and targeting others - without getting to know them - caused the groups rarely to socialise together.

The IPC still does not understand the needs of deaf athletes. In the build-up to the 2012 London Paralympics, Laurentian Tan, a Deaf CP Paralympic equestrian representing Singapore but based in the UK, approached UK Deaf Sport for assistance. The issue was that during the Beijing Paralympics, she was the only equestrian rider in her team, but in preparations for London, the team had grown and it had become increasingly difficult for her to prepare and compete without the use of sign language interpreters. Tan had sourced her interpreters but needed assistance in obtaining accreditation for them. When UK Deaf Sport investigated the matter and learnt from the London Olympic Games Committee that it was a problem for Singapore to resolve and not something for the British. On another occasion, a hearing woman who works as a teaching assistant in Deaf education spoke to me about her experiences of volunteering in the 2012 Paralympic Village. She quickly noted that a number of Deaf athletes were isolated, because there were no interpreters provided. After consulting the athletes, she approached her supervisors and suggested that she would be able to accompany the Deaf athletes into the Closing Ceremony to help them to access the celebrations. This was turned down. A senior IAAF official also reported that Deaf athletes were not able to access any recall signals if a race was false-started. Future Paralympic Games Organisers need to build in processes to enable deaf Paralympians to resolve such basic needs more easily. Perhaps the IPC could make a start by putting deafness on the agenda of the IPC High Support Needs Committee?

Conclusion

Before we can consider taking Deaflympic athletes into the Paralympics we should ensure that the organisers are able to meet their needs as elite athletes. Sebastian Coe's template for organising any sports event is to;

> ***"put competitors at the centre, because if you succeed in doing that, then so much else falls into place"***
> (Coe 2012).

There are many opportunities for this to be worked on at other events within the Paralympic programme. Things can be tried out on a smaller scale and then built up from there. It requires both the ICSD and IPC to work together, pooling their expertise. Only through this process can we find out the answers, one way or another.

Baines (in Whalley 2010) and others (Crowley, Kaufman and Ammons) recognise that change is always inevitable; otherwise the Deaflympics will become unsustainable. This chapter has already highlighted some changes that would have to be made to the Paralympics in order that they could be deemed suitable to accommodate Deaflympic competitors. Unfortunately, the matter is complex; as is explored in the next chapter.

8

Logistics

The withdrawal of the CISS from the International Paralympic Committee (IPC) in 1995 was partly down to the fact that the IPC had not replied to six questions from the Comité International des Sports des Sourds (CISS) about including deaf athletes into the Paralympics. There were two key logistical issues that could not be resolved: firstly, the number of athletes allowed to compete; and, secondly, the requirement for interpreters (Jordan 1996; Ammons & Eikman 2011). In addition to bringing these two issues up to date, this chapter also deals with the other considerations of optimum environments, costs, classification and timescales.

Number of Athletes

Ever since the establishment of the IPC, many National Olympic Committees and corresponding sport authorities (including UK Sport) have argued that they will not support deaf athletes entering the Deaflympics and that they must enter the Paralympics, which would then entitle them to conditional

World Class funding and support.

In Athens 2004, the International Olympic Committee (IOC) indefinitely restricted the size of the Paralympics to 4,000 athletes. Therefore, if the IPC were put under pressure to admit deaf athletes, other disabilities would have to 'make way' for what they see as a lesser disabling impairment and one that is more attractive to mainstream media, which, ultimately, attract sponsorship (Howe 2008:83). There is a hierarchy of disablement within the IPC with regards to each group's inclusion entitlement. I experienced this when I was working for UK Deaf Sport. I persuaded two sports to compete successfully in Pan-disabled events. Unfortunately, there were comments and decisions made that some might class as discrimination (see next chapter). Since 1994, the IPC has also had pressure from the more severely disabled athletes, who compete in 'race runner' chairs (these are athletes who propel their own chair using their feet) and who wished to return to the Paralympics programme (Howe 2008:51).

The CISS's withdrawal from the IPC was because the IOC advised the IPC to start with seven sports disciplines; but the CISS already had 17 and therefore could not commit itself to reducing opportunities for athletes (Hussain 2012; Ammons & Eikman 2011). The Summer Paralympics has now grown to an event offering 21 disciplines and the Summer Deaflympics covers 22 and is growing. According to LOCOG publications (Kilgallon 2012), there were over 4,000 athletes competing in the 2012 Paralympics, which suggests that the IOC may have now relaxed their limit set for Athens 2004.

To include Deaf athletes in the Paralympics, either some disability classifications would have to be removed from some events or the IPC would have to introduce extra events. There are many possibilities, but some examples to consider would be: adding the 10,000 metres & Steeplechase in athletics; and including additional classifications in Marathon, Road Cycling, Sailing and Shooting. Alternatively, on the basis that communication in team sports is a major disabling factor, they could introduce new disciplines; for example, 11-a-side football, volleyball, basketball, handball or golf (a new Olympic sport in 2016).

If Deaf events or competitors were brought into the Paralympics, the concern for international deaf sport federations such as basketball and football would be the implications for their sports if they were not included in the IPC. Would these events remain outside the support of the IPC movement or, at worst, lead to the demise of sign language in deaf sport (Ammons & Eikman 2011:1154)?

One suggested preference would be to see the Deaflympics come under the Paralympic movement (e.g. IPC World Championships, Commonwealth Games) and act as a feeder to the Paralympics and the Olympics. The major concern is the risk of losing the two blue ribbon sports of athletics and swimming. It is not beyond our imagination to envisage that, over time, as the characteristic of the deaf athlete (Stewart & Ammons 2001) evolves we might see classifications for these two sports 'creep' in.

Communications Requirements

Critics argue that the Deaflympics should be able to manage with volunteer sign language interpreters to keep costs to a minimum (Carpe Diem 2012). What is not widely understood is that interpreting in sign language requires higher levels of skills and longer, more intensive training than spoken language interpreting. The quality and standard of interpreters need to be proficient to cope with the linguistic intricacies of International Sign Language. The 2007 Winter Deaflympics recruited approximately 325 interpreters for 298 competitors and officials, delegates and spectators (Gorrell 2007). The 2009 Summer Deaflympics recruited 2,800 sign language volunteers and 50 from overseas who spoke higher level English and sign language (The China Post 17.12.08).

The costs of providing training for all the volunteers would be justified by the increase in the number of people who would then have useful sign language skills that could be developed further and applied widely within or outside sport. The New Zealand Deaf community benefitted from a sign language interpreters' training programme set up after the Christchurch Deaflympics. Other agencies serving the Olympics/Paralympics could also be involved. The city bus services in Taiwan provided sign language training for all its drivers to meet the demands of the 2009 Deaflympics. The number of interpreters required for the Paralympics would be in proportion to the number of athletes involved and the number of sports provided. With the expected increase in Deaf spectators, additional provision would be required to meet their needs. Whatever is decided with regard to communication support, World Class sports events organisers can now refer to the list of recommendations provided by the London Organising Committee of the Olympic and Paralympic Games' (LOCOG) review for Deaf and Deafblind people (LOCOG 2012) *Learning Legacy: lessons learned from planning and staging the London 2012 Games.* This report lists no fewer than eleven recommendations with 58 key performance indicators. These recommendations ensure that event organisers meet equality legislation and stress the importance of involving Deaf-led organisations, and organisations which then work closely with Deaf people, from the very beginning of the planning process to the execution of the event, in order to minimise problems.

Optimum Environments

ICSD states that the Deaflympics require no modifications to playing surfaces and equipment or rules of sport. But this is not strictly true, as the environment needs modifying. Starter lights for each athlete in some races are required (a traffic light system) to provide an optimum start. Unfortunately, the systems failed at both the 2009 (Polk 2008) and 2012 Paralympics as the organisers were not experienced enough to cope. The competitors were then directed to re-run races alone; or they wasted energy, because of missed call-backs. Teething problems are to be expected, but at the highest levels of performance they cannot be tolerated.

The Athletes' Village would have to be modified to ensure that athletes have the best down-time experiences possible, avoiding the stress associated with dealing with a lack of interpreters, subtitles on television screens or inaccessible PA systems. Fire safety systems are all additional investments that require modifications. Communication in warm up and holding areas need to be accessible as would access to sign language interpreters to relay information from officials, judges, referees, doping staff etc. We must have one thing paramount at the front of our minds and that is that the use of sign language interpreters still only provides a second-hand access to speaking and listening. I have already mentioned the lack of awareness by LOCOG when dealing with an enquiry from Laurentian Tan for interpreter's accreditation.

Using assistive technology in the Paralympics has the potential to attract media attention; and this use of technology further down the sports pathway should be encouraged, to give deaf athletes equality at lower level competitions. Ideally, this should be something that becomes an integral part of mainstream sport, because it could also improve performances there too. The ICSD should become the first port of call when planning for Deaf sports in the Paralympics; it has the experience and expertise required with the foresight to prevent problems occurring. Likewise, with overall event planning and co-ordination, there would be an influx of deaf and hearing volunteers with the skills to help optimise the Paralympic environment.

Costs

The actual costs for including Deaf sport into the Paralympics cannot be calculated here. When I interviewed Crowley, he observed that facilities in the athletes' village were underused at the London 2012 Paralympics and suggested that including deaf athletes there would help to achieve the greatest return on investment in temporary venues. The increased media coverage of Deaflympic athletes in the Paralympics would, perhaps, have the potential to attract corporate sponsorship and government funding into the Deaflympic Movement. Increased media profile would also encourage budding sports persons to consider joining national Deaf sports organisations.

Would the IPC consider Deaf athletes to be worthy enough of media attention and therefore to attract more commercial resources to the Paralympics? It is interesting to consider one opinion from Colin Rains, a former President of the CP-ISRA, who thinks that certain forms of physical disability are more acceptable than others at getting across messages through the media:

> ***"It is tough to say, but I believe that people think that athletes with CP are not totally media friendly, visually. They can be slightly uncoordinated both in their running and their visual expression. It is possible that people find this off-putting."***
> (From Mott 2000, in Howe 2008:142)

Classification

The classification for Deaf athletes into the Paralympics would be the 55dB threshold or whatever its derivative might be in the future. The problem is finding a way to include this class without impinging on existing competitions or jumping the queue in front of other athletes, such as the chair-runners, who have been trying to get re-instated since 1994.

In addition to classification, there would have to be decisions made on eligibility based on performance standards. There would be an expectation that, being less physically disabled, Deaf athletes competing at the Paralympics would be reaching the higher performance standards of Parkin and others. In time, these margins would be reduced as performance funding and resources become available.

How would the IPC make decisions about athletes, who were deemed to be 'cheaters'? At the Barcelona Olympics they expelled intellectually disabled athletes from the games indefinitely on the basis of the basketball cheating scandal, until the INAS-FID had introduced more stringent protocols. Would the IPC apply this when they discover a 'deaf cheat'? My observations of the practice in the Deaflympics is that technical meetings are hotbeds of passionate debate, as coaches and athletes accuse the technical officers of either bending IF rules or creating ICSD versions. Breivik et al give an illustration of this from a Deaflympic football match between Iran and the USA. During the game, an Iranian player was found to be wearing his hearing aid and the officials decided to stop the game and award the USA with a walk-over. Apparently, the USA players felt the punishment was too severe and only the individual should have been penalised (Breivik et al 2002:34).

Another consideration is how much the ICSD would tolerate the ongoing 'evolution' of classification within the IPC itself, which classification was created in accordance with the concept of providing a level playing field, but is now designed to attract the attention of the media and commerce (Howe 2008:81).

Timescales

Stewart and Ammons anticipated that the Deaflympics would transition into a new cultural event for Deaf sport but, at the same time, ICSD wants to protect competitive opportunities for those who need it most. The IPC is not likely to want to rush into things; and would place stringent conditions on classifications and performance requirements, as they have done with the re-instatement of the Intellectual Disability competitors.

There have always been suggestions to the ICSD that it consider staging events as part of mainstream, International Federation-sanctioned competitions. ICSD recently approached the Glasgow 2014 Commonwealth Games organisers about hosting Deaf test events, but this was declined; whilst the organising committee have increased the number of IPC sanctioned sports. This is another indication that things are going to take some time to resolve.

Whilst the inclusion of high performance Deaf events has not yet been achieved, another opportunity has been created in the wake of the 2013 Deaflympics, which Greece abandoned after entering into deep economic decline. The new hosts, Sofia, were unable to provide the resources to hold the Marathon event at such short notice and so the ICSD moved to secure the Deaflympic Marathon into the Konigsschlosser Romantik Marathon in Fussen, Germany, just over a week before the Opening Ceremony. Although not a world class sanctioned event, it was a very successful partnership, highlighting the elite talents of Deaflympic athletes, who dominated all the top ranking finish places in both the men's and women's categories; and it should be seen as a stepping-stone for more opportunities in the future.

If agreements could be reached, the timing for introducing Deaf sports into the Paralympics would have to be scheduled many years in advance. It would have to be incorporated into an event that has not yet been identified; the earliest would be 2024. Bidding for the host city would begin in 2015 with the winner announced in 2017; but even this is optimistic. Alternatively, the IPC and ICSD could turn their attention to including Deaflympic athletes into the Winter Paralympics, as this may prove to be logistically easier to introduce.

But even before all this could happen, the IPC would need to work out how the ICSD would become a member, because the old governance system led by the International Organisations of Sport for the Disabled was replaced with members from the National Paralympic Committees in 2002. There would be a matter of resolving NPC membership for NDSFs alongside this.

Whatever the outcome, in the meantime, governments, National Olympic and Paralympic Committees should recognise equally, and respect the status of, the Deaflympics and provide proportional performance funding and resources until, at some time in the future, all avenues have been exhausted by the IOC, ICSD and IPC to come to a resolution.

SECTION 3

How does Deafness affect Sports Performance?

"The hearing impaired is no difference from regular people in their appearance. We just endure more silence inside."

(Chang Yao-Chien, in Deaflympics09 9/9/09b)

9

How Deafness affects athletes

When interviewed by the BBC World Service, Rajeev Bagga stated that his deafness did not affect his performance. Other deaf sportsmen and women share this high level of self-belief (Parkin in 21st Deaflympics 4/9/09c & Zakladnyi in Deaflympics09 8/9/09a) However, these personal perspectives create confusion and give reasoning to those, who claim that the Deaflympics are unworthy of the support they deserve. In this chapter, I argue that exceptional individuals like Bagga have been fortunate enough to have developed their skills in an environment, which has counteracted possible barriers facing deaf people in sport and that, to an extent, some high performance athletes are so affected by the stigmatisation of deafness, that they downplay its impact on them in a way that is detrimental to their development as high-performance athletes. Terence Parkin (RSA), Olympic silver medallist, recognises the potential impact of non-congenital deafness and the difficulties that people have adjusting. Tony Ally (GB), Commonwealth Games and Olympics diver described his deafness as being the greatest weakness in his life, creating many communication problems both in and out of the pool. (In Achieve Sept 2006: 21)

What is affected by Deafness?

Before I continue, it is imperative to point out that individual deaf people are unique from each other. No two deaf athletes are the same, even if they have the same degree, type, pattern and onset of hearing loss. It does not mean they hear and understand the same thing or benefit from a hearing aid or cochlear implant in the same way. Each athlete's hearing and speaking capabilities are unique.

Balance

Balance depends on the nerves in three systems synchronising with each other; eyes, legs/torso and inner ear balance organs. This is our vestibular system. Nerve signals are sent to the brain to help us stay upright. When something goes wrong with one of these systems, we lose our balance. Researchers at John Hopkins University studied 40 deaf children with cochlear implants and found that one third of them had vestibular and balance dysfunction.

Those whose deafness was caused by meningitis had worse balance than others (Cushing et al 2008). The National Institute on Deafness and Other Communication Disorders identified that 4% (8 million) American adults report a chronic problem with balance (NIDCD 2006). Athletes with Ushers Syndrome, a condition causing visual and hearing loss, are also greatly affected.

Taiwanese shooter, Huang Cheng-hao has Menieres Disease, an inner-ear disorder that affects his balance, but which also causes episodes of dizziness, tinnitus and a progressive hearing loss (Deaflympics09 7/9/09). Lin Bo-Chong's deafness was caused by a childhood fever. He can barely hear with hearing aids and has a gradually progressive deafness; *"I had to readjust to everything after I became deaf. I doubled my training to cope with situations and in the Games".* Dizziness occurs when he does quick turning movements and he also suffers from Thalasemia, which makes progressing tougher (Deaflympics09 8/9/09b).

Dean Barton-Smith went on to become an Olympic decathlete and retired from athletics due to a balance-related illness.

Ability to hear

There are three types of deafness: conductive, sensori-neural and mixed deafness.

- Conductive Deafness: sound cannot pass efficiently through the ear to the cochlea and the auditory nerve. *Otisis Media*, the build up of fluid in the middle ear, is the most common cause of conductive deafness, which is usually temporary; but it can also cause permanent deafness.
- Sensori-neural deafness: a fault in the inner ear or the auditory nerve. The most common cause of sensori-neural deafness is the failure of hair cells in the cochlea to grow or function properly. This causes permanent deafness.
- Mixed deafness: is a combination of both conductive and sensori-neural deafness and can be temporary or permanent.
- The degree of deafness is measured using audiometers (audiograms) and it is graded mild, moderate, severe or profound.

In sport, deaf people cannot hear the calls or plays from teammates or their coaches and referees. Deaf players have to make greater use of their sight and look around to determine their own position on the field of play and that of their teammates. In football (soccer) deaf players have to learn how to look ahead when dribbling (moving with the ball) rather than at the ball so he/she knows who is 'open', unlike hearing players, who can also rely on auditory cues.

In table tennis and badminton, a deaf player cannot hear how hard a ball or shuttle has been hit by themselves or opponent. The cut of a ball cannot be heard to determine the type of return the opponent has played (Tamil Deaf Sports 2013)

The support of spectators cannot be heard to spur and motivate players. Kelly Duran explained that, when she reached the finish line in mainstream skiing events, the spectators looked at her and clapped with smiles on their faces but there was no direct feedback on how she had competed. After her first Deaflympic event, she felt more like an elite athlete, because she got a rush from the crowd who came up to her and shared her successes and failures of competition through direct communication (in Lockhart 2003).

Players in the Taipei 2009 basketball competition could not hear the 2,000 spectators cheering them on, but they could feel the support, because of the close proximity (Deaflympics09 15/09/09). In some sports it is considered an advantage to be unable to hear the crowd and disruptive noises from opponents or the surrounding environment. For swimmer Terence Parkin, his deafness is his strength. Undisrupted by background noises and distractions, he can concentrate better in the water and focus on the finish (21st Deaflympics 4/9/09a).

Deaf athletes are disadvantaged in competition, because they cannot hear start pistols, whistles, bells, or other auditory signals. This causes the athlete to start with a small delay and, for some sports, the smallest fraction of a second can make the difference between a gold medal and a silver medal. Hartley Bressler (in Dummer & Stewart 1991) analysed the differences in starting positions between deaf and hearing sprinters. The first problem is visual orientation - on the command 'on your mark', the hearing sprinters are in a position where they look down at the track surface. The deaf sprinter has to look at the starter, in an uncomfortable position with contracted neck muscles. They might also be dazzled by the sun or distracted visually by movement in the background. On the 'get set' command, the deaf runner has to continue looking at the starter and cannot assume the ideal position. Stability is affected, because the body is not squared to the blocks. Hearing sprinters have their head in a relaxed position with the body balanced. A deaf sprinter's start is therefore slower, because of the inefficient start position and also because hearing sprinters are coached to lift an arm when the gun is fired. Deaf sprinters must first concentrate on the starting gun, then looking at the ground, then on arm action. Driving away from the blocks the head needs to be lifted slowly and gradually. They lift their head too early and too fast. The solution to this is a starting unit with a set of three coloured lights positioned on the track in the sprinters lane. This has also been adapted for use in swimming and other sports. Unfortunately, this equipment is only available at the Deaflympics and at the European and World Deaf championships and is not used in mainstream competitions.

In the run up to the 2009 Taipei Deaflympics, a public fun-run attracted 3,000 runners, who were encouraged to wear ear-plugs to simulate what is was like playing sport without being able to hear. A senior state official taking part described how he felt unsafe, because he could not hear (8.6.09 China Times). A Taiwanese bowler explained that Deaf athletes look no different in appearance from regular people – they just endure more silence inside (Deaflympics09 9/9/09b)

Being unable to hear a referee's whistle has caused many Deaf players to be penalised and often sent off the field of play. There has also been an incident reported to a helpline where a rugby player was not allowed to wear his hearing aids because the referee called it a communication device (Palmer, in AoHL Forum 2012). Water Polo is a game where the play is controlled by very frequent blowing of the referees whistle. Jordan Eikman and his Deaf team challenged a hearing team to a re-match after losing their game, this time the game was controlled by referee using hand signals instead of the whistle; the opposing team was disadvantaged and lost comprehensively. (Eikman in Lockhart 2003)

Predisposition to use spoken language.

As the Swiss Deaf sports website explains, society is built on the cultures of speaking and hearing, which is why Deaf are the only disabled group with their own culture and language. Because of their communication problems, the Deaf cannot talk to other disabled persons and non-disabled persons and this puts them at a disadvantage in sport (SDSF 2013). Spectators at the 2009 Deaflympics, experiencing the event for the first time, observed how Deaf footballers expressed themselves with body language and facial expressions (forumosa.com 6/9/09)

A hearing man recollected how difficult it was to play in a Deaf softball team. Playing at second base, he could not rely on a team mate to call when running backwards to catch a ball – the calls never came. He also explained how umpires would approach him to discuss an incident during play instead of approaching the Deaf pitcher, who was the nominated team representative; presumably because the official thought it would be easier. (Stewart & Nulf 1996)

Not contributing to team meetings and mid-play discussions would give the impression that a Deaf player was unable to articulate and make effective contributions, so making them more disposable at higher performance levels or when the stakes are higher.

For those of you who know me, I have what my teachers and speech therapists described as 'intelligible speech'; and people often tell me that they would not have known I was deaf if I had not mentioned it to them. These people also assume that, because I can speak clearly, I can 'hear well'. This forms the basis of 'communication breakdown', because I have to remind people constantly that I cannot hear them. However, if I introduce myself to someone and immediately declare my deafness, I have a comparatively better communication rapport with that person. But, as the majority of people I tutor in sports coach CPD programmes would testify, they are surprised to discover that I have a severe/profound deafness in both ears and when I ask them why they thought otherwise, it is always because of the intelligibility of my speech. They make this assumption despite the fact that I also have an interpreter working for me.

To Darren Dunne, captain of the Ireland football team communication is like:

> ***"dribbling past an opponent – difficult but worthwhile".***
>
> (in 21st Deaflympics 4/9/09b)

Ability to understand – training

The inability to hear and speak in the mainstream sports environment has different degrees of influence on an athlete's learning of skills, movement forms and tactics (SDSF 2013). Lockhart (2006) describes this as compromised or diluted access to quality coaching or training, which affects technique and strategy. On a personal level, I have two degrees - in Physical Education and Deaf Education - but I cannot understand what is being said in mainstream coaching sessions unless the coach is using effective communication tactics, signing to me or working through a sign language interpreter. All I can do is mimic the coach and follow the other players.

Dummer, Haubenstriker and Stewart used the Test of Gross Motor Development (TGMD) with a group of deaf children. They analysed 93 girls and 117 boys aged 3 to 22 years with an average hearing loss in their better ear at 97.12 dB. They were all students at two schools for the Deaf. The presentation of administering the procedures of the TGMD was modified and delivered using sign language interpreters, who were also trained in TGMD administration. The test assesses the ability to perform seven locomotor skills (run, slide, gallop, hop, horizontal jump, leap and skip) and five object-control skills (throw, catch, bounce, strike and kick). Deaf children's performances were comparative to hearing children for run, slide and gallop but there were delays in acquisition for four of the locomotor skills (hop, leap, horizontal jump and skip) and in each of the five object-control skills (two-hand strike, stationary bounce, catch, kick and overhand throw). The deficiencies in the performances were attributed to (a) the subject's performance abilities (b) difficulties in communicating test instructions to the subjects, and (c) inadequately specified performance criteria on the TGMD. (Dummer. G. & Stewart D.A. 1991)

I agree with Eikman (in Lockhart), that training and technique development for elite athletes is significant at world-class level and share his theorising that skills development in some sports is designed specifically to suit deaf players, either as a by-product of their deafness or as a compensatory measure towards competitiveness, such as the *Dave Smith Rule* used by the US Olympic Volleyball squad. When elite deaf athletes have been interviewed in *Achieve* magazine they have been asked if communication was ever an issue when working with coaches. Diver, Tony Ally, found it difficult when he was working in the water and they had to use a form of body language that was very frustrating for both himself and his coaches. When instructions were not fully understood, it took longer to correct a problem (UKDS 2006a). Squash player Rebecca Macree found it difficult when she had to take her hearing aids off to play or practice and there were difficulties with the court layout or the positions of player and coaches. More often than not, the coaches positioned themselves at the back of the court, but each time they spotted a problem in training they couldn't call out a correction. They had to stop the flow of play in order to give feedback, which was frustrating and something that they had to get used to (UKDS 2006b).

We need Sports Science studies that examine the knowledge and experience gained by Olympic and Paralympic athletes so that they can be applied to Deaflympic sport. For example, the proprioception feedback loop enhances the ability of Visually Impaired athletes to understand what is happening in their immediate environment and thereby use the feedback to adjust their movements accordingly (Burkett in Gilbert & Schantz 2008:116). Deaf athletes are unable to benefit from auditory feedback and thus should be examined in terms of developed enhanced visual perception and non-verbal communication. Do we really understand the adaptations that deaf performers are making when they play sport? A good place to start would be Stewart's discussion on the concept of *Symbolic Interactionism,* the study of understanding human interactions through analysis of symbols and meaning. (Stewart 1991a: 89-92). What adaptations can we make to linguistic techniques of visualisation to enable athletes to modify their moods or follow a race plan?

The loss of hearing needs to be compensated with support from another of the senses. We need to understand the rehabilitation processes for the deafened athlete who needs to be retrained, not just in their listening and other sensory perceptions, but also in their social, communication and Deaf *Gain* skills.

How far have Deaf athletes got?

A very small number of deaf athletes have competed at Olympic and world-class levels. Some have also had a professional playing career. Valery Sushkevich, President of the National Committee of Sport of Invalids of Ukraine was asked if Deaflympic athletes competed in 'normal' sports competitions. His reply was that they are capable of demonstrating great results, describing how a team of Deaflympic skiers had competed in an official Olympic level tournament and the majority took top-ten positions (Sushkevych 2013). The 2005 Deaflympics patron, Cindy-Lou Fitzpatrick, who held national swimming titles in the 100m and 200m breaststroke and represented Australia at two Commonwealth Games and two Pan Pacific Games, is profoundly deaf and has 19 Deaflympic gold medals. In 2005 Dean Barton-Smith, who represented Australia in the 1992 Olympic Decathlon, came out of retirement to compete in the Deaflympic once again in the discus, javelin and shot-put (Paxinos 2005b). The previous year's Olympics, in Athens, saw the following deaf athletes compete: Terence Parkin (RSA) Silver medal in swimming; Frank Bartolillo (AUS) Fencing Foil reached the 32nd round; Tony Ally (GBR) reached 5th in the pairs and 15th in individual Diving; Hugo Passos (POR) 60k Greco –Roman (results unknown) and Jueri Jaanson (EST) Single Sculls Silver medallist. These athletes were recognised in an ICSD report either because they were known Deaflympic competitors - they wore hearing aids - or declared themselves as deaf (ICSD 2004b).

In almost all of the examples given above, and in all known instances, elite-world class deaf athletes are usually found in sports for individuals and extremely rarely in team sports. The compounded impact of deafness on the inability to hear and communicate with others, along with dependence on the synergy of a team, means we usually find that the deaf athletes in world-class team sports are those who are able to make very effective use of hearing aids. Of the majority of athletes, featured in the newsletters reporting the back-stories of medal winners at the 2009 Deaflympics, nearly all had a post-congenital hearing loss, more commonly occurring in childhood. The congenitally, pre-lingual, deaf high performance athlete is a very rare specimen indeed.

Individual Sports

There is very little research into the relationship between deaf athletes and coaches, who practice individual sports. However, there was a comprehensive coverage of the 2009 Deaflympics in Taiwan, through a locally produced set of newsletters created specifically for the event. Most articles featured Taiwanese competitors and provided interesting insights from their coaches about the relationships they have with deaf athletes.

Karate coach Chuang Yu-hao explained that time spent training deaf athletes has to be almost double that for hearing athletes. The athletes themselves also have to double their efforts to improve their skills and performances. To help develop talent in deaf athletes, Yu-hao suggests that coaches should focus on strong qualities of discipline, fortitude and determination not to yield (Her 2009). This also helps the athlete to build respect with others in a world outside of sport. The bowling and shooting coaches recognised their athletes' work ethic to study their sport and training (Deaflympics09 12/9/09a and b).

British Deaflympic cyclist Tom Smith left his native Wales to live and train with a Belgian professional cycling team, which already had another Deaflympic cyclist Jean-Pierre Fauconnier on its books. The two riders met when they were sole representatives of their countries at the 2012 European Deaf Championships in Russia. All the other nations had 3 or more riders, so they formed an alliance to help each other. After performing well in Russia, Smith decided to get back into cycling properly (he almost gave up the sport after fracturing his vertebrae in an accident). He spoke to Fauconnier's manager Jan van den Braembussche and asked him if he knew of any teams looking for riders. Jan explained the set-up in Belgium and described the team that his own company sponsored, and eventually Smith joined up with *Lumet VDBG Steenhouwerji Racing Team* to prepare for the 2013 Deaflympics.

The two riders have different dynamics as part of a professional cycling team. Smith is able to communicate by speech using a cochlear implant and Fauconnier is a sign language user. Both used their sense of humour to build relationships with the other teammates and Smith has had to learn to speak Dutch in order to get by. It has been more difficult for Fauconnier, because he is of French-speaking origin (Wallonia) and there is only one other person on the team who can speak fluent French. Ideally, he should have a sign language interpreter, but Smith translates for him if they are at the same races. The team dynamic of getting to know all the personalities is very important, more so than the technical side of the sport; and this is what makes it more difficult for athletes like Fauconnier. Smith described his own relationship with his Belgian professional team manager as being limited only by his lack of Dutch. The situation is more difficult for Fauconnier, because of the dual barrier of not being able to speak Dutch and the manager not being able to use sign language; but they are all passionate about their sport and they all look out for each other.

The British/Belgian alliance continued at the Deaflympics, with both riders sharing resources and transportation. Smith's father, Ian, was his mechanic and Jan, being his guardian for his year in Belgium and a team sponsor, wanted the best for both riders. They both knew what they had to do in races and how to help each other when opportunities presented themselves. Smith won a bronze and silver medal.

Australian Deaflympic swimmer, Cindy-Lu Fitzpatrick, was also a national champion and competed at two Commonwealth Games and the Pan Pacific Games. At the 1985 Pan Pacs, she was roomed with a younger swimmer, Nicole Livingstone, who was hearing. Paxinos (2005a) interviewed them both about their relationship together as teammates. Livingstone looked up to Fitzpatrick as a role model for 'stability, guidance and level-headedness' and described Fitzpatrick as someone who 'speaks very well and is easy to understand', but signing is her first language; so she taught Livingstone 'all the swear words' in sign, first. Fitzpatrick said that teaching Livingstone to sign was very useful because she helped her to understand what was going on at meetings. But being a member of a hearing team was always difficult for Fitzpatrick and at the 1986 Commonwealth Games, she was having a difficult time communicating with the rest of the team and felt left out; but wondered if that was because they were not aware of how she was feeling, she thought that, if an interpreter had been available, she would have had a 'better connection to the team or the coaches' (from Paxinos 2005a).

Team Sports (All team sports)

Without the closer relationship between athletes and their coaches practicing individual sports, deaf athletes who choose to compete in team sports have challenges that push the effects of their deafness to the limit. Darren Dunne, captain of the Ireland men's Deaflympic football team, described how the limitations of communication in team sports can lead to misunderstandings with officials, teammates and coaches. When play breaks down, a deaf player is unable to get direction from the team manager/coach and thus has to rely on experience to find a way past difficulties. Being unable to make a living out of playing football professionally, he instils discipline in his teammates by reminding them of their pride and honour in representing their country (21st Deaflympics 4/9/09b).

In 2005, the Italian men's Deaflympic volleyball team, which had won gold at the previous three Games, drew its players from those who played in mainstream competition in Italy and who only came together for the international Deaf competitions (Paxinos 2005b). This is a growing and common trend in Deaf sport now that mainstreaming in education has reduced the number of hubs in schools and local Deaf community clubs, which would previously have provided grassroots sources of talent. Those wishing to compete at the highest levels now seek their everyday training and competition within mainstream sport.

Professional rugby player Matthew Gilbert was diagnosed with deafness at the age of five and has a hearing loss that would qualify him to compete at the Deaflympics. However, according to Jim White (2013), Gilbert prefers that his club and teammates do not make anything of his deafness; and he would prefer no special treatment. Could we consider for a moment that Matthew might be doing himself a great disservice and that, by not acknowledging his deafness more openly, he's not giving himself and his club the opportunity to help him rise to the very top of his game?

A good example of where this has worked in practice is within the US Olympic Men's Volleyball team, where Coach John Speraw describes the 'Dave Smith Rule' that applies to their middle blocker who is deaf. *'The rule applies: when Dave wants the ball he takes it because he cannot be called off in the middle of a play"*. Like Gilbert, Smith wears his hearing aids during competitions and suffers from a common problem across all sport disciplines when sweat runs into the hearing aids and causes them to malfunction (Peterson 2012). David Smith has a long-standing relationship with the Olympic team coach, who persuaded him to join his squad at UC Irvine. Thus their relationship has established an understanding, so that team tactics have developed as a by-product of the deafness. My research also uncovered Brian Thornton, a team setter in the Olympic squad, who also played with Smith at UCI. Their attacking partnership would have been honed out of an understanding between players that takes Smith's deafness into account (Daily Pilot 2012).

At the present time, Matthew Gilbert has a promising career ahead of him in professional rugby, and he could take it further if, as proposed, he embraces his deafness. According to White's article, he has been told that Gilbert can cope on the field of play and does not want special consideration. If we look back at his personal history, we learn that he was diagnosed with deafness at the age of 5 and coped by learning to lip-read, whilst also sticking to his older brother for support. His parents felt that he was a slow developer as he communicated with his mother through his older brother. At school, he had short sessions once a week with support to make sure that he was keeping up academically. His rugby developed naturally; he was the biggest child at school and, at college, and he took his sport more seriously. He used his deafness to get around the rules, to give himself more time to compose himself during play; but this stopped when an astute referee caught him out. It's clear that he could not have got to the position he is in today without the support of secondary agents; people who are essential to the development of high performance athletes. He should not be afraid to continue to develop his Deaf-identity and should seek to work with others to push his talent further. According to White, Matthew admits that he does miss the 'odd thing' when the game plan breaks down, so he has to look around to work out what changes have been made. This is the kind of vulnerability that may, conceivably, prevent him from reaching the very peak of his potential. A high performance coach will make some very tough decisions and therefore Gilbert should not put himself in a position where he is compromised. It would be interesting to know if he has worked with his team coach to experiment with the use of alternative means of communication support, which can be applied to both the training ground and the real-time match situation. Once again we lack the hindsight of high performance research in Deaf sport and should consider the benefits of creating an optimum environment that will allow sports teams to bring out the very best in talented deaf players.

What we do not want to see is the repetition of a story similar to that of David Hamilton. It was during a basketball game in his freshman year at Southern Illinois, when his team was losing early in the game, that the coach was angry and put Hamilton in for 'garbage' time to penalise the starters. Hamilton went on to score eight points and gave six assists and brought the game to a tie at half time. The coach then benched Hamilton for the rest of the game, because he wanted to remain competitive and win. After that game, Hamilton left the college and moved to Gallaudet University for the Deaf where he competed in the NCAA division III. He left Illinois, not because he was in trouble with the coach, but because the playing environment was not right for him. He shared no connection with the coach and conversed not even small talk. The coach knew no sign language and Hamilton was unable hear or speak effectively, so the stunted relationship with the coach lowered his self-confidence and created a psychological barrier (Lockhart 2003). Reading up on Gilbert's story does not suggest that there are communication or relationship problems at Bath Rugby but, when the status of the club is at stake in a high-pressure game, decisions could be made that become detrimental to his career. I suggest, therefore, he has nothing to lose by trying out some new changes.

I draw here on the example of Michael Lizarraga, when he was playing in the NCAA Division 1 basketball league for Cal State Northridge (Markazi 2010). He had an interpreter available for practice and games, but her time with him was limited owing to budget cuts. Fortunately, he had struck up a friendship with teammate Willie Gallick, who started informally to learn to sign with Michael; and then, during the summer camp of their second year, became technically competent and fluent enough to stand in when the regular interpreter was not available. Lizarraga described it being difficult not having the interpreter available; "I want to know what coach said but he talks for a really long time and I want to know everything he is saying but I have to be patient and just get the summary version from Willie." CSUN Coach Brawell noticed Lizarraga at an AAU tournament, where he had gone to scout another player. He did not realise Lizarraga was deaf until he saw him signing with his father. Brawell later found out that Michael was planning to study at CSUN, because of the large cohort of deaf students at the University, and because there were already other deaf athletes training there - Ashley Griffith on the track team and Danielle Berman on the women's water polo team. He chose CSUN over Gallaudet University, because he wanted to play Div 1 basketball.

In a short documentary about his time at CSUN, Lizarraga's interpreter explained that it was important first to observe practice and games as much as possible to get a feel for the environment and how everyone interacted. It was the off-court communications where interpreting was essential, since it was important for the player to be involved in daily banter/jokes, as much as the serious work of training. All of this helped Lizarraga learn about the personalities and dynamics within the team: knowledge that is essential, because, without such, a player cannot bond with others. Technically, interpreters should review practice schedules in order to be prepared for which sessions are likely to be conducted in any given period and which might involve filming. During play and match situations, the position of the interpreter is usually behind the coach on the bench, in a position to help with transitioning, so as not to slow things down. Most feedback is given once the player is on the bench. It is important for the interpreter to become a trusted member of the team, so that everyone is comfortable having him around. Michael graduated from CSUN in 2012 and his currently playing for Soles de Mexicali in the LNBP.

We know from the experience of others (Stewart 1991a: 81) and in the example above, that, in team sports, athlete-coach relationships are harder to develop than in one-to-one working relationships. The coach's perspective of deafness and disability becomes more generalised and the specific specialised differences, that are likely to be picked up in an individual sport, go unused and unrefined. The players and coach have less time together. My evidence lies in the comment made by the USA Paralympic and Deaflympic Ice Hockey coach, Jeff Sauer, who declared that: there is no difference between disabled and non-disabled athletes; it's just their handicap they have to deal with (Mackay 2013). Sauer's comments could be seen as a modest oversimplification of the intricacies of his work and skills with Deaf and disabled athletes and I suggest that the ICSD and other partners find the means to research and extract the knowledge that he holds for the greater benefit of Deaf sport and its high performance athletes.

Optimal Environments

It is important for all levels of sport, especially at the high performance end, that organisers ensure that the very best training and competition environment is provided for all athletes; so that they can optimise their performance. Sebastian Coe's (2012:400, 432 & 454) principles are that we should create the right environment and then leave the rest up to the athletes. The London 2012 LOCOG review of deaf people's involvement in major sports events (authored by Josef Baines 2012) is likely to be the first of its kind to be written under the auspices of an Olympic Games Organising Committee. It makes recommendations for the accessibility of world-class sports events for deaf athletes, officials, volunteers and spectators. The most significant lesson learnt is that the Olympic and Paralympic Committees, International Sports Federations and all other event organisers need to work with Deaf organisations at the very early stages of event planning and preparation, to avoid negative experiences at later stages.

Organising committees of the Deaflympics plan at length for the provision of: technical equipment for sports; sign language interpreters; technical and other environmental systems; and resources. The organisers of the 2007 Salt Lake Winter Deaflympics focused on creating the right environment, enabling the competitors to perform at their best (Gorrell 2007). As mentioned elsewhere, at the 2005 Summer Deaflympics the Taiwanese organising committee of the 2009 Deaflympics, sent a large team of observers to Australia to observe, make notes and begin planning.

The scientific discipline of occupational biomechanics may have a use here, in evaluating the environment of the elite athlete and creating the optional environment for best possible performances. Can we use Sports Psychology to answer the following questions: How does the involvement in sport affect the psychological make-up of deaf athletes? What affects their motivation and brings on moments of anxiety?

Starting signals

I have already discussed the importance of providing starting lights in races to make sure that deaf athletes have the best possible start. Dean Barton-Smith had a bad experience during the 1994 Commonwealth Games, which forced him out of medal contention. He has since been lobbying organisers to incorporate starting signals into IAAF sanctioned events. There was no mention of this technology in the LOCOG report, but the failures to give such systems priority would not be tolerated by other competitors and so deaf athletes should not be treated any differently. Barton-Smith competed in the Olympics and Commonwealth Games without the assistance of technology and had to, either, feel the vibration of the starting gun, or watch his opponents launch from the corner of his eye. He always started at a serious disadvantage.

Deaflympic martial arts events provide flashing red lights after each round or temporary stop in the contest. The lights flash to signal for the contestants to stop. The electronic scoreboard has one red and one blue light on each side. These lights flash at five seconds before the end of round intermissions to signal that the contest is about to resume.

Interpreters

Although not all deaf competitors use sign language, it is an important fundamental in sport for deaf people. This is often cited as the main reason why they are discouraged from participating in mainstream sport and why they opt for the more effective environment of Deaf sport. In preparation for the Taipei Deaflympics, organisers set out to recruit 4,000 volunteers who would be given training in sign language. The level at which they were trained depended on their role in the event. For the majority, they were deployed to assist at venue reception points and in guidance roles. The enthusiasm of volunteering took the city by surprise, as 8,000 were eventually enrolled (Her 2009). The 2007 Winter Deaflympics in Salt Lake City used approximately 325 interpreters to support an event hosting 365 athletes (Gorrell 2007). We have to bear in mind, of course, that the Deaflympics also needs to provide for the secondary agents (coaches, sports officials, team entourages and supporters). In Taipei, it was estimated that the ratio of volunteers to athlete was 2:1. (Her 2009).

Rajeev Bagga and other high performance athletes rarely mention the support of secondary agents that help them with training and thereby assist their participation at elite levels. Parents and siblings devote incredible amounts of time, poolside or courtside, interpreting/communicating for their children/ siblings. Dean Barton-Smith explained that it is not the deafness that limited his capacity to train; it was the necessity of making 'adjustments' (The Australian, 1992). I have spoken to many deaf athletes (both sign language and non-sign language users), who have been, or who are currently, on the cusp of maintaining their presence in world-class sport. When I ask them to describe the issues that prevent them from reaching their true potential, I am probably the first person to ask them the right questions to get them thinking about issues that they have momentarily recognised, but never resolved, because they are forgotten amongst the many other facets of their lives.

The use of interpreters in a training or competition environment has received very little attention in relation to the potential of high performance deaf athletes. There are guidelines and publications available to help coaches understand the value of using interpreters/communicators appropriately, but this is mainly in relation to making sport accessible to children and young people. In the UK, the National Deaf Children's Society (NDCS) and The Football Association (FA) have collaborated to create the "Coaching Deaf Footballers Course". They have also made similar resources for Rugby, Swimming and other sports. However, costs of learning and the time it takes to acquire sign language fluency, puts this skill beyond the average club coach, whose time is already at a premium. UK Deaf Sport and sport coach UK, in partnership with the NDCS, have created an accredited workshop for sports coaches: *'Effective Communication: Working with Deaf people in sport"* (scUK 2013). These resources give coaches and sports organisers the basic communication skills required to make their coaching more accessible.

In the competition environment, there are rules and regulations regarding the positioning of coaches and others during play. During international Deaf competitions, interpreters are utilised when the coaching staff are hearing. Ideally, deaf athletes at the high-performance level should consider the option of using interpreters, or other forms of communication assistance, in order to enhance their interaction with coaches and teammates to discuss tactics, techniques or for socialising during competitions. To be effective, Sign Language interpreters (SLIs) have to be trained to communicate in the sports environment, because standardised, accredited interpreter training does not prepare them for the language of sport: jargon, acronyms, player identification, scoring, tactics and so on. Ideally, sports would do well to recruit SLIs who already have coaching qualifications and experience of sport.

We can now look at examples of using interpreters in Baseball/Softball and Soccer as given by David Bar-Tzur (2001).

In Baseball/Softball, SLIs need to stay in the dugout with the coach but take positions within eye-line of the deaf player. The SLI and player need to learn the signs and signals used by umpires and 1st and 3rd base coaches. The catcher and pitcher also communicate in signs. Time-outs, that involve a deaf catcher or pitcher and the coach, need to involve an SLI. There will be occasional on-field 'meetings' and the SLI will have to make a judgment whether or not to join in; usually the deaf player will indicate to the SLI when needed. In soccer, the SLI or a team representative should approach the officials and the opponents' coach, to explain that they have deaf players in the team - to avoid confusion and conflicts later on – encouraging all players to raise a hand when the whistle is blown to prevent the loss of time that occurs when deaf players continue running with, or off, the ball. In one example, the Deaf soccer coach, who was giving advice, indicated that he would prefer it if the SLI did not come on to the field of play. It is not clear what this meant; the article suggested that he did not want young players to become too dependent on SLIs and needed to learn cope without; but in the case of Baseball/Softball, there should be no reason for SLIs not entering the field of play for team meetings and time-outs, providing that it is done within the rules and regulation of each sport. In the training environment, the use of SLIs is actively encouraged, because coaches are unable to give deaf players their undivided attention in team sports. During an average a one-hour training session, an SLI is probably needed for only 10 minutes, at the most.

Baines' report for LOCOG highlighted that deaf athletes had no access to SLIs, or personally had to pay for their own, for use in competitions and team meetings during the 2012 Olympics and Paralympics. Agencies and organisations providing SLI services need advanced notice to book interpreting assignments, because the resource is in short supply. The report stated that the last-minute accreditation process for interpreters did not allow time to source quality interpreters and recommended that organisers should make sure that there are no issues regarding SLI accreditation, and that all future world-class event organisers should recognise the flexibility of using SLIs; providing a pool of roaming interpreters for ad hoc situations. Finally, organisers should check that only SLIs recognised by national registration bodies are used.

Media and other systems

The LOCOG report cited the difficulty that Deaf Paralympian swimmer, Tadhg Slattery, had when he was interviewed live on TV. He was unable to engage with journalists, because an SLI was not available, and this prevented him from gaining full media exposure. The report recommended that organising committees remind NOCs and NPCs about the communication needs of their athletes. Role models need to relate their stories effectively in order to help reduce the stigma and discrimination associated with disability (Niyogy & Bhalla 2012).

For the Deaflympics, accessible telecoms and services in airports, hotels and sports venues are required. Training seminars for facilities, emergency situations, transportation, venue personnel and volunteers are essential.

The International Committee of Sport for the Deaf (ICSD) has recently appointed Dean Barton-Smith and Terence Parkin as joint chairs of the new ICSD Athletes Commission (Mackay 2012). This enables ICSD to leverage the knowledge, that the Olympic and International Federations network have of Dean and Terence, to raise the profile of Deaflympic competitors within the Olympic Movement. In addition, their roles champion ICSD as an athlete-driven organisation and allow for the highlighting of many of the issues and needs that have been given a brief introduction in this chapter and elsewhere.

Having looked at how deafness impacts on the ability of the high-performance athlete to train and perform at the highest level, the next three chapters examine the external influences of stigmatisation, the organisations of disability sport and pathways for Deaf sport.

10

Stigmatisation

Stewart (1991a: 99-101) described the stigmatisation of Deaf sport as a 'penalty for being different'. Stigma is described in *Harnessing the Power of Sport for Development and Peace* as: unfounded stereotypes, inaccurate assumptions, negative perceptions and prejudice about people with disabilities. Stigma is deeply rooted in societies; and the creation of external practices and policies that form barriers to disabled people are based on stigma (Right to Play 2008). The Right to Play report encourages the use of sport to tackle stigmatism by placing a disabled person in a position where their sports skills are highlighted. But stigma is also an internally constructed psychological barrier, causing a person to question their worth in society, and is generally based on their parents' notion of deafness and disability. Over 80-90% of deaf children are born to parents with little or no previous experience of living with a Deaf person (NDCS). If families have a stigma about deafness, it is likely to impact upon children's access to sport and their access to Deaf sport pathways.

Education

Stigma is attributing characteristics which suggest failure, handicap and shortcomings; a symbolic representation of inferiority (Stewart 1991a). In the 1880s, sign language was abolished in schools and it became stigmatised. The stigma of special education was dealt with by the mainstreaming policies of the 1970s and 1980s. The impact of all this is that students in mainstream education internalise a stigmatisation of sign language and segregation so, when they face difficulties in sport, they choose not to tackle them by declaring their deafness, because of the negative connotations that have become part of their self-belief.

But there are those who can be assertive: Kelly Duran, transferred to a skiing school so she could train consistently whilst still in full-time education. Unfortunately, she had to endure a legal battle with the school over its initial refusal to pay for the provision of sign language support. Eventually winning her case, she went on to become a two-time collegiate All-American skier. There are assumptions that deaf children will take up sport alongside their hearing peers, but for the vast majority, mainstreaming means isolation. (Lockhart 2003)

In September 2011, Deaf Sport Australia lodged a discrimination claim with the Australian Human Rights Commission on behalf of 11-year-old athlete Sekou Kanneh; who had qualified to compete in the School Sports Australia athletics 100m and 200m events, but was not being allowed to use visual prompts in a mainstream race, and would have to compete in AWD (Athletes With Disabilities) races instead. Fortunately, the matter was resolved and Kanneh has since gone on to break the Queensland's Schools 100m record, which had previously stood untouched for 21 years (Dodson 2011; Boswell 2013).

Howe (2008) noticed the manifestation of stigmatisation when he compared the attitudes of high-performance athletes in the 1980s, who had been either special-school or mainstream educated. The socialisation skills of those from special schools were distinct from those who had been mainstreamed. Special school adaptations of PE were 'normal', whereas mainstream PE 'adaptations' labelled individuals as 'other' and thus stigmatised. An interesting observation from Howe is that: whilst special schools can be advantageous for selecting Paralympians, since most of the students are likely to be more engaged in sport; by and large school staff steered clear of the possibility that their students could be high performance athletes (Howe 2008:141).

Chapter 13 discusses at length how 1970s education reform has contributed to the decline of Deaf sport by disrupting the pathway into sport for deaf children. We know from experience that the number of disabled children participating in Physical Education remains low, and non-PE sport has become an increasingly lower priority for staff in Deaf mainstream education. This has, in turn, influenced young people's attitudes when considering sport as a life-long activity. The Ukrainians speak more positively about Deaf sport and the Deaflympics and so actively promote it when they talk of making public sports facilities available to all. They recognise the barriers facing deaf people in sport and have consequently developed a unique system of physical education and sport for people with disabilities, despite the fact that they claim not to be as well funded as other nations (Sushkevych 2013).

Family

A main obstacle to the participation of disabled children in sport is their parents. Over 80 - 90% of deaf children are born to parents, who have no prior experience of having ever lived with deafness. In the first years of their child's life, the professional advice of medical experts and Teachers of the Deaf, and the prevailing educational trend towards mainstreaming, heavily influence the parents of deaf children. We know that, where schools have a low priority towards PE and community sport, the impact is further compounded for deaf and disabled children.

Children can internalise parental attitudes and the stigmatisation of deafness, along with the inferiority associated with it. In many cases this has a lasting impact on them, even long after they have become members of the Deaf community as adults. I have been told stories of parents patronising their adult children's driving skills by praising them at the completion of manoeuvres and journey.

Parents with an interest in sport may see Deaf sport as an undesirable social activity and might discourage their children from participating;, instead encouraging them towards mainstream sport, without providing a balanced experience of both. Even in more enlightened parents, their comments reveal the deep-rooted influence of stigmatisation as they describe their 'amazement' at their child's successes. (Clydebank Post 2012).

There are some great examples of 'hope', in that we can look forward in our current information-age to a time when stigmatisation might have a weaker influence on decisions made by parents and families. For example, a mother of a deaf child researched Deaf sport on the Internet when she was watching the Opening Ceremony of the 2012 Paralympics. Her son had asked how he could compete in the Paralympics (NANHM 2012). Information is now instantly available on-line; unlike 15 or 20 years ago, when a child would have asked the same question, but the mother's drive to provide an answer would have been lost in the moment, because it would have taken considerable effort to research the matter.

Deafness

Stewart (2001:122-123) discussed how media coverage of deafness in sport focuses more on the overt indicators of deafness - such as hearing aids, sign language and speech - instead of the athletics skills and sportsmanship. However, work produced by mass-media sources reveals an undercurrent of the influence of the stigma of deafness upon the athletes themselves. The author of the Dave Smith article wrote about the sweat-resistant benefits of the hearing aid and then described Smith as having an 80% to 90% hearing loss and being nearly deaf (Peterson 2012). Is the use of the term 'nearly deaf' suggesting that Smith and his team wished to avoid the stigma of deafness and its associated inferiority? Is there a fear that 'coming out' as 'Deaf' would have affected his professional volleyball career?

It is generally agreed within the Deaflympic movement, and backed up by the research I have undertaken for this book, that the media coverage of 2009 Deaflympics was, by far, the most extensive to date. But it is striking to discover that in almost every article, the term 'hearing-impaired' was used instead of 'Deaf'. The Deaf culture lobby argues that the term 'hearing impaired' is a reinforcement of the inability that is associated with deafness. The psychologist and advocate of Deaf culture, Harlan Lane, proclaimed when writing in 2002 that defining deaf people as hearing-impaired is like redefining women as non-men (Young 2002).

Deaf sport should not overly concern itself with defending itself from such issues; it should embrace and accept that the characteristics of Deaflympic competitors have now changed. The impact of educational mainstreaming and the advancement of hearing aid technology and cochlear implants cannot be reversed, and those who benefit from such developments should not be stigmatised for it.

Role models in sport are powerful agents for change and more should be done to promote those who are deaf. One blogger suggests that, because of the greater media coverage of the Paralympics, the IOC now ignores deafness, because it is no longer taboo or the 'elephant in the room' (Bart 2012). I would suggest that the IOC and ICSD realise that there is a great deal of work to be done, because society now has more obvious overt disabilities to focus on and it continues to misunderstand deafness. Therefore, as Stewart (1991:123) confirms, it maintains the stigma of deafness.

There are some in the Deaf community, who ostracise those who do not conform to the Deaf cultural norms. For example, the Deaf community dismissed Heather Whistone, who won Miss USA in 1995, because she could speak. The English Deaf Golf Association has seen a steady drop in numbers participating in its national championships, because there is a perception amongst the Deaf golfing community that the event is dominated by oral-deaf. The 2012 Deaf Sports Personality of the Year Awards (Great Britain) opened up its categories to include people who also competed in mainstream and Paralympic sport – this being aimed at encouraging Deaf people to be more empathic of each other, to recognise sporting achievements and not to be distracted by cultural perspectives.

It is interesting to understand the impact of Paralympic classifications and how they stigmatise individuals. Howe (2008) discussed the treatment of visually impaired, cerebral palsy athletes with intellectual disabilities, and athletes, who do not rely on technology (e.g. prosthetics, wheelchairs) to compete. Their sporting performances are considered within the realms of 'normality' and this "can be seen to be detrimental to how these groups may be treated both inside and outside the Paralympic communitas.' (Howe 2008: 134) The public has empathy with visually impaired athletes, because many people wear spectacles and contact lenses and, to a certain degree, most people are visually impaired through age-related sight loss. These athletes are not marginalised to the same extent as cerebral palsy or intellectually disabled athletes, who, like deaf people, have a hidden disability that only manifests itself in the social environment and not in the sports arena. (Howe 2008:134-136)

This hierarchy of disablement within the Paralympic movement, with regard to each disability's entitlement to be included in the Paralympics, can be demonstrated by two encounters I experienced in my capacity as Development Manager for UK Deaf Sport. I had persuaded Deaf sports organisations to compete in multi-disabled events, only to be knocked back with comments and decisions that some would class as prejudice. After successfully taking part in a multi-disability tournament, the Deaf sports organisation concerned wanted to enter a team the following year, only to be told that the organisers could no longer fit them in, because they would be taking up places of other more-disabled players. On another occasion during a multi-disabled competition, a disabled competitor was heard saying that it was not right to have Deaf players competing, because they were 'able bodied'. This unfortunately, dissuaded both Deaf organisations from further engagement.

Politicians

A classic example of stigmatisation on the basis of prejudice occurred in a debate in the UK parliament in June 2009. The Parliamentary Under-Secretary for Culture, Media and Sport at the time, Mr Gerry Sutcliffe, argued that the government was not discriminating against the Deaflympics and implied that deaf athletes did not require separate Games, because they already compete in the Olympics. The minister cited Antonio Ally as his example (Hansard 2009). Unfortunately, Sutcliffe's challenger at the time, Mr Ian Duncan–Smith, was not armed with the following facts provided by Thomas & Smith (2009):

- Disabled people have competed in the Olympics since 1904, starting with George Eyser, a left leg amputee who won three golds and two silvers in Gymnastics.
- This was followed by Karoly Takacs winning his first Shooting gold in 1948 (his right hand had been injured by a grenade, so he shot with his left);
- Lis Hartel, Dressage Silver in 1956 (below knees paralysis);
- Marla Runyan 1500m athletics 2000 (legally blind);
- Natalie Du Toit 10km swim 2008 (amputee) and
- Matalia Partyka (born with no right hand and forearm) who competed in 2008 and 2012.

This information was only discovered during research for this book and has yet to be introduced into the ongoing debate. On the basis of the above evidence it could be argued that to continue funding the Paralympics but not the Deaflympics is discriminatory against the Deaflympics.

We should take heed of what Howe has concluded: that, because governments make policies for the disabled, including provisions for sport, we should not see this as a hallmark of 'enlightened society', because disabled people still feel that politicians are just appeasing them, and it is in their best interest to appear more compliant to the needs of marginalised groups than they actually are:

> ***'their posture is more calculating and manipulative rather than grudging and conciliatory'***
> (Howe 2008:126-127)

If our politicians are going to do their utmost to force Deaf sports organisations to merge into Paralympic structures, in order to benefit from elite performance funding, we are in danger of radically affecting the quality of life of individuals, if Deaf sport is forced to merge or fold altogether.

Empowerment and self-governance

Is there a risk for the International Committee of Sport for the Deaf (ICSD) if it continues its determination to be Deaf-led? The ICSD is stigmatised as socially undesirable, because it is not allowing non-deaf people to take the lead. Stewart & Ammons suggested that the ICSD is not ready to give up its autonomy, because society is not ready. Society has not yet learnt how it affects deaf people (Stewart & Ammons 2001). Deaf people are not assertive by nature and, for example, allow public bodies like schools, doctors and hospitals to ignore their responsibilities by using their own children as interpreters. Deaf sport has produced. and continues to produce, confident, self-assured and assertive young Deaf people, like Oliver Monksfield, who used the UK political system to encourage the Duncan-Smith v Sutcliffe debate cited above.

Far from being isolationist and exclusive, Deaf-lead Deaf sport teaches both deaf and non-deaf people about effective communication, the significance of team work and co-operation, goal setting, self discipline, respect for others and the importance of roles. It allows people to take risks and to learn how best to manage failure and success in a safe supportive environment. Therefore, it needs to be a Deaf-led, Deaf-inspired integrated environment. The ICSD Congress designates the responsibility for organising the Deaflympics to local organising committees where non-deaf people hold lead posts, because they hold the necessary credibility and influence locally (Melbourne 2005, Taipei 2009). National teams which are competing send both deaf and hearing coaches and other secondary agents who, with officers from the national federations, provide positive role models of deaf and hearing collaboration and inspire deaf and hearing people to apply these skills to other arenas of life, such as employment and advocacy.

Other Assumptions & Perceptions

My experience of working with Deaf and non-deaf people leads me to believe that promoting the Deaflympics as a sports event, in which Sign Language is the dominating feature in legitimising an athlete's eligibility to compete, is perpetuating the stigma of the Deaflympics. The ICSD and its Congress should learn not to rely on the Deaf culture militancy of Sign Language and more on 'sport for sports' sake', in a way that it brings social and economic benefits to host nations and those yet to come.

Despite sign language being legally recognised by a growing number of nations, and being the preferred language of the Deaf community, not all profoundly deaf people (or those classified as 55dB hearing loss) use sign language. It is reasonable to conceive that potential deaf athletes are not coming forward, and their parents, teachers and coaches are not introducing new competitors into the Deaflympic Movement, because they have a stereotype of who is eligible to compete and do not consider themselves or their athletes worthy of selection, because they do not use sign language.

Deafness is a hidden and low–prevalence disability. It is likely that many sports coaches and teachers go through their entire careers without working with or recognising a potential Deaflympic competitor. When I was undertaking some post-graduate research, I followed up with schools that had responded to my initial questionnaires. I was surprised to notice that many did not register any deaf students on their response forms and, when I made enquiries, the most common answer I received was that they registered students as 'hearing aid wearers' and not as 'deaf'.

A Rotarian named Lou Marino, the founder of the Silent Knights baseball programme, believes that baseball coaches were not encouraging young deaf people to take up the game because they thought that their deafness would affect their performance. (Guzman 2006).

Religious and cultural beliefs in some developing countries still designate deaf and disabled people as 'sinners who deserve to be punished' (a deaf sports administrator quoted in Lauff. (2007:17)).

Recommendations

Stewart (2001a) recommended that Deaf sport needed to do more to engage with deaf children in schools and Dean Barton-Smith (2009) has reinforced this. There needs to be far greater involvement of Deaf sport role models in schools and, where appropriate, mentoring programmes for deaf people to consider sport as a life-long activity.

It is my recommendation that Deaf sport must engage more with the parents and families of deaf children, by working in partnership with other organisations that specialise in working with children and young people, and with those who provide support to families. Information on the Internet needs to capture the imagination of parents, about the potential for their children through sport, and compel them to encourage participation.

Deaf sport needs to embrace all types of deaf role models so as to encourage greater cohesion between those who see themselves as culturally Deaf and those who do not. Sport has to become a primary common ground for collaboration to achieve equality.

Deaf sport needs to demonstrate how self-governance and Deaf-led sport is the best way to ensure a more optimal and effective model of inclusion. Dean Barton-Smith credits his participation in the 1985 Deaflympics as helping to focus his route to the Olympic and Commonwealth Games (Paxinos 2005c).

Other Deaf people, who have also gone from Deaf sport and broken into the realms of mainstream, world-class, professional sport, should follow his lead and learn to understand the wider benefits to society of accepting their deafness.

11

Long Term Athlete Development

Introduction

The UK government's implied position that the Deaflympic Movement did not require recognition and funding, because deaf athletes can compete at the Olympics (Hansard 2009), dismisses the fact that talent alone does not achieve high performance sport; that it has to be developed and maintained through a Long-Term Athlete Development programmes (LTAD). The principles of LTAD are based on the work of Istvan Balyi, who sought to produce the largest possible number of athletes capable of competing at World Class level. One of the oft-challenged principles of LTAD is based on the need for 10 years of extensive practice to excel (Stafford 2005).

This 10 year lead-up period is currently not available to the Deaf, because the pathways are not well known or clearly identified. It is not clear how to 'enter' Deaf sport and LTAD raises conflicts within Deaf sport around communication needs. If resources are to be provided, they need to be funded and -

with LTAD systems - coaches and significant others need to be trained and aware of deaf athletes' needs. Casual observers of Deaf sport, suggest that the 'bar' of performance is low, because of the low number of athletes coming through. Despite this, year on year, Deaflympic and Deaf World records continue to be broken. I would like to propose what needs to be done to allow this talent pool to grow.

Pathways

LTAD pathways provide a road map and a menu of activity towards the ultimate performance goal. The pathway of Deaf sport has never been officially documented and is therefore not well known or clearly identified. To begin with, we need to 'classify' a Deaflympic athlete. The Deaflympic classification is "a hearing loss of at least 55dB pure tone average (PTA) in the better ear (three tone pure tone average at 500, 1000 and 2000 Hertz, air conduction, ISO 1969 Standard)".[8]

I have mentioned earlier that the cause or onset of deafness varies for each individual, as they are either: congenitally or prelingually deaf; or deafened by trauma/illness or disease or by natural causes. Research has shown that the onset of natural deafness, post-birth, usually begins in the late teens and early twenties (Mathers et al 2000). Not every athlete will reach the 55dB benchmark within a timeframe that allows them to compete in Deaf sport, but they will still have a significant hearing loss that can impact on performance and, therefore, are able to benefit from the services and resources available within an LTAD programme designed to support deaf athletes.

Stewart (1991a) explains that deaf athletes have a choice of where they wish to play sport: mainstream, Deaf specific or a combination of both. An LTAD pathway for deaf people needs

---

[8] ICSD Audiogram Regulations can be downloaded at http://www.deaflympics.com/pdf/AudiogramRegulations.pdf

to maintain a flexible approach in order for the individual to peak at their maximum potential.

At the 13th World Winter Games for the Deaf, the Canadian Ice Hockey team had several junior 'A" level players, regularly competing just below professional hockey (Stewart & Ojalas 1995). The Italian Deaf Volleyball team all play in mainstream sport and come together for international matches (Paxinos 2005b). Their LTAD is covered through mainstream sport. This is much more commonplace now, since the advent of educational mainstreaming programmes.

However, there is a problem with a reliance on mainstream sport to provide LTAD pathways, owing to the lack of access to communication. This has been discussed elsewhere in the book, but the emphasis should be that deafness is a communication problem and therefore, once it is overcome, a deaf athlete is, for all intents and purposes, able-bodied; and should be coached within the deaf/mainstream pathways. There are systems which embed deaf athletes into pan-disability or disability sport activity; but this must be examined carefully to ensure that the individual is not further isolated, because it is assumed that their communication needs are met. There are further opportunities for organisations within the Deaflympic and the Paralympic pathways to reinforce their MoU commitments by jointly supporting athletes, who are eligible for both Deaflympic and Paralympic competitions by virtue of their multi-disability. Two examples of this in Australia are track sprinter Lara Hollow-Williams, and swimmer Megan Grant, who both have visual impairments also.

Deaf people are concerned about embedding Deaf sport into mainstream structures, thereby effectively handing over administration roles. Both the Canadian and the American Hearing Impaired Hockey Associations (AHIHA) are administered by hearing people. In the 1990s, Stewart wrote that these arrangements disenfranchised Deaf leaders and sports directors.

A visit to the AHIHA website today (2013) shows no less than eight former players are now on the 20-strong coaching staff under the management of Jeff Sauer.

There are now more Deaf sports organisations working in partnership with mainstream sport in a way that enables them to maintain Deaf-lead autonomy. However, many would agree that this makes economic sense; as isolated, segregated provision is now much harder to sustain. Another issue that affects Deaf sport is the impact of IPC dominance on government policy, which in turn determines how public money is distributed. This could be seen to be preventing the construction of a separate Deaf pathway.

The argument for maintaining deaf autonomy is based on a concern that the larger group of oral deaf could dominate the Deaf sports environment and marginalise sign language users (Ammons & Eikman 2011). This is a very important and valid argument and one that must be taken seriously. In order to strike a balance, Deaf sport needs to provide examples of good practice where the welfare of sign language users is considered. I return to the AHIHA website, where there are seven interpreters listed and some of the administrative staff are also fluent signers.

Where it is mutually beneficial, national Deaf sports organisations have affiliated with federations of disability sport, in order to benefit mutually from, and contribute to, the continuing development of sport. It is beyond the scope of this book to examine the effectiveness of these relationships. Stewart and Ammons in *Awakenings* (1994) recognised that there is a benefit to the partnerships with mainstream organisations – the calibre of the athlete can be found to be higher.

If Olympic legacy is about inspiring young people to take up sport locally, then sports coaches need to be supported and trained in order that they can work effectively with deaf athletes in both mainstream and specialist provision. There are currently not enough coaches with the basic skills and knowledge, with which to accommodate deaf people into sport. Deaf sport is an excellent place for coaches looking to specialise and develop their communication skills, which can then be transferred into mainstream settings. I suggest that national Deaf sport organisations collaborate with their national coaching COD programmes and organise workshops and clinics, where inexperienced coaches can learn the basics and the more experienced can pool their experiences to raise the performance 'bar' higher.

Entry into Sport

For most people in developed countries, their first experience of sport is Physical Education in school. But, of course, not every young person decides or wishes to maintain their interest in sport when they leave full-time education It is a personal choice after all. However, children's experiences at school are likely to have a strong bearing on their decisions to continue. In the 1980s, when mainstreaming was legislated, deaf children were not considered to have Special Educational Needs (SEN) when it came to PE; and many, who had communication support in the classroom, were expected to cope in PE independently. This problem is still prevalent today, as cuts in education budgets are impacting on the quality and quantity of teaching and the support staff available to support students effectively (NDCS 2009).

Schools that have a good understanding and awareness of the life-long opportunities for disabled people in sport will do their best to ensure that they provide a good start. Unfortunately for Deaf sport, government policies do tend to have a strong Paralympic bias and therefore information, advice and guidance to school staff will reflect this. This cannot be allowed to continue, and therefore both full-time education and Deaf sports organisations should seek each other out, to connect in different ways. These can be curriculum connections through PE, and through the use of Deaf awareness opportunities to bring in role models to inspire and mentor; or they can be more informal, through information and networking, in order that opportunities can be taken up when needed. Currently, Deaf sport is not sufficiently resourced to meet all the demands. A long-term strategy is required to make more effective use of the resources that are already available.

Deaf people and teachers, who have tried all of the above actions tell me that these approaches do not always work. From my own experience and of others, the problem is that, most of the time, there's not enough consultation with the children, their parents and school staff in the first instance, to determine what the needs are. After consultation, plans can be put into place to deliver activities, even if they are only to support one or two pupils who show an initial interest and are then primed to report back to their peers that they have had positive experiences. Activity providers should promote their good practice and successes to attract more interest. Dean Barton-Smith has the right idea by suggesting that mentoring programmes should be set up to link current and former Deaflympic competitors to schools (Barton-Smith 2009).

Stewart and Ammons (1994) examined statistics for the Canadian team in the World Games for the Deaf (WGD) to assess the impact that 1970s-1980s mainstreaming had on team demographics. The result showed that in the 1969 WGD team, 97% of athletes were from specialist schools for the Deaf and that in 1989, 45% were from mainstream schools. It would be interesting to carry out further analysis of this, to determine the composition of each team and to analyse participants by sport, as understanding these trends would be helpful to inform decision-making.

As in all areas of sport, familial interest and a background in sport can be a positive influence on young deaf people.

Barbara Odonne (ITA), undefeated in the Deaflympic Tennis singles since 1989, lost her hearing from pneumonia when she was 9 years old. Her parents are tennis players and Barbara concentrated on her sport after the illness. With her family's support she progressed to compete on the European ITF tour, until injury forced her to stop and she focused on Deaf tennis (Deaflympics09 10/9/09).

The grandfather of Thomas Moesching (SWI), Deaflympic gold medallist, was a Swiss national 50m-rifle champion. Moesching's father became his coach when his son was 10 years old. He attended shooting schools at 21; and, after three previous Deaflympic bronzes, he won gold in 2009 aged 36. At the time, he ranked 6th in Switzerland, and only needed to rank 5th to be in with a chance for the Olympic team (21st Deaflympics 6/9/09).

Terence Parkin and Dean Barton-Smith were both encouraged by their peers; Parkin joined a swimming club aged 12 and his peers encouraged him to make the pool his 'kingdom'. It was just for fun to begin with and then he realised how well he could do when he competed (21st Deaflympics 4/9/09a). Barton-Smith was discussing with his school friends his frustrations at losing time over sprint starts when it was suggested that if he was able to do 13 events at one school's sports day, then why not specialise in the Decathlon and do 10 events over two? (Paxinos 2005c).

People often come into disability sport and Deaf sport at a late age, because their disability has been caused by trauma/disease, illness or a natural onset as in the case of deafness or blindness. Howe (2008:103) discusses how trauma survivors come to terms with their disability through the 'vehicle' of sport. They have a second chance to re-think their bodies and are given the opportunity to remake their bodies in different or less restrictive ways. Lauren Newton (GBR) was a competitive swimmer, whose degenerative hearing loss was diagnosed at the age of 15 during a medical examination for an ear infection (Holland 2004). Her mother sought out and contacted UK Deaf Sport, which was able to register her into the GB team, just in time for the 2009 Deaflympics. Her LTAD background was enough to bring her 3 gold medals. There is a similar story for David Ewan, a Scottish golfer, whose adult life was badly affected by this dramatic loss of hearing. I recall him telling me that Deaf golf had been his safety net, giving him the inspiration he needed in life, and which culminated in a Deaf World Championship win for him on 2010.

Several martial arts competitors have been motivated to take up their sports in order to defend themselves against school bullies (Deaflympics09 9/9/09a). I am not aware if this is a trend, but one could anticipate that bullying is a particular problem facing young deaf people; and sport presents them with a greater incentive to address the challenge of bullying and their own well being.

A fundamental point to note, here, is that many coaches are reporting that, when sign language users or profoundly deaf athletes become involved in high performance sport after leaving school or later as young adults, they have to be taken back to basics; because they have not had access to quality skill fundamentals, even though they may have already been playing their sport for several years. David Hamilton describes how a new college basketball season usually begins with an influx of new lower skilled deaf and hard of hearing players, who have had a late introduction to sport, and how a ‘steep learning curve’ awaits players who were unable to communicate well with their previous coaches (Lockhart 2003).

LTAD Funding

Deaf athletes do not have access to LTAD funding, which is predominantly allocated by government sports policy to Paralympic athletes. There are families, schools, coaches and other secondary agents, who are supportive of Deaflympic sport, and who are frustrated that government recognition and funding is not in place to send potential medal winners to the Deaflympics for experience, with a view to performing at higher standards in the next cycle. It has been mentioned elsewhere how Kelly Duran entered into a lengthy legal battle with her school to cover the costs for interpreters to allow her to attend and pursue her skiing career. Young deaf people, who require communication support, should be given all the assistance they need to achieve their true potential. I personally share the views of Dean Barton-Smith and the late John Lovett, who see the Deaflympics as an important pathway event for deaf athletes to step up into other world-class events and ultimately the Olympic themselves.

The amount of funding denied to the British Deaflympic programme, over two quadrennial cycles leading up to the London 2012 Paralympics, would only have represented 0.6% of the total spent on the GB Paralympic team. When UK Sport justified their decision, because they also cut out other sports, what they were overlooking was the fact that it was not only a single sport that was being penalised but also a complete multi-sports pathway of several sports. The situation is similar in the USA, where the US Olympic Committee is focused on Olympic, Paralympic or Pan-American interest and only recognises the USA Deaf Sport Federation as a lower-status Community-Based Multi-Sports Organisation; which in my view is an insult. The UK, American and many other governments worldwide either do not understand or choose to ignore the equal recognition of the Deaflympics and Paralympics in the eyes of the IOC, IPC and ICSD.

Governments in Russia, Taiwan, Ukraine, and some others elsewhere award their Deaflympic athletes with funding in the same manner as Olympians and Paralympians. The systems there are to provide LTAD and coaching support and an incentive to remunerate expenses for medal winners by awarding cash prizes. In 2010, an appeal was made by Hungarian Deaflympic medal winners for their entitlement to equal treatment of pecuniary awards in line with Olympians and Paralympians. The appeal was upheld and the respondent was found in breach of equal treatment as there was no reasonable ground for the differentiation from either sport or fiscal point of view (Kadar 2010).

LTAD specialists

The habitual nature of elite sport means that the elite performer has a support team which provides a social environment distinctive to each sport (Howe 2008:66) The coach and the support team become the controllers of the regime, and sport is a disciplinary institution where the body is partly controlled through the training process (Howe 2008:67)

Because of communication problems, you have to take a different approach when coaching deaf athletes. During a practice game, orders cannot be given verbally from the touchlines. The inclusion of an interpreter alongside a coach can only provide a momentary bit of information, because it requires athletes to take their visual focus off the game. Time is required to give instruction and then restart the game.

There are not enough specialists involved in Deaf sport, primarily because of historical trends of Deaf sport operating in isolation. Change is progressing and more collaboration between deaf and mainstream specialists is bringing results.

Many coaches, like Dong Jiong, are still coming into Deaf sport by chance. Jiong, a badminton silver medallist at the 1996

Atlanta Olympics and winner of the 1997 British Open, owns a badminton club in Beijing where he employs deaf athletes as workers. Once he began to understand the difficulties that deaf players experienced in training and the lack of competitive opportunities, he decided to take on the role as China's Deaflympic badminton coach. Communication with players is a difficulty that he is learning to overcome. His enthusiasm for his players is reflected in his desire to overhaul the team for future success (Deaflympics09 11/9/09a).

Will Garrow retired from professional snowboarding in 1999 and was studying to be a Teacher of the Deaf at Gallaudet University when he was offered the opportunity to be Head snowboard coach of the US Deaf Ski and Snowboard Association (Kaftan 2011). If LTAD programmes for the deaf are going to mean anything, there must be commitment from mainstream sport to build in financial provision drawn from government-sponsored sources. Either that, or they work in partnership with National Deaf Sports Federations to bid for the funds required. Deaf sport can no longer rely on attracting high-performance sport funding by maintaining a tradition of using Deaf coaches, unless they are of the highest calibre. 'Participation-level' coaches, and not enough 'Performance specialists', are still supporting too many teams and individual athletes. The rationale to compromise quality of technical experience for communication is a difficult one to handle. Deaf coaches need to accept that, if circumstances will not allow collaborative coaching, the alternative is to work as assistants and build up their experience. LTAD cannot be limited to 4-year quadrennial cycles; we must start looking at deaf athletes with 10-year perspectives.

Training time

Deaf athletes train equally as hard as Paralympians; but without the resources in place they are limited to the amount of time they can put in, either because they cannot afford full time coaching, or because they cannot afford to give up work on the off chance; given that, even though they are likely to qualify for the Deaflympics, the lack of funds would mean that they would not be able to attend. (Clydebank Post 2012)

Lack of available time may not be a concern for some, but lack of financial support means that resources have to be limited. The Taiwan shooting team had to train with air pistols right up until Deaflympic year when they switched to live bullets. They began with 5 bullets a day and then moved up to 50 in July and then 120 shots a day in the closing preparations and during the Deaflympic competition (Deaflympics09 11/9/09b).

All the German handball players at the 2009 Deaflympics worked full time and could only manage to get together for three practice weekends, because they had to cover large distances to be together and they were also in high demand by their home clubs (21st Deaflympics 7/9/09).

Will Garrow had to adapt the training regimen for his snowboard athletes in the run-up to competitions, because of the lack of time available, and because they also had to take time out to fundraise; so he directed his athletes to focus on strength and conditioning as well as hill training. He also asked them to compete in their own time in local events.

LTAD Systems and Coaching

Ron Stern addressed the 1989 Canadian Deaf Sport Conference on the difficulties of recruiting and training deaf athletes and coaches. After-school practice is no longer available to groups of deaf children, because they are isolated in mainstream education. They may also not be aware of opportunities available locally to get involved in Deaf-friendly sport. Deaf sports administrators face 'red-tape' restrictions when trying to pass information on to students via school staff. Teachers of the Deaf in specialist schools often take on coaching responsibilities.

Because training and coaching are becoming more complex and demanding, not only do athletes have to specialise but coaches also have to develop their communication skills. Stern would like to see Deaf and hearing coaches working together to share their skills and knowledge. Longer-term commitment to developing teams and athletes needs to be given support to allow coaches to build a rapport and develop their communications skills (Dummer & Stewart 1991). Barton-Smith (2009) recommended that Deaf sports organisations needed to establish 12 year plans in order to be effective.

Antoine Hays, judo coach to Cyril Jonard (FRA) explained that, whilst they are both 'forced' to communicate in sign language, Jonard has been practicing Judo since he was 5 years old and then became deaf/blind when he was 12. His 30 years of judo experience means that he can easily understand what Hays wants him to do (21st Deaflympics 12/9/09).

Virender Singh (IND) lives and trains with India's elite wrestlers. He has medalled at the 2005 and 2009 Deaflympics and the 2012 Deaf World Championships. However, he is denied the opportunity to enter the 'hearing' World Championships, because officials say there is no provision for disabilities. His interpreter lives with him to ensure long-term commitment. (Sengupta 2012)

Are there specially designed systems for LTAD for the deaf? The principles and guidelines established by Balyi are applicable to deaf athletes in the same way as 'hearing'. Nations like the Ukraine and Russia have made provisions for their Deaflympic athletes to use the same facilities and resources as their Paralympians, namely, specialist centres with accommodation and resources. In Scotland, swimmer

Lucy Walkup has transferred to a Paralympic Swimming Club, where she has access to three squad sessions a year with the Scottish Swimming Youth Development Squad (SDS 2013). However, I would like to suggest that modifications are made to the delivery and communication environment in which LTAD is provided, in order that we can serve larger groups of athletes simultaneously and more economically in terms of human resources and financial outlay.

The model I envisage is based on the principles of the Friends for Young Deaf People (FYD). In the early 1980s, the activities of the FYD, regardless of whether it was a one–day sports Festival, weekend or week-long sports activity or camp, always catered for both deaf and hard of hearing children and young people who were coached and taught alongside their hearing peers. The ratios of deaf to hearing were always strictly controlled at 3:1, which ensured that the deaf person had the opportunity to be in the majority – a rare experience in everyday life. Coaching teams and support staff were also a mixture of deaf and hearing adults, with co-leadership and mentoring in place to develop future sustainability. Interpreters were also available at all times. The majority of the GB Deaflympic athletes at the 1985 and 1989 Deaflympics came through the FYD programme. The FYD leadership and Training programme also found its way to New Zealand and was fundamental in establishing services for young deaf and hearing people. I was pleased to come across a report of a variation of the FYD Sports Festivals organised by the Japanese Federation of the Deaf. Deaflympic Mini-Festivals - one-day introductions to the Deaflympics for 70 young people, of whom 30 were deaf - took place. The day began with a lecture "What is the Deaflympics?" and a video showing the event, followed by introductory sessions with members of the Japanese Deaflympics squads for table tennis, volleyball and a 20m shuttle run where sound was converted into lights. (JFD 2010) This is a very simple and repeatable model of introducing the Deaflympic Movement into local schools.

I would like to finish off here and make a comparison between the most recent medals tables of the Deaflympics and Paralympics in Tables E-G below.

Table E: 2009 Summer Deaflympics medals table

	Country	Gold	Silver	Bronze	Total
1	Russian Federation	29	41	28	98
2	Ukraine	20	22	25	67
3	Korea	14	13	7	34
4	Peoples Republic of China	12	9	17	38
5	Chinese Taipei	11	11	11	33
7	United States of America	10	5	7	22
12	Italy	4	5	5	14
13	France	4	2	6	12
18	Australia	3	2	1	6
21	Latvia	2	3	0	5
22	Hungary	2	0	3	5
26	Great Britain	1	4	5	10
27	Poland	1	2	1	4
35	Netherlands	1	0	0	1
DNS	Belgium				
DNS	Romania				

Table F: 2012 Summer Paralympics medals table

	Country	Gold	Silver	Bronze	Total
1	Peoples Republic of China	95	71	65	231
2	Russian Federation	36	38	28	102
3	Great Britain	34	43	43	120
4	Ukraine	32	24	28	84
5	Australia	32	23	30	85
6	United States of America	31	29	38	98

9	Poland	14	13	9	36
10	Netherlands	10	10	19	39
12	Korea	9	9	9	27
13	Italy	9	8	11	28
16	France	8	19	18	45
36	Belgium	3	1	3	7
38	Hungary	2	6	6	14
47	Latvia	1	1	0	2
47	Romania	1	1	0	2
63	Chinese Taipei	0	1	2	3

Table G: 2013 Summer Deaflympics medals table

	Country	Gold	Silver	Bronze	Total
1	Russian Federation	67	52	58	177
2	Ukraine	21	30	37	88
3	Korea	19	11	12	42
4	Belarus	12	11	4	27
5	Peoples Republic of China	12	5	8	25
6	United States of America	9	8	12	29
7	Turkey	7	9	17	33
8	Iran	7	4	21	32
9	Kenya	6	5	5	16
10	Lithuania	4	5	4	13
12	Italy	4	3	5	12
13	Chinese Taipei	3	12	9	24
15	Hungary	3	0	1	4
17	France	2	6	3	11
18	Poland	2	1	1	4
25	Australia	1	1	1	3
33	Great Britain	0	2	3	5

46	Latvia	0	0	1	1
53	Netherlands	0	0	0	0
60	Belgium	0	0	0	0
DNS	Romania				

I would argue that there is a correlation between the rankings on medal tables and the level of State-funded support. Unlike the Deaf community in Russia, Western Deaf communities have been less tolerant of the benefits of 'Oralism' as a 'solution'. The Russians, by maintaining and preferring sign language amongst each other, accepted the need to work with Oralism and the wider community in order to survive (Burch 2000). The 'Russian approach' to LTAD appears to have delivered a greater sense of understanding and justification of Deaflympic and Paralympic athletes as equals and this philosophy has been inherited by former Soviet states (Sushkevych 2013). It has been demonstrated at length in Chapters 1 and 16 how Taiwan has also been able to understand and grasp the notions of the Deaflympics, Deaf Culture and Sign Language and its potential as a form of empowerment for everyone.

I have included the founding members of the Deaflympics in the tables above to demonstrate that on the whole, the founder members are not currently supported as well as their Paralympic counterparts in terms of the overall share of medals available. The United States, I would argue, has been able to maintain her higher Deaflympic status on the strength of the grassroots sports structures, particularly with the nucleus of college-level sport at Gallaudet and Northridge Universities. Belgium (in 2009) and Romania (in 2009 and 2013) failed to send Deaflympic teams. Australia were the Deaflympic hosts in 2005 but post 2005 their government's contribution to its Deaflympics structure was only AUS$80-$100,000 per year compared to its four year investment of AUS$20m+ for its Paralympians.

SECTION 4

Why Have I Not Heard of the Deaflympics?

"Use the term Paralympic instead
of disabled," he said understatedly
"If you avoid using the word Paralympic,
no one will know what it is."

**(Charlie Huebner, in Emener June 2006,
in Gilbert & Schantz 2008:79)**

Competitors of the 1924 International Silent Games
(copyright A Dimmock/ B Whalley)

Closing Ceremony Taipei Summer Deaflympics 2009
(courtesy of Sam Perkins)

Starting equipment at the 1924 International Silent Games
compared to the technology used today (see below)
(courtesy of ICSD)

Starting lights as used in 100m athletics today
(courtesy of ICSD)

Eugene Rubens-Alcais, founder of the Deaflympic Movement
(courtesy of ICSD)

Ludwig Guttman, Founder of the Paralympic Movement
(copyright Godfrey Argent Studio supplied by the Royal Society)

Pierre de Coubertin, Founder of the Olympic Movement
(copyright IOC)

Mens Cycling road race, Sofia 2013 (l to r)
Smith (GBR) Makaron (RUS) Carbone (ITA)
(courtesy of Joanne Harrison)

Emerging number of nations are now rewarding Deaflympic
medalists on par with Olympics and Paralympics
(courtesy of Joanne Harrison)

'Time Out', Women's Volleyball, Taipei Deaflympics 2009
(courtesy of Sam Perkins)

Mens 4x100m relay Taipei Deaflympics 2009
(courtesy of Sam Perkins)

Jerald M. Jordan CISS President (1971 – 1995) received the Olympic Order in 1995
(courtesy of ICSD)

John Lovett CISS President (1995-2004) his first task was to inform the world of the CISS withdrawal from the IPC
(courtesy of ICSD)

Antonio Samaranch IOC President (1980-2001) oversaw the financial stability of the IOC and the creation of the IPC is amongst his legacies
(copyright IOC/Jean Jacques Strahm)

Crowley ICSD meets Rogge IOC during the 2013 Deaflympic Torch Relay visit to IOC headquarters
(courtesy of Craig Crowley)

Craven IPC and Ammons ICSD agreeing on the Memorandum of Understanding 2004
(courtesy of ICSD)

Public transport livery promoting 2009 Deaflympics, Taipei City metro
(courtesy of Sam Perkins)

Torches used for the first international Deaflympic Torch Relay 2013
(courtesy of ICSD)

Extensive promotion of the Deaflympics during the 2009 Taipei Dragon Boat Festival
(copyright Daniel M Shih)

12

Leadership Profiles

This section of the book covers some of the main reasons why the majority of society has not yet heard of the Deaflympics. This Chapter focuses on the notion that movements and organisations within society are highly dependent on the political and public profile that the leaders inherit, cultivate or acquire. The founding of the Olympic, Deaflympic and Paralympic movements all originate from the ideals, beliefs, innovations and leadership of three individuals who have been credited as 'founding fathers' of their respective events. They were Baron de Coubertin, Eugene Rubens-Alcais and Ludwig Guttmann. These three men are the central subjects of the following discussion.

Socio-economic backgrounds

By the time their first Games were inaugurated, Coubertin and Guttmann had enjoyed professional success in their careers and were highly celebrated. In contrast Rubens-Alcais, in his lifetime, never progressed to become anything more than a car-mechanic in a Paris suburb. This surely suggests that the legacy of Eugene Rubens-Alcais is remarkable. Without a comparable high-standing in society, Rubens-Alcais was unable to call upon networks or influential political support when most needed. Described as a 'brilliant' man of modest habits, he spent the whole of his adult life in a sparsely furnished and simple attic apartment. He gave all his time and everything he had to the cause of his friends and others. He was decorated several times; *Officier d'Académie* 1930 (Silver Palms) – awarded in France for contributions to national education and culture, *Médaille d'Or de l'Education Physique* (1930), a Gold Medal for Physical Education, *Chevalier du Mérite Norvegien* (1960), *Chevalier du Mérite Social* and the *Commandeur du Mérite Sportif* (1962). (Lovett et al 2001 p16-17)

Howe (2008:20-23) notes, however, that Guttmann on the other hand was able to call upon the support of many influential people. One of his spinal-cord associates was Professor Maglio, who ran an Italian research centre on impairments. They collaborated and worked to ensure their Games followed on from the 1960 Olympics in Rome. Dr Nakamura, a Japanese medical researcher worked with Mr Kasai, Chairman of the Japanese Sports Association for the Disabled who, through him, had close ties to the Japanese government. And Kasai's further influence secured funding for the 1964 Games from both public and private sector sources. When the Mexican government cited 'technical difficulties' as their reason for not hosting the Paralympics in 1968, the Israeli Government was lobbied by the ILAN Society (a group of disability activists); and this resulted in the event being hosted near Tel Aviv.

Political Influences

The political influence accessible to Coubertin and Guttmann placed them in a position of influence that Rubens-Alcais could never hope to achieve. To demonstrate this, we can examine the origins of the Modern Olympics; a certain Dr Brookes attempted to revive the concept of the original Olympic Games but was studiously ignored by the British sports establishment, despite having contacts within the Greek government and with the Greek Olympic philanthropists, the Zappas cousins. Brookes then began to collaborate with Coubertin who used his international society contacts to persuade the King of Greece and its government, along with others, to fund the 1896 Olympics in Athens.

Guttmann's research work was government-funded so he already had the political backing he required. The idea of using sport as a motivator came to Guttmann when he observed patients playing a game in their wheelchairs utilising a puck and an up-turned walking stick. The Disabled Persons (Employment) Act was passed by the British government in 1944 and members of Parliament who were war-veterans themselves *'insisted that the act give preference to those injured as a result of war service'* (Anderson in Howe 2008: 18). This, however, focused on those who had become disabled by the trauma of war and did nothing to help the congenitally disabled who had not been injured in the line of duty.

It is necessary to digress here, whilst on the subject of political influence, and introduce a fourth pioneer - Eunice Kennedy Shriver, founder of the Special Olympics. Her first "Shriver Camp" was set up in 1962 and was an indelible part of the philanthropic Joseph P. Kennedy Jr. Foundation and the political drive of President John Kennedy towards the needs of children and the field of intellectual disability. The Kennedy legacy still remains a large attribute of the Special Olympics today.

Eugene Rubens-Alcais, who was born with normal hearing but became deaf at an early age due to fever, already had odds stocked against him when, in the 1920s, he began his far-reaching friendship with Antoine Dresse. Antoine came from a family of Belgian bankers and industrialists in Liege. These two men formed a unique alliance of interests as they began to build a federation of pan European Deaf sports organisations. They had small networks to draw upon and neither had the credibility of a highly respected international social/professional position. But, nevertheless, what they had was an opportunity to empower disabled people in a society that largely ostracised them.

Eugene Rubens-Alcais resigned as the President of the *Comité International des Sports Silencieux (CISS)* in 1953 and was succeeded by four other leaders who had to compete with Guttmann's political standing until Robert Steadward in turn succeeded him. Rubens-Alcais' successors were also people of modest socio-economic standing (See Table A)

Table A: CISS Presidents during the time Guttmann led the International Stoke Mandeville Games Federation (ISMGF)	
Rubens Alcais FRA (1924-1953)	Car mechanic
Oscar Ryden SWE (1953-1955)	Joiner, woodcarver, sculptor, editor and lecturer.
J.P Neilsen DEN (1955-1961)	Carpenter
Pierre Bernhard FRA (1961-1971)	Carpenter, wood sculptor, coffin maker and WW2 resistance fighter.
Jerald Jordan USA (1971-1995)	Printer, teacher, administrator at Gallaudet University for the Deaf.
Further details and biographies can be found in CISS 2001: A Review.	

Empowerment of the disabled

The self-determination of disabled people in sport is still a difficult concept for the non-disabled to grasp. Providing disabled people with positions of leadership in sport has often been seen as tokenistic or taken up by those who are not congenitally disabled. This has presented challenges for the CISS and the International Committee of Sports for the Deaf (ICSD), which receive less recognition, support and resources than disabled organisations that are led by non-disabled people for the disabled.

The Paralympic Movement did not elect its first disabled leader until Philip Craven succeeded Dr Steadward in 2001, by which stage, the IPC were already on the crux of signing its binding agreement with the IOC to bring the two events together. The Deaflympics, by contrast, has been a disability-led sports movement since its inception and one that has attracted the envy of other congenitally disabled groups who aspire to be similarly 'user-led'.

Major decision-making *in the best interests* of disabled people in sport is still being made by the non-congenitally disabled and is still largely non-representative, with most leaderships being comparatively autocratic. To date, the International Olympic Committee (IOC) has been presided over by 9 Presidents, the ICSD by 9 Deaf Presidents and only three people have led throughout the combined history of the International Stoke Mandeville Games Federation (ISMGF), the International Coordinating Committee (ICC) and the IPC to date (September 2013).

The political influence of non-disabled people in disability sport is discussed elsewhere, but a number of disabled athletes have described Guttmann as an 'exceedingly strong character', who did not like change unless he instigated it. A number have even suggested that his respect for disabled athletes was limited (in Howe 2008:36).

Howe (2008) suggests that those in positions of power in the IPC have not subscribed to the ideal of disability sport being led by disabled people themselves. He states that there has not been enough proactive recruitment of ex-Paralympians into positions of influence and suggests that some people in power have been reluctant to give up their positions. There is no denying that liaising with the IOC gives a President considerable power and influence (Howe 2008:44). The CISS stated that its withdrawal from the IPC in 1995 occurred as a result of the practical and logistical difficulties of including Deaf athletes. But my research suggests that elements within the IPC saw President Jordan and the Deaf sport movement as lacking gravitas. This was not a reflection of Jordan's abilities as a negotiator and diplomat, but rather as a result of the leadership 'pecking order' of disabilities within the IPC and their perception of who is 'disabled' and who is 'normal' (Howe 2008:11). Indeed, whilst Samaranch was persuading his friend Jordan to consider joining the ICC, it seems other leaders of the International Organisations of Sport for the Disabled (IOSDs) were manoeuvring for position so as to become key players in the IPC (Howe 2008:44). Given the experience of those governing the CISS at the time, it can be assumed that Jordan was far from impressed with the ICC, as an organisation with which Samaranch wanted the CISS to work in partnership. Dr Steadward, who rose from the ICC to become the first president of the IPC, later reflected:

> ***"The ICC was not a democratic organisation, did not report to national members, had no constitution and was in fact only an agreement between four federations. The presidency (pro tem) changed every six months or every executive meeting, and decisions had to be taken unanimously."***
>
> (In Howe 2008:27)

Current Leadership in Deaf Sport

Prior to the 1989 Dusseldorf Agreement (which formed the IPC), Olympic sport in general was largely an amateur concern and all its athletes, along with the majority of administrators and officials retained amateur status. From the late 1980s onwards, a more professional high–performance ethos emerged, with athletes seeking commercial sponsorship to cover the costs of training and event participation. Event organisers themselves increasingly sought academic, economic and scientific justification for sponsorship, government and commercial funding for elite sport.

In progressing the professionalism of disability sport, the newly created IPC appointed Dr Robert Steadward as its leader. A sports scientist, who founded the Canadian Research and Training Centre for Athletes with Disability, Steadward's expertise in sport development, science and coaching gave him an instant standing. In perusing the full biographical list of CISS/ICSD Presidents and General Secretaries to date, whilst many had the professional and academic backgrounds proficient enough to run a large international organisation, there has certainly not been anyone with Steadward's credibility.

Yet in the last 25 years or so, an increasing number of deaf and disabled people have undertaken academic studies in sport. A number have gone on to teach PE professionally and administer sport on a local level. But very few have attained or currently hold any key positions in National Governing Bodies or National Disability Sports Organisations. Tiffany Granfors was appointed as the CISS/ICSD's first, full-time, Secretary General in 2004. During her term of office, she studied for a Master of Science degree in Sport Administration and Technology at the International Academy of Sport Science and Technology, University of Lausanne, Switzerland. She undertook her internship in the Games Department of the IOC headquarters in Lausanne, under the supervision of Mr Gilbert Felli, Executive Director of the Olympic Games. Whilst this was obviously a very productive placement, it did, however, leave ICSD with an operational vacuum in the short and medium term, without any managers with substantive experience of international sports administration.

It has been seen that many young deaf people take up academic foundation studies in sport, often because the course is vocationally structured and considered less academically challenging for those with a lower level of literacy. However, once out in the employment market place and competing for jobs, deaf young people are usually disadvantaged. In the United Kingdom, there are a small number of Deaf people, who have qualified at degree level in sports administration but only a fraction of this group have gone on to hold programme management positions in local government sports departments. One of them currently holds a senior position within a national disability sports organisation. This bodes well for the future; but without a continuing programme of opportunity for young Deaf people, enabling them to progress on the sports career ladder, it is unlikely that, without recognising Deaf sport at national level, the vision of it being lead by Deaf sports professionals will develop.

When Crowley sought to recruit a replacement for Granfors in 2010, he was criticised within the Deaf sports community for externally appointing the services of a professional recruitment agency, *Sports Recruitment International.* Crowley was looking for someone, with experience in working with international or national sports governing bodies, who could progress the ICSD further. In March 2011, the organisation appointed its first non-deaf senior administrator, Mark Cooper, who brought high level-experience of sport and sport policy from his previous role as Head of Communications for the IOC. Crowley's drive to ensure a collaborative leadership approach saw a number of personnel changes within the ICSD Executive Committee. Cooper also recruited Deaf staff onto his team who had professional experience and knowledge of sports coaching and development.

The critics of Crowley and Cooper would do well to note that throughout its long and illustrious history, the success of the CISS / ICSD has been largely due to the collaborative partnership of Deaf and hearing people. Examples include Noel Curtis-Bennett at the 1935 International Silent Games in London; the German Government and its military at the Köln 1981 World Games for the Deaf; The KRES Marketing Agency – Sofia WGD 1993; Trish Tracey - Melbourne 2005 Deaflympics; Mary Rusznak - Salt Lake City 2007 Winter Deaflympics; Emile C.J. Sheng - Taipei 2009 Summer Deaflympics; and the rescue of the 2013 Summer Deaflympics in Sofia.

Another example of successful Deaf-hearing collaboration is Ammon's visit to Japan in 2006 and her meetings with Princess Akishinomiya, the Japanese Olympic Committee and the Japanese Paralympic Committee. After much negotiation, the Japanese pledged their support to the Deaflympics and other possible events (ICSD 2006). Since then, Japan has hosted the 2011 World Deaf Golf and the World Deaf Table Tennis Championships, both of which enjoyed considerable domestic exposure. Although it is difficult to evaluate by exactly how much those early meetings influenced support, it is evident that, as a result of collaborative discussion, much was achieved.

One of the biggest challenges to Deaf-hearing collaboration in the post Dusseldorf / IPC era has been the attitude of National Olympic Committees and National Paralympic Committees towards the constitutional status of the CISS / ICSD. Few seem to understand or recognise its mandate and role, despite the published written agreements with the IOC and IPC. In hindsight, it seems that ICSD can do more to foster collaboration with its national deaf sport federations and respective, partner, mainstream sports bodies. By way of illustration, the relationship between Sanford Robey Burns (CISS) and Avery Brundage (IOC) according to Bailey (2008) was the main reason for the IOC recognition of the CISS as an International Federation in 1955. Both men were from Illinois USA, and their paths will undoubtedly have crossed locally as both men were prominent in their respective fields of sport. By the time that Brundage became IOC President in 1952 he would have understood the value of the CISS through his correspondence with Robey Burns, who had become President of the AAAD. Similarly, in 1935 at the International Silent Games in London, the Chair of the Organising Committee, Noel Curtis-Bennett was a member of the IOC and his relationship with the deaf sports community at the time was illustrated through his letter to The Times. National deaf sports organisations should therefore be making every effort to build a relationship with its national IOC members if there is going to be any real influence or understanding between ICSD and IOC. But, to do this effectively, there has to be a commonly agreed message that ICSD wants its members to pass on in order to avoid the ambiguity and confusion that currently prevails.

Athletes Commission

In December 2012, ICSD appointed Olympians Dean Barton-Smith (AUS) and Terence Parkin (RSA) as interim joint Chairs of the newly created ICSD Athletes Commission. Both men bring high–performance experience to the table and are ideally placed to evaluate the Deaflympics – Olympics pathway, ensuring that Deaf athletes are best able to maximise their potentials. Suffice to say, we are waiting to see what impact the ICSD Athletes Commission has on future Deaflympics.

13

The Decline of Deaf Sport

Civil society has limited awareness and understanding of Deaf sport, since the Deaflympic Movement has not been able to establish and engage with public profile. In spite of the continuous increase in the number of nations and athletes participating in the Deaflympics, there has been a sharp decline in the number of Deaf people participating in sport at grassroots level. This has obviously had an impact on interest in, and the visibility of, the Deaflympics. This chapter demonstrates how the Education Acts of the 1970s have had contrasting influences on the development of sport for disabled people: on one hand, an apparent positive impact for Paralympians; and on the other, a negative impact for Deaflympic athletes.

Since the 1980s, there has been an increase in the number of countries and athletes participating in the Deaflympics, Olympics and the Paralympics. This is partly a result of the breakup of the former Soviet Union and other political changes in Eastern Europe. With support from the three movements, the developing nations of the world have, over time, become members of the Olympic family. Within Western nations, the integration of disabled people into society has had contrasting effects on the development of sport for disabled people. Whilst there is now greater provision and awareness of Paralympic sport at local and national level, there has been a contrasting and steady decline of Deaf sport. The largest single influence of this contrasting growth/decline within Disability sport has been the impact of the 1970s education reforms in the UK, USA, Canada and Western Europe. These reforms saw disabled children integrated into mainstream education.

The effects of these reforms are still being felt almost 40 years on as they have had a significant impact upon the funding of disability sport and, in particular, perceptions of deafness as a disability. Both of these have contributed to a decline in Deaf sport at grassroots level (Atherton etc al 1999, Dummer & Stewart 1991; Stewart 2001a).

With the closing down of segregated institutions and the integration of disabled children into mainstream schools, attitudes towards disability began to change. All of this, in turn, led to positive embracement of the Paralympian ideal and helped to move the Paralympics towards the global brand they are today. However, there is evidence that not everything has changed for the better, because, for the majority of disabled people, sport and civil society are two very different, very contrasting environments.

Although statistics still show that the number of disabled children participating in PE remains low, it appears that an even lower number of deaf children are participating in PE and sport. Many deaf children have few opportunities for sport and lack the self-esteem to participate. This situation has its origins in the 1880 Milan Congress and the attempt to eradicate Sign Language in Deaf education.

In the 1970s, a thriving network of Deaf schools in the UK, USA and Canada worked to provide a series of inter-school sports competitions for deaf children. In the UK,

PE teachers in schools for the Deaf developed an annual programme of regional and national sport competitions, which were administered by the National Deaf Children's Sports Association (NDCSA). In its heyday, there were competitions in athletics, cross-country running, football and swimming. These four sports enabled Deaf schools to field large teams and the programme gave the participating deaf children a positive experience of sport that they continued to sustain by joining Deaf sport after leaving school.

Education reform continued to push for an ever-greater integration of disabled children into mainstream education. Whilst this was seen as a welcome move for some disabilities, especially those which had been institutionalised and with little interaction with local civil society (Howe 2008, Stewart 1991a), the impact upon Deaf communities was the break up and disruption of what was a thriving economic and social base, with Deaf sport at its foundation.

For Deaf schools, these reforms saw the movement of children, who were being educated orally, into local mainstream schools; whereas schools for the Deaf remained the placement of choice for sign language users. Much of the decision-making as to where individual deaf children are placed has been determined by hearing educationalists. What this has led to is the closure of 79 specialist Deaf schools, with just 19 remaining. Today, more than 95% of deaf children in England are educated in mainstream schools (NDCS 2009)

By the 1990s, sign language was making a re-appearance in public (Stewart 1991a: 14) and a small number of mainstream settings began to teach through sign language. This resulted in the closure of even more Deaf schools. This, in turn, led to a fall in the numbers of schools taking part in NDCSA events such that only the respective national championships remained. By 1992, the NDCSA was reduced to only running a national football and cross-country event. The swimming competition was sporadic and the athletics had been reduced to two regional events. Today all that remains is the national 5-a-side football and the cross-country competitions.

The remaining Deaf schools continue to work hard to include their students in local mainstream sports events. They give their pupils access to information about the Deaf community and it ensures that the Deaf sport inflow from Deaf schools (and to a lesser extent from mainstream schools with Deaf resource bases) is maintained. But clearly, as Paralympics New Zealand (PNZ) have warned, increased 'integration' into society's systems results in fewer avenues available for talent identification, as labelling students in education is dropped (Bradbury in Gilbert & Schantz 2008:203).

Stewart (2001a: 149) observed that the majority of deaf children, educated in mainstream schools by staff who would have no idea or understanding of the opportunities available in the Deaf sports pathway, would as a consequence become ever more remote from the Deaf sport experience. I know from experience that, in mainstream schools, teachers and teaching assistants are trained to focus on the correct use of wearing hearing aids and are primarily focused on the development of language across the curriculum. Most of the teachers coming into this training were language and English specialists, with no prior knowledge or experience of Deaf children, Deaf adults or the parents of Deaf children. There was nothing in the syllabus about the importance of the Deaf community and the benefits of socialisation into society through sport. The focus was purely on providing deaf children with access into their local community, with no constructive attempts to develop relationships with adults in the Deaf community. In short, mainstreaming deaf children into local schools, many of whom had an insulated journey by car or taxi, further removed them from the local Deaf community and the Deaf sport experience. (Stewart 1991a: 3 & Harrison 1995: 47-53).

Research suggests that a lack of association with a sports-orientated peer group tends to reduce an individual's participation in sport (Stewart 1991a: 141). In 1994/95, I was teaching in a mainstream school that had three large resources bases for Deaf primary (5-11) and secondary (12-16) students. An after-school youth club was established, since it was felt that the constraints of the school environment were not enabling the students to fully develop and utilise their socialisation skills (Harrison 1995:30-37). Whilst some of the older students had tried to organise a series of after-hours social activities, such as shopping and cinema visits, they were hampered by their inability to plan. Furthermore, they had little experience of public transport and so were not sure how to get from school to places of leisure. What became apparent was that the practice of providing local authority transport to and from school isolated the children from each other. Consequently, they missed out on valuable opportunities to socialise amongst themselves and their non-deaf peers.

This is where the youth club came into its own – it enabled the students to participate in organised activities and to socialise with each other, especially as there was very little other structured provision in place. Both deaf and disabled children struggle to participate in extra-curricular sport and would welcome access to the many opportunities local clubs and organisations offer. The club was the only after-school club of its kind in the UK for Deaf children attending mainstream schools. At this time and elsewhere, the PE departments of the specialised residential/day schools provided the only other provision for Deaf children to access local sport for the Deaf, who were also still involved with the NDCSA.

It would have been unrealistic to expect Teachers of the Deaf in other local schools to work after hours to provide a youth club. Many were hearing and, not being trained as PE teachers, they simply didn't have the motivation. The subject was not a priority and, therefore, through to today, as others have commented, Special Needs education continues to pay lip service to PE.

The concern for Deaf sports organisations was that they would eventually become redundant, as fewer and fewer young people came into sport through schools (Atherton et al 1999:55). In my work, I encouraged Deaf sports representatives to contact their local schools to offer coaching support to students and to introduce them to Deaf sport. Unfortunately, though, increasing legislation aimed at safeguarding vulnerable children and adults and increasing health and safety requirements presented new barriers. Deaf adults who run sports clubs and organisations for the Deaf are volunteers. They are usually unqualified and lack any formal or professional training. When they contacted local schools and offered assistance, teachers and other staff were not prepared to take risks, and matters ground to a halt. To overcome such obstacles, the Canadian Deaf Sports Association once employed a Youth Recreation Officer, who worked to make students aware of the positive benefits of Deaf sport and to encourage them to develop a positive attitude towards physical activity (Stewart 1991a: 163). Stewart also highlighted the notable case of Jeffrey King, whose parents successfully sued their local education authority, forcing it make his school's extra-curricular provision accessible. The family won the right to have extracurricular sport discussed on his Individual Education Plan as an integral part of this education (Stewart 2001).

My first experience of collaborative leadership between Deaf sport and mainstream sport came in the mid-1980s, through an organisation, which was then well ahead of its time – Friends for Young Deaf People (FYD). This organisation aimed to demonstrate to young deaf people how collaborative leadership between deaf and hearing young people and adults could result in positive outcomes for all. Before studying to be a teacher and qualifying as a PE specialist, I worked for a couple of years as a volunteer in the FYD programme, helping to organise sports and leadership programmes for deaf and hearing children and young people. This developed a new and exciting pathway for Deaf children, from both mainstream and specialist schools, into sports organisations. These activities included multi-sport events, sports festivals, coaching days, weekends and summer residential camps at specialised sports schools.

There have been several beneficial outcomes from the FYD programme, and two of them directly impacted upon Deaflympic sport. The first of these was the 1984 Los Angeles World Games for the Deaf. It has been reported that the bulk of the new and emerging talent across almost all the sports in the GB camp were products of the FYD programme. Secondly, the programme influenced and inspired young deaf people to follow careers in either Physical Education or sport.

When it became apparent that the British Deaf Sports Council was no longer involving itself actively in the collaborative governance of Disability sport in the UK, I collaborated with several other Deaf sports volunteers and community professionals; and the Deaf Sports Strategy Group was created to consult on a new way forward. UK Deaf Sport (UKDS) was established in 2003 and has now entered its second decade of operation. Although UKDS has not used the term 'collaborative leadership' to describe its ethos, this is one of its operating fundamentals. With limited success with the more traditional British Deaflympic sports, UKDS has worked in partnership with others to foster the initial developments of new pathway models to sustain the involvement of Deaf people in life-long sport.

Returning to the beginning of this chapter, it was suggested that the Paralympic movement gained much from the Education Reforms of the 1970s. Chapter 5 took us through the global developments that have led to confusion amongst many nation states as to where Deaflympic sport sits within the Olympic

Family. The close relationship between the International Olympic Committee (IOC) and the International Paralympic Committee (IPC), resulting in the collaborative organisation of the Olympics and Paralympics, has led to the UK government and its sports authorities aligning their approach to disability sport in a similar manner and thus disability sport is seen as synonymous with Paralympic sport. Funding for the national governing bodies of sport has been ring-fenced for Paralympians only, with these agencies subscribing, by default, to Paralympic definitions of disability sport. PE/Sport in school has therefore become geared towards the needs and ideals of the community rather than that of the physical, psychological and social needs of the individual. It was shown in chapter 7 that, when it comes to the question of integration, being Deaf cannot be compromised by imposing standards on Deaf people derived from a hearing and speaking society (Stewart 1991a: 43).

Worldwide, national deaf sport federations and their sports organisations look for new athletic talent not just within Deaf schools but also in the wider sports community, where eligibility is fulfilled through an individual's hearing loss matching the required classification of 'Deaf'. Some commentators argue that adolescents and young people today are less interested in sport as they have other more exciting, but sedentary, pursuits to pursue. But we cannot assume that young deaf people are affected in the same way as their hearing peers and we must ensure that all opportunities to inform and attract young people are pursued and made accessible.

Now that there are no longer concentrations of Deaf talent located around schools for the Deaf, deafness has become a low incidence disability. Grassroots sports coaches now have little opportunity to work with and be equitable with Deaf people (Stewart 1991a: 102). This low incidence of deafness has also meant that, in the UK, Deaf football teams now concentrate on playing in hearing leagues despite facing prejudice from their hearing opponents. Atherton et al (1999) correctly predicted that this was how Deaf football would survive in the future.

The majority of young deaf people rely heavily on their mainstream schools to socialise them into sport. But they face challenges, as my study (Harrison 1995) illustrated; there is very little in the way of information being passed between hearing and deaf students about sports opportunities in mainstream schools. There is a correlation between the amount of time a student is physically integrated into the mainstream teaching programme and the chances that they will become involved within school sport. When taking part in PE lessons or playing in school teams, hearing students can be reluctant to partner up with deaf students. They see them as a hindrance and so are reluctant to make deaf players integral to team strategy. There is hesitation about passing the ball to deaf teammates and a lack of interactive communication during play, which work against the inclusion of deaf players (Stewart 1991a: 147-48). However, if we look hard enough, we can discover good examples of where team management has been inclusive for deaf players as illustrated by the *Dave Smith Rule* (Chapter 9 & 10).

PE teachers fail to assess fully the potential of their deaf students and inaccurately attribute a lesser ability to them (Stewart 1991a: 148; Guzman 2006). As a result, Bruce Gross from the World Recreation Association of the Deaf and others have sought to encourage schools to form working relationships with Deaf sports organisations by inviting Deaf role models to speak to both deaf and hearing students. Despite fears about the possibility of mainstreaming diluting Deaf culture, such partnership can provide opportunities for greater understanding and learning (Gross, in Dummer & Stewart 1991).

Educational mainstreaming has also created conflicting ideas about what deafness is and whether or not Deaf people see themselves as having a disability or rather as members of a language and cultural minority. The closing down of special schools for the Deaf was noticeably seen by Deaf people as a negative action, because it contributed to the breakup of community structures that had taken decades to develop. Other sports service providers have attempted to engage Deaf people in 'pan-disability' activities (coaching, training or competitions), but this does not work effectively for the recreational deaf athlete; and a lack of awareness of the needs of deaf people in PE and sport has restricted the funding made available to Deaf sports projects, where they are seen to be less cost effective than those that deliver a 'pan-disability' opportunity.

The size of the Russian team attending the last four Deaflympics may suggest that they have found a way of reversing the decline. Since 1990 when they entered 90 athletes, the team has grown; 2005 – 130 athletes; 2009 – 220 athletes; and in 2013 the team had grown to over 500. Approximately 300 were athletes and 200 were coaches, support personnel and interpreters. Valery Rukhledev, the newly appointed Deaflympics President from Russia, has made it one of his goals to halt the decline of Deaf sport worldwide by ensuring that deaf children and young people are participating in sport at the highest levels of their potential.

The next Chapter explores other factors influencing decision-making about participating in sport that have contributed to a decline in deaf sport. The socialising agents of this are the family, peers, the school community and mass media. The Deaf parents of Deaf children themselves are often unaware of what opportunities are available for young people, as one Deaf mother explained on an Internet forum. She noted how she had grown up with sport and had developed a love for it that she had instilled into her own children. On remembering times when there used to be sports events, which drew together Deaf school children, she asked whether these were still happening or not (AoHL Forum 2012). Atherton et al (1999:55) suggested that the survival of some Deaf sports at grassroots level is likely to be due to teams and individuals choosing to compete in mainstream competitions. However, in order for international Deaf sport to be sustained, a greater emphasis has to be placed on making mainstream sport accessible for the individual, whilst at the same time supporting a pathway framework for performance sport.

In May 2001, the IOC granted permission for the World Deaf Games to be known as the 'Deaflympics'. Yet a number of National Olympic Committees and National Paralympic Committees seem reluctant to respect the Olympic status of the International Committee of Sports for the Deaf (ICSD) and the Deaflympics themselves. In response, Ammons created and led an ICSD special commission titled *Deaf Sports Reform*. A symposium was held in Zagreb, Croatia in July 2007 where ICSD members, technical directors and other individuals were invited to contribute thinking, with which to address the governance and management of Deaf sports pathways. This work continues today.

14

Society has misunderstood the Deaflympics

The evolution of organised Deaf Sport has, from its beginnings in the 1800s, mirrored mainstream sport; a social construct based on mutual interest and needs. Deaf people form teams, clubs and groups as any other group in society – reflecting a common interest in a particular activity and sharing a common language and culture (Atherton et al 1999). By contrast, the evolution of organised Disabled sport is largely a creation of the able-bodied or those who have become disabled through traumatic events. This evolution began in the 1940s with the conception of the Stoke Mandeville Games, which were aimed at motivating, and rehabilitating spinal cord injured ex-soldiers back into society as contributing taxpayers (Anderson in Howe 2008:137). Its central focus was medically/economically motivated and there was very little interest in the welfare of the congenitally disabled. (Howe 2008:141).

Sport at every level requires volunteers, facilities, athletes, spectators and funding in order to be sustainable. Governments classify people according to common denominators to enable policies, funding and provision to be managed and controlled as efficiently as possible (Ammons 1990). Other institutions in society follow the same rationale. During the 1980s, the International Olympic Committee (IOC) found itself under increasing pressure to react to the growth of international disabled sport. Under the leadership of Samaranch, the IOC used its supreme status to wrestle control of disabled sport in an attempt to streamline its administration, funding and support. In doing so, they marshalled together the two mainstays of international disability sport, the Comité International des Sports des Sourds' (CISS) and the International Coordinating Committee (ICC), which led to the creation of the IPC, based on future promises and agreements with the CISS and other members of the ICC as founder members.

Unfortunately, many sports decision-makers and commentators struggle to understand why the CISS withdrew from the IPC. Society fails to understand deafness as a disability and how it differs from other disabilities. On the whole, Deaf people favour segregated schooling, marriage within the Deaf community and place a high priority on socialising with other Deaf people. (Stewart 1991a: 86 & Ladd 2003). Society has attempted to merge Deaf sports into disability sport – without success. By withdrawing from the IPC in 1993, Deaf sport has become an inconvenience to political decision-makers responsible for sport and physical activity, becoming a source of frustration for sports administrators and those governing sport at national and international level. Some commentators believe that the self-imposed isolation engineered by the Deaf community is both uncomfortable and unwelcome.

The power of sport to reduce stigma, discrimination and to empower disabled people was harnessed by the Deaf community long before the existence of all the other organisations that now make up the Paralympic Movement. It is only in the last few decades that society has grown to understand how it can interact with disabled people through sport and thereby change assumptions about what disabled people can, or cannot, do. Eugene Rubens-Alcais and Antoine Dresse have demonstrated that empowerment through sport enables individuals to acquire social skills whilst, in turn, allowing them to advocate for changes in society by acting as agents for change. Unfortunately, Deaf sport has always been Deaf-led and this has led to an impasse, as civil society institutions have always wanted to control change in a way that suits them.

The influence of the IOC on international and national sports politics is all encompassing and their spotlight on the Paralympics; and not giving equal consideration to the Deaflympics, could be described as being in defiance of the recommendations of IOC Congress 2009 and the guidance of the United Nations (UN) Convention on the Rights of Persons with Disabilities, a legally binding international instrument to address the rights of persons with disabilities within sport. Article 30 of the Convention stipulates that:

> ***"States parties shall take appropriate measures to encourage and promote the participation, to the fullest extent possible, of persons with disabilities in mainstream sporting activities at all levels."***

This is also extended to include access to sports venues as spectators and participants and extra-curricular PE, all to the *'fullest extent possible".* Article 30 protects the rights of disabled people by recognising the concept of integration and inclusion; but this is a difficult concept and, whilst it can be defined at policy level, it is less easy to define in reality. (Howe 2008:146)

The Silent Games were created to engineer inclusion and integration. Over time, and through both the World Games for the Deaf and now the Deaflympics, this has continued to evolve to the "fullest extent possible". Yet further evolution has been hampered by the influence of Deaf politics. A number of Deaf individuals and Deaf organisations have allowed Deaf politics, that are less appropriate to Deaf sport, to permeate the Deaf sports agenda and so confuse mainstream sport further. This is touched on in the next chapter under the context of marketing and the media.

UN Article 30 also reinforces the notion that sport can reduce the dependence of disabled people by developing their independence and enabling them to become physically and mentally stronger. These skills are then transferred into other areas of life, such as employment, that help ensure self-sufficiency (UN 2011). Once again, this is a critical path that Deaf sport has pioneered. Deaf sport is unique, because it is Deaf-led and there is a democratic process of empowerment within the constitution of the International Committee of Sports for the Deaf (ICSD) that, through due process, allows any deaf individual to be represented at Congress and have the opportunity to sit on the Executive Board. Unfortunately, hearing people have accused Deaf sport of discriminating against them by not allowing them to hold positions of power. Is this a reflection of society's reluctance to afford power to its disabled minorities? We should remind ourselves of the UN Convention:

> ***Article 5 (Equality and non-discrimination)***
> ***Where specific measures which are necessary to accelerate or achieve de facto equality of persons with disabilities shall not be considered discrimination under the terms of the present convention.***

There has been much political rhetoric against Deaf sport. During a UK parliamentary debate on Deaf sport in 2003, the Sports Minister at the time, implied that the Deaflympics and its British athletes were not worthy of high-performance funding support, because it was deemed a 'social' event (see below).

This is a common prevailing perception amongst hearing people, because Deaf sport has largely promoted itself under the guidance of the ICSD, who have stressed the importance of the socialisation benefits of Deaf sport. This, allied with the cultural and linguistic arguments put forward by Jerald Jordan in his paper *World Games for the Deaf and Paralympic Games* (1996), has shifted focus away from the issue of deaf people accessing and participating in high-performance sport. However, had it not been for Deaf sport empowering disabled people to acquire the knowledge, skills and confidence with which to become effective advocates for themselves and others, Oliver Monksfield would not have approached his constituency Member of Parliament, Ian Duncan-Smith, and inspired him to open up the Parliamentary debate (Hansard 2009). This is what the Deaflympic athletes, and Paralympians like Linda Mastandrea (in *Right to Play* (2003)), mean by the positive impacts of socialisation. As a result, the Deaflympics serve an advocacy and political role. It is not within the realms of possibility to guess this is what non-disabled governments, politicians and their respective National Olympic/Paralympic Committees are afraid of?

Since the ICSD withdrew from the IPC, national deaf sport federations have come under increasing pressure from their respective National Olympic Committees, who are trying to channel deaf athletes into the Paralympics. When the UK won the bid to host the London 2012 Olympics, UK Sport, the government quango representing elite sport, withdrew funding from UK Deaf Sport, because its priorities had shifted to supporting Olympic and Paralympic excellence - specifically for 2008 and 2012 (which has now been extended to 2016). UK Deaf Sport challenged this policy and after a series of exchanges, Liz Nichol, CEO of UK Sport argued that for her organisation to fund Deaflympic athletes:

> ***"The best route for the longer term is to align with the Paralympics to the extent that perhaps discussions with the IPC about recognising deafness as a classification within the Paralympic movement because then if it was formally part of the Paralympic Games and we will have deaf athletes with medal potential in those Paralympic Games, it would absolutely come under UK Sports funding radar."***
>
> (Liz Nichol, interviewed on BBC See Hear, March 2009)

In hindsight, the former Chair of UK Deaf Sport, Crowley, believes that the UKDS argument to support British Deaflympic competitors was weak and poorly evidenced. This, in turn, reflects the lack of guidance from ICSD at the time. UK Sport has never properly understood the intricacy of Deafness as a disability and this is reflected in Nichol's statement, which is simplistic at best and fails to understand how international disability sport is organised. This book brings forward evidence and arguments to support the case for supporting the Deaflympics in Chapter 19.

It is important to note that the Deaflympic Movement, like the Deaf community as a whole, is not at odds with the world but rather seeks a relationship with wider civil society based on mutual respect and understanding (Stewart 1991; Ladd 2003). There are many examples where Deaf sport has come out in support of wider society. Going back as far as the First World War a Deaf football match between Warrington and Liverpool drew a crowd of 500 spectators who all donated money to the War Effort (Atherton et al 1999). Because Deaf sport is Deaf-led, it nurtures and develops leadership skills in Deaf people, who then go on to become positive role models for young deaf people. This approach is practiced in disability sport the world over by advocates like Handicap International (Ikelberg et al). However, through this book, I have argued that if Deaf sport is to progress, its leadership needs to be more collaborative with non-deaf people and it should be more confident about bringing in outside expertise to fulfil supportive roles at the higher strategic level.

For inclusion and integration to occur, deaf and hearing people have to develop mutual understanding and trust. Deaf sport has historically been wary of allowing the non-deaf to contribute to Deaf sport, because it is one of the last remaining social institutions in the Deaf community and one where they still have full empowerment and self-determination. Whilst relationships can be built by bringing strangers together through the common medium of sports activities, it still takes time for trust to develop. However, once this trust is in place, new and further activities can be introduced (Ikelberg et al). This, clearly, has to work both ways. Siv Fosshaug explains that it is the relationship between Deaf sport and majority sport that brings about empowerment and that this system should enable a deaf person to choose how, where and when they want to be involved in sport. They have the right to be given the freedom of choice to decide on the degree of integration and segregation that they wish to experience (Fosshaug 2004).

The ICSD has established a number of effective relationships with national governments that have been of immense value to Deaf sport. In the years leading up to the Taipei 2009 Deaflympics, the city government undertook a wide- ranging and all-encompassing Deaf awareness programme. Aimed at creating access for deaf people, this programme saw local schools twinned with one of the visiting national teams, along with visits by schoolchildren to some of the Deaflympic events. Given the inevitability that most of these young people are going to experience hearing loss in later life, this exposure is significantly important. They will have been given an insight as to how they might use sport as a vehicle for integration:

> ***"In the world of wheelchair sports.... I realized... I wasn't different, but very much like everyone else out on the floor. Through my years of competition, I found the strength and drive to pursue goals that I never would have before. I learned that people with disabilities worldwide had the same struggles I had, trying to fit in, trying to get around, trying to learn, to do, to be"***
>
> Linda Mastandrea, Paralympian and Lawyer
> in Right to Play (2003)

Disability-specific, segregated sport can help people build knowledge and understanding of the needs of disabled athletes. The instance when 3,000 disabled people from across Iran came together for a "Paralympic Day" is particularly interesting. As well as being introduced to sports, they learnt about physical fitness, nutrition and preventive health (Right to Play 2003) It is my opinion that observers do not see such events as being segregated, because all the participants were hearing. For these types of event, there need to be modifications to the delivery of seminars, including interpreter provision and other communication support resources.

Deaf sport knows from experience that elite athlete training and education is more effective when delivered to deaf–specific audiences, because the language and pace of delivery has to be tailored to suit Deaf people and also to make cost-effective use of expensive interpreters, palantypists and the like. Unfortunately, when requesting funds to cover such events, Deaf sport has to overcome the donor community's entrenched perceptions that funding such activity is not cost-effective, because pan-disability Paralympic events represent better value for money.

Following the success of the Russians at the 2009 Deaflympics, where they dominated the medals table, the Russian Government led the celebrations with a series of letters that lauded the dynamic integration of national sports organisations and Russian Deaf people. This partnership was cited for working to 'involve, interest and give equal possibilities for all citizens of Russia' and through sport they can bring to public attention the 'problems of Deaf people' (RCDS 2009). The Russians consider their Deaflympic athletes to be on a par with their Paralympians and Olympians. The Russian Deaf Sport Union (RDSU) website explains that when the IOC bestowed the name 'Deaflympics' to the ICSD in 2001, the RDSU formed the Russian Committee of Deaf Sports and this organisation improved co-operation with state organisations to bring in funding for events and their participation on state-run initiatives.

Society, sport and disabled sport have been built on the cultures of hearing and speaking. This culture may never be accessible to deaf people unless changes in attitude and practice occur. Deaf people want to see hearing people (both disabled and able-bodied) change their perspective about deafness so that deaf people can become full and participant members of civil society. Hearing people should not be trying to synchronise the lives of deaf people with that of their own and should instead look to respect the communication needs of deaf people, within the institutions of society. The ability to hear should not be conductive to a superior lifestyle (Stewart 1991a: 15)

Stewart (1991a: 18) advocated two principles as guidance for hearing people who wish to work with deaf people. The first is that it should not become a mission to associate with deaf people; they don't need *zealots* – deaf people need equal opportunities in order to succeed. They don't need to be *helped*. The provision of interpreters, palantypists, note-takers, captioned subtitles and in-vision sign language[9] are

[9] In-vision sign language – the image of an interpreter/translator is superimposed onto the corner of a TV or video screen

provided to access auditory information and not to *overcome* deafness in the battle against deafness; instead, it is a way of living. The second is that Deaf people should not have to be placed on the defensive to fight or preserve their human rights of access to Deaf sport, sign language, social cohesiveness, heritage and culture. The existence of Deaf people is justification enough, because the Deaf community is seeking awareness, not approval from society.

15

Marketing the Deaflympics

Often, the first glimpse that anyone has into the Deaf world occurs when the Deaflympics arrives in his or her hometown (Stewart & Ojalas 1995). It is, therefore, the responsibility of the International Committee of Sport for the Deaf (ICSD), Games Organising Committees and national deaf sport federations (NDSFs) to make sure that sports marketers have an understanding and awareness of what the Deaflympics is about and what it is seeking to achieve. The challenge for the ICSD is that the 2001 Treaty between the International Olympic Committee (IOC) and International Paralympic Committee (IPC) has enabled the Paralympics to monopolise the disability sport market. The IOC is heavily reliant on income from TV and corporate sponsorship rights and is, understandably, very protective of this. Although it is permissible to hold a dominant position, it could be suggested that the behaviour of the IOC and IPC has been highly detrimental to the Deaflympics. Some commentators (Baines 2010, Gold & Gold 2007, Stewart & Ammons 2001) would suggest that by withdrawing from the IPC, the Deaflympics has missed the opportunity to build its market share.

However, as mentioned in the last chapter, there have been Deaf individuals and those employed by Deaf organisations, who have allowed the politics of deafness to permeate Deaf sports and thus confuse mainstream sport further. This also includes sports marketers, who are often at a loss as to where Deaf sport sits in the disability spectrum. What should the ICSD and its NDSFs be doing to tackle this challenge?

Marketing is self-promotion for the greatest exposure of a product or service. The earliest example of this in the Deaflympics Movement was the letter written to *The Times* newspaper in 1935 by Noel Curtis-Bennett, a member of the IOC, who wrote in his capacity as Chairman of the 4th International Games for the Deaf. The letter is reproduced below in full, as found in *The History of British Deaf Tennis*.(Whalley 2010:233-235). What is remarkable is that, despite the use of terminology that would not be acceptable today, this letter still encapsulates the contemporary spirit and values of the Deaflympics.

> *"Sir – London has recently witnessed an athletics festival unique in the history of this country in the fourth international games for the deaf, held at Wembley, White City and Arsenal FC. Their success has been remarkable and the goodwill risen from them is widespread. Never before have so many athletes of the silent world met together, and one and all from all over the world are grateful to this country for staging the games for such a high standard. Many feel, too, that the prominence given to the games will go far to helping to bring their cause and their ideals before the hearing world.*
>
> *The born deaf- deaf mutes- start life with closed gates. For them, no reiteration promotes imitative speech or creates thought and it's 'clothing' which is called language. The deaf meet life through their eyes alone and, except for the intervention of modern special education, there would result from them confusion and chaos. Slowly they equip themselves*

with language and speech – and yet there remains for them a silence and a sense of social isolation, which is practically impossible for hearing people to comprehend. The theatre, the wireless and the cinema mean nothing to them. The deaf need courage, persistency and optimism but because their affliction is not readily apparent to the general public, the help and sympathy, which is so generously given to other afflicted classes, is often thoughtlessly withheld from them.

In 1922, two deaf mutes Mr Alcais of France and Mr A Dresse of Belgium met to discuss what could be done to co-ordinate international effort to alleviate the disabilities, both material and social, of the deaf mutes of the world. They realised that it was only through the deaf youth that they could attain success and to achieve that end they decided to attempt to federate the sports clubs of the various nations into an international body. This they did, and in 1924 the first international games were held in Paris. The second games were held in Amsterdam in 1928 and in 1931 the third games took place in Nuremburg. It was only this year, when the fourth international games were held in London that the nations outside Europe were federated – when Japan and USA became members of the Association of the Silent World.

In order to overcome the difficulty of languages of the deaf all of these nations converse by pictorial expressive signs and gestures which convey ideas without the use of words. These signs and gestures are so efficient that the business of Congress which follows each games can be conducted quite easily. The Congress has to be seen to be believed. Its work is carried out as efficiently and with the same due form as that of any big business organisation. And what manner of men are these representatives? The British representative is as good an example as any. A deaf mute, Mr Baird has given 40 of his 60 years to the betterment of his fellows in this country. His own time and his own money mean nothing to him. A man of high intelligence and indomitable courage, he travels at his own expense throughout the country, working and helping. A sportsman in his youth, he sees that it is through the medium of sports that he will get the youth of the Silent World organised and, 'til the end, he will go on with his work with all the fiery enthusiasm of the Irish race from which he sprang.

What the deaf need from the state are a Deaf Persons Act on the lines of the Blind persons Acts, better educational facilities till a later age than the present, and better 'after care'.

They need from the hearing world a little more sympathy and patience, and from employers a few more facilities for obtaining employment and from their hearing fellow-workers a little more help and forbearance.

They do not desire charity, but only ask that their special problems should be sympathetically considered in order that they may work and become useful citizens of their respective countries. So much has been done – and rightly done- for their fellow sufferers, the blind and I am confident that the apparent indifference shown to these tragic people in this country is not in any sense due to lack of sympathy and desire to help, but solely to the fact that their sufferings, their courage, and their ideals are insufficiently widely known.

These games have done much, not only to give happiness and joy to the deaf, but, what is far more important, to bring about that much-needed closer and more sympathetic understanding between the hearing and the silent people of the world.

The welfare of the deaf is a great human problem which concerns us all, and one which must be tackled with compassion and understanding in order that the future of these splendid men and women may be more sympathetically looked after and guided than it has been in the past. Let us see to it that we do not fail in the duty to them."

This letter raises several issues that remain contemporary today: that sport is a tool for raising awareness and for educating people; deafness 'has to be seen to be believed'; and that it has to be a 'lived-in' experience. It notes that deaf people lack support in employment, education, and from government and they seek to improve this by working in collaboration with hearing people.

Twenty years later, in 1955, the IOC recognised the *Comité International des Sports Silencieux (CISS)* as an International Federation of Olympic Standing. Whilst the IOC and its National Olympic Committees noted this in passing at the time, this recognition now appears to have been 'forgotten' and the visibility of Deaf sport has fallen. National Olympic Committees have made up their minds to grant supreme status to the Paralympics thus causing problems for the development of Deaf sport. In order to counteract this problem, the ICSD recently received a letter from the IOC, dated 29th November 2012, which confirms that their recognition still remains and that it recognises that the Deaf withdrawal from the IPC in 1996 was legitimate, on account of the specific nature of the disability. The letter ends by confirming that the IPC and ICSD are both Recognised Organisations by the IOC. However, my study of some correspondence between the CISS/ICSD and the IOC, notes/minutes of their joint meetings and IOC publications (in Chapters 5 and 6) indicates that the IOC has, in the past, protected itself against the promotion of the ICSD.

Barbara J Evener's essay on marketing disability sport in *Innovative Marketing for the Paralympics* published in *The Paralympic Games: Empowerment or Slide Show* (in Gilbert & Schantz 2008:79-89) is a useful reference point in this consideration, where she notes financial and resource support are the overriding components for a successful marketing programme. The Treaty signed by the IOC and IPC in 2001 tabled a shared responsibility for the marketing, media, licensing and sponsorship of the Olympic and Paralympics. Funding commitments several years ahead backed these plans. In 2001, the IOC contributed US$9m to the IPC for the marketing of the 2008 Paralympics and US$14m for the 2010 and 2012 events. Despite formally recognising the legitimacy of the Deaflympics, the IOC only contributed 150,000 CHF (Swiss francs) to the ICSD for the four year period 2005 -2009. This suggests further evidence of an historical bias on the part of IOC towards the IPC in spite of their assurances to uphold the status CISS/ICSD.

The Treaty is also likely to have influenced the bias of National Olympic Committees towards Paralympic athletes at the expense of Deaflympic athletes. On one occasion, the American Olympic Committee had projected contributions of US$23m to the US Paralympic programme but nothing at all to the US Deaflympic programme. Emener suggested that the reason for the tripling of contributions to the US programme was partly because 54m Americans are registered disabled, with US$1.2 trillion in total income. On that basis, should the USA Deaf Sports Federation and all other NDSFs be promoting the percentage of incomes attributed to deaf citizens and argue that a proportionate contribution is due? The financial support, given to the Paralympics for broadcasting and marketing by the IOC, could be seen by the offended parties to be contravening Recommendations 3, 15, 39 and 62, of the IOC 2009 Congress and Article 30 of the UN Convention on the Rights of People with Disabilities. Indeed, Deaf people might perceive the financial marginalisation of the Deaflympics as both oppressive and detrimental, despite the IOC and IPC having declared the Deaflympics to be equal to the Paralympics.

Emener's work also notes that it is essential for disability sport marketers to identify their 'target audience' and to build a baseline of awareness for the audiences identified. These audiences are invariably global, national and local. Therefore, with the Deaflympics, the audience would be composed of four segments. The primary audience is the hard-core Deaflympics fan. This segment includes Deaflympic competitors, associated families, friends, coaches, media, volunteers and industry members. The Olympic fans are next. They are 'consumers', who already have an affinity for world-class athletic events such as the Olympics and may have already heard of the Deaflympics. The casual sports fans are next and they would make up the tertiary target audience. And, finally, there are the 'new fans' that may have chanced upon the Deaflympics. It can be suggested that the main obstacle preventing the ICSD from reaching these audiences is that the IOC has imposed marketing limitations on the ICSD (Gorrell 2007), which could be interpreted by Deaf people as an abuse of power, by the IOC, in favour of themselves and Paralympics.

When researching for her essay, Emener consulted with Charlie Huebner, who was then Chief of Staff for the US Olympic Committee and former CEO of the US Paralympics Committee. The future of Paralympic marketing, he explained was simple – substitute the word *disabled* and use *Paralympic*. The challenge is that, by avoiding the use of the term Paralympic, no one knows what precisely the event is and which sporting constituency is involved. The CISS/ICSD has been unable to develop a scalable marketing plan for the Deaflympics, as it lacks financial support from the IOC and because the IOC has not allowed the development of a Deaflympics brand. The term 'Deaflympics' is restricted by the IOC to just the title of the event. There has been legal pressure forced upon the ICSD by the IOC, preventing it from using derivatives of the word 'Deaflympics" (Deaflympian, National Deaflympic Committee, International Deaflympic Committee and so on) thus depriving the ICSD of an essential means for marketing.

Others would, however, argue that, regardless of the bias and pressures from the IOC, it is the CISS/ICSD that has failed to market Deaf sport and the Deaflympics effectively. Some argue that CISS should have done more at a national level to capitalise on the support it received from the IOC in 1955, which would have in turn been maximised by the NDSFs. However, the situation is more complicated that it first appears. Emener comments on the need to attract the attention of Chief Marketing Officers with visual impact, human-interest stories and the 'wow' factor. The IPC has capitalised on this for sure. For example, in 2012, it allowed Channel 4, a national UK TV network, to market its blanket coverage of the London Paralympics by using the '19th century freak show phenomenon' (Popham 2012). Channel 4's promotion of its Paralympic coverage featured a series of adverts which whilst portraying 'superhuman' Paralympians, also reinforced disability as something tragic and horrible. Unlike physical disabilities, deafness is hidden; its athletes are able-bodied and have no deformity. There is nothing visually attractive (hypervisible) about Deaf sport for the 'casual sports fan'. On first impressions, people naturally compare the performance results of Deaf sport with that of Olympians and decide that there is no entertainment value to be had. The IOC and IPC marketing has, since the Barcelona Paralympics, steadily increased the number of spectators attending the Paralympics, but they weren't there to watch sport and the athletic prowess of disabled people (in Gilbert & Schantz 2008:66), they were there to see something else. Peers (2012) describes the IOC choice to use *hypervisible* wheelchair sport instead of blind sport as its demonstration event at the 1980 Olympics, because it supported a disability sport structure that was more in line with the ways that freak shows differentiate bodies. If they had exhibited with blind sport, the athletes could have been mistaken as being *able-bodied* and their results would have been too easily compared with those of *normal* Olympians;

> ***Hypervisibility provides a text against which the spectators and non-patient competitors 'indistinguishable bodies' can be reaffirmed as neutral, normal and invulnerable, and the sporting context provides a venue for gawking that allows it to be discursively reframed as a sporting and/or charitable interest.***
>
> (Thomson p10 in Peers 2012)

Deafness is a difficult disability for people to understand and empathise with. Profound deafness is usually a congenital and genetic disability, which affects a small number of people, whereas age-induced hearing loss affects a greater number of people as they succumb to the aging process. Compare this to the largest and most prolific group of elite Paralympians today. They are a group of people, who have suffered major physical trauma through accident, terrorism or war. The associated marketing creates powerful human-interest stories of 'making a comeback'. The rehabilitative benefits of sport as seen the creation of organisations such as *Battleback*[10] in the UK, which proactively promote the power of national pride and the debt owed to disabled war veterans.

So, what has stopped NDSFs from taking the same approach and recruiting deafened war veterans into the Deaflympics? It has been the politics of Deaf culture creeping into Deaf sport and the confusing repetition of mixed messages emanating from the 1980-90s perceptions of Jerald Jordan. The social politics of deafness argues that, although deafened war veterans might meet the 55dB classification required for participation in the Deaflympics, their presence should not be encouraged, as they are not culturally Deaf. I would hope that the Deaf community

[10] Battle Back is an adaptive sport and adventurous training programme for wounded, injured and sick (WIS) personnel from across the British Armed Forces, including mobilised reservists. It is is an MOD initiative delivered in partnership with Help for Heroes and The Royal British Legion.

would now see the fatality of their argument.

Another example of the permeation of social politics into Deaf sport is the conflict in terms of using the word 'disabled' to describe deaf people. In response to the IOC/IPC Treaty of 2000, the ICSD signed a Memorandum of Understanding separately with the IPC in an attempt to safeguard and reaffirm its market position in disability sport. In the ICSD / IPC MoU, there is a commitment by both sides to support each other as equal providers of Olympic–style events for the disabled. Unfortunately, when Jordan, Ammons and others in the Deaflympic leadership articulated the view that Deaf people do not see themselves as disabled, the IPC then, rightly or wrongly, declared itself to be the world's leading disability sport organisation. The resultant IPC marketing has affirmed this position and most people now see the Paralympics as an event that represents all disabled people. This has, in turn, created a public perception that the ICSD is stubborn, awkward and difficult; that it takes advantage of the 'disabled' moniker when it chooses to.

Despite these difficulties, the ICSD and its NDSFs have tried their best, with the very limited resources at their disposal, to market the Deaflympics brand. These resources have been limited to the small number of organisations and companies, which are associated with Deafness; those for which the international Deaf community is their target market.

What the ICSD could do to address matters is to seek out potential host nations whose governments and NOCs would be prepared to assist with the marketing of the event. The key motivation for the Taiwan Olympic Committee in 2009 was its desire to redevelop the sporting infrastructure of Taipei so that it could contend hosting a future Olympics. The city government set aside NT$1.1 billion for advertising and marketing. Every sporting and accommodation venue was branded to the Deaflympics, and branded livery appeared on all public transport. There was extensive national news coverage of the Deaflympics and several local Internet forums were set up, which discussed and debated all manner of issues around the politics of staging Olympic-status events. More importantly, these discussions facilitated dialogue and debate on deafness in society as well as in sport.[1]

This investment by the host of 2009 was exponential when compared with the previous Summer Deaflympics in 2005. Melbourne attracted 12,000 spectators whereas Taipei brought in 278,884. The total costs are estimated to be have been US$200m (NT$7 billion), with 14 flagship sponsors bringing in US$4.34m. It is worth noting that; unlike the organisers of the 2005 Melbourne Summer Deaflympics, who were embroiled in a trademark lawsuit with the IOC, and the 2007 Salt Lake City Winter Deaflympics, who were challenged by the US Olympic Committee over its rights to the '-lympic' brand (Gorrell 2007); the issues faced by the Taipei Organising Committee were of an internal political nature, as one would normally anticipate with any Olympic-standard event, where the investment of public funds is subject to scrutiny.

On limited budgets, previous Deaflympic organising committees have done as much as they can to promote and market their events. The reality is that the Deaflympics are usually low-impact and marketed internally as a domestic event rather than one of Olympic standing (Stewart 1991b). A Chinese National Party (KMT) City Councillor in Taipei argued that the city needed to take its lead from the city government of Kaohsiung; which visited China, Hong Kong and Japan to promote the World Games, which were held ten weeks before the Deaflympics. She argued that, for the Deaflympics, greater efforts should have been made to increase international visibility (Yan-chi Mo. 2009).

For the build up to the 2013 Deaflympics, the ICSD organised its inaugural international flame relay starting from the Pershing

Stadium in Paris in celebration of the original 1924 Silent Games. The flame was then carried by cyclists, to the host city of Sofia, making scheduled stops at key locations on the journey. The secondary aims of the relay were about creating awareness of Deaf sport in general, Deaf cycling and safer cycling lanes (ICSD 2013a). Melbourne 2005 was the first Deaflympics to organise a formal Torch Relay, which was launched, to acclaim, on 14th July 2004 in the presence of the Australian Prime Minister John Howard with the promise of a local relay within Melbourne (ICSD 2004a). As far as I can make out, the relay was eight Australians representing the States and Territories, who did a lap of honour at the Opening Ceremony before Cindy Lou Fitzpatrick had the honour of lighting the cauldron. The feat was repeated in 2009 in Taiwan with the relay restricted to within the bounds of the opening ceremony. I have wondered if the previous year's controversy, over Taiwan not agreeing to participate in the Beijing Olympics torch relay, had any bearing on this.

The Opening Ceremonies of the Olympic-family events are predominantly a marketing opportunity to celebrate the host nations. The Deaflympic opening ceremony also serves to increase awareness of deaf people (Taipei Times Editorial 2009). The 1989 World Games for the Deaf (WGD) in Christchurch, New Zealand, opened at a time when there were just two full-time sign language interpreters for the entire national population. The interpreters were prominently displayed throughout the ceremony and this resulted in an interpreter education programme being established in New Zealand. (Stewart & Bressler 1997). In 1997, Stewart observed how the ceremony for the 18th WGD in Copenhagen was geared towards a hearing audience with a predominance of musical performances, despite the wishes of the Deaf community, who wished the ceremony to be visual and less auditory.

Stewart has warned the CISS not to be blinkered by Deaf cultural politics and to consider embracing the wider hearing world so as to financially advance the Deaflympic cause. Therefore, opening ceremonies need to attract a hearing audience and be supported by known commercial brands (Stewart & Bressler 1997). The Taipei 2009 opening was designed and orchestrated by the celebrated poet and playwright, Stan Lei, and featured a range of international artists and celebrities. The promoters also invited spectators to attend the dress rehearsal, which was unprecedented in Deaflympic history.

Some commercial sponsorship of Deaf sport is known. The hearing-aid manufacturer WIDEX sponsors the annual ICSD sportsman and sportswoman of the year awards. Candidates are nominated by their own NDSF and then the ICSD Executive elects the winners. WIDEX also sponsors the Fair Play award for the Summer and Winter Deaflympics. This partnership is almost a contradiction in terms, given that WIDEX mainly serves hard of hearing / severely deaf people, the very cohort the Deaf community suggests is trying to take over Deaf sport. All of this, again, demonstrates why the Deaf Culture lobby must not dictate to the ICSD.

Despite the difficulties experienced by the ICSD and its NDSFs, the need to maintain a continuous year-round projection of the Deaflympic brand is paramount. In addition, there is a need to build wider partnerships with both the global Deaf community and external hearing stakeholders. This and further discussions on the competition for commercial rights are covered in chapter 20.

16

How the media portrays the Deaflympics

There is very little coverage of the Deaflympics in the media. It has already been stated that the marketing of disability sport is currently monopolised by the financial contributions made by the International Olympic Committee (IOC) towards the International Paralympic Committee (IPC). Schantz and Gilbert (2008) have examined at length the importance of media coverage for disability sport. Their research concludes that media representation informs and shapes public attitudes to disability sport. News selected and constructed by journalists and their editors reflects how they wish to get the attention of consumers. The thoughts, behaviours, styles and opinions of consumers are hugely influenced by the mass media's construction and presentation of 'knowledge'. Furthermore, exposure to mass media plays a significant role in reinforcing existing norms and attitudes that might serve to change public attitudes (p34-35). Family and peer opinions can also be strong, but these too are mass media influenced. Journalists have the power to inform or not inform and they construct reality from their particular perspectives.

De Pauw (1997 in Howe 2008) described the evolution of media coverage of disability sport occurring in three phases, having:

1. been invisible and excluded from sport
2. become visible in sport as disabled athletes and then;
3. increasingly become visible in sports as athletes.

Howe suggests that media coverage is attempting to go though the third phase at the moment; but still has a long way to go, and he is concerned that the media coverage of the more severely disabled athlete may already be entering a fourth phase, where they are becoming less visible in the Paralympics and, if the games were integrated into the Olympics, then it would come a lot sooner (Howe 2008:143).

Simply put, the less the coverage of the Deaflympics, the more that people will remain unaware. Whatever coverage is realised, it does influence attitudes towards the Deaflympics brand; and so it is important that the ICSD interacts with the media as much as it possibly can; to present a positive and attractive brand to future athletes, target audiences, corporate supporters and others who are essential to the sustainability of the event.

There is not enough scope in this book to examine all aspects of mass media (television, radio, newspapers, magazines and internet media), where the most influential is television (TV). Studies show that viewers of sports on TV are invariably over 14 years old and regularly consult newspapers and magazines to get further information. Newspapers are the common source of information about minority sports and marginalised sports groups (Gilbert & Schantz 2008:34-57). This chapter, therefore, is limited to an examination of two newspapers in Taipei that were collected during the 2009 Deaflympics. The analysis that follows has used some of the methods employed in a similar study by Schantz and Gilbert, who assessed the coverage of the 1996 Atlanta Paralympics by the French and German press.

Visiting the 2009 Deaflympics as a spectator, I collected copies of 'The China Post' and the 'Taipei Times', published during the period of 6th – 15th September 2009. These are two of the three English-language newspapers published in Taiwan; the other being 'Taiwan News'. For the purpose of finding answers to the main questions posed in this book, I took my lead from the Gilbert/Schantz methodology. I examined the coverage to try and answer the following questions:

- How much coverage was there of the Deaflympics?
- Which themes and facts were considered newsworthy?
- Was the discourse sports-specific or did it consider athletes as victims of deafness?
- How were the ideals of the Deaflympics reflected in the coverage?
- How did the photographic coverage portray the athletes?

How much coverage was there, of the Deaflympics?

Table B: Newspaper Coverage of the 2009 Deaflympics (6th – 15th September 2009)

	Coverage within each newspaper		
Newspapers	Front	Inside	Back (Sports)
The China Post	(2) 30%	(2) 10%	(9) 20%
Taipei Times	(8) 45%	(1) 33%	(15) 72%
Total	(10) 38%	(3) 22%	(24) 46%

The combined number of headlined articles produced by the two newspapers and the approximated column inches per page were measured. The positioning of the articles was also studied to determine how much was placed as front-page headlines and how much space was given over in the sports pages. Other articles, usually non-sports specific, but event related, were also measured.

We can see in Table B above that there were a total of 10 headlined articles on the front pages, taking up an average page space of 38%. Colour photographs, showing Taiwanese athletes, accompanied all but one. As expected, there was greater coverage in the sports pages; all 24 articles were placed on the back page and covered an average of 46% page space. There was one article and two reader's letters found in the inside pages with an average space coverage of 22%

It was also important to know how much interest there was in the pre-Deaflympics build up, follow up and coverage in non-Deaflympic years. To ascertain this, the on-line archives of both papers were analysed.

Table C: Number of Articles written in Pre and Post games Coverage of the 2009 Deaflympics (2003-2013)

Time-line	The China Post	Taipei Times	Totals
2003		1	1
2006		1	1
2007	1		1
2008	10	3	13
Jan – March 2009	6	2	8
April – June 2009	24	4	28
July – Aug 2009	5	7	12
1st – 5th Sept 2009	6	5	65
6th – 16th Sept 2009	26	25	
17th – 30th Sept 2009		3	
Oct – Dec 2009		1	1

2010 - 2013	21	0	21
Total	99	52	151

Following on from the previous chapter, where it was considered vital to promote the terms 'Paralympic' and 'Deaflympic', our on-line archive search of *The China Post* and the *Taipei Times* sought to discover how many articles used the term 'Deaflympic' in their headlines or written text. The search was broadened as widely as possible, to find the earliest mentions of the 2009 Deaflympics and then followed through to the 2009 event and beyond, continuing up to the Spring of 2013. The results are shown in Table C above.

The first mention of the Deaflympics came in March 2003 with the announcement at the ICSD Congress in Sweden, that Taiwan had won the bid to host the 2009 version. There is nothing further for two years until 2006, after which there is then a gradual build up with peaks in 2008, April 2009, and September 2009. It is encouraging to note that in the four years preceding the event, there were 21 articles making references to the Deaflympics.

Which themes and facts were considered newsworthy?

The coverage followed a similar focus of Olympics coverage where a bias occurs in favour of the host country's athletes. This was especially evident in newspapers during the period 6th – 16th September 2009. The biggest stories were celebrating the success of domestic medal winners and the disappointments when they fared less successfully.

During the period examined (2003 – 2013) the prominent themes covered were;

Marketing

- The City of Taipei declared 2009 'Deaflympic year' and a number of major civic events were held in the build up to the event ('The China Post' 2/1 and 13/2/09)
- The Organising Committee featured prominent citizens ('The China Post' 26/2/08)
- There were celebrity appearances, statements and declarations from politicians, joint marketing ventures with other events ('The China Post' 17/5/08 & 2/1/09)
- Information for the target audience about the size and content of the event ('The China Post' 17/12/08)
- This coverage prompted new sponsors and demonstrated the Taiwanese government's commitment to providing an Olympic standard event.

Athletes

- As expected, home-based athletes enjoyed a high profile. 'Celebrity' athletes also made headlines and were to be found adorning event banners, posters and regalia at all venues.

Impact

- A professional table tennis tournament, the Taipei Open, was cancelled because the Taipei Gymnasium was undergoing refurbishment for the Deaflympics ('The China Post' 29/5/08).
- Schools each adopted a competing team and school curricula were adapted to work on deafness and the Deaflympics ('The China Post' 6/9/08).

- Tourist accommodation was made deaf-friendly ('The China Post' 3/3/09).
- There was an instance of sexual harassment involving a participant at the events. (Forumosa.com 2012)

Finance

- Direct government financing ('The China Post' 19/9/09).
- The Deaflympics were a major event to help attract tourism ('The China Post' 20/12/07).
- The government agency for sport supported and provided funding for the Deaflympics ('The China Post' 23/01/08)
- The event was incorporated into integrated citywide services ('The China Post' 31/5/08)

Political

- The Taiwan/Chinese Taipei President Ma used the event to promote positive relations between China and Taiwan ('The China Post' 6/9/08) and;
- To make Taiwan more disabled friendly ('The China Post' 5/2/09).
- Political parties used the profile of the Deaflympics to make statements ('The China Post' 18/2/09) and:
- There was controversy surrounding a Deaflympics ambassador Jackie Chan ('The China Post' 21/4 and 22/4/09)

ICSD

- Coverage specifically about the ICSD and the ideals of the Deaflympics were limited (see later in this chapter).

One article 'Countdown to the Deaflympics' ('The China Post') published three days before the Opening Ceremony explored the notion that the Deaflympics were a case of political correctness gone overboard by discussing whether or not Deaf athletes should be competing in the regular Olympics instead.

Was the discourse sports-specific or did it consider athletes as victims of Deafness?

During the Deaflympics the discourse was entirely sports specific, focusing on the action, records, results and statistics. Occasionally, and particularly for the 'celebrity' home-nation athletes, there were a few by-lines about the onset of their deafness, how they became involved in sport and the benefits it brought them.

The information appeared to be based on how athletes perceived their deafness – one deafened female athlete mentioned how she had hoped to avoid the 'family curse' of progressive deafness. Through all the coverage researched, the term 'Hearing-impaired' was used instead of "Deaf'; this is indicative of framing deafness in terms of a physical deficit as opposed to the cultural and linguistic.

Comments from coaches were interesting, as they tended to focus on the technicalities of participating in sport as a deaf person and how it impacted on coaching styles. This has been expanded on in Section 3.

There was an interest in the economic and professional backgrounds of the non-domestic athletes as opportunities were taken to highlight their professional occupations, possibly in an attempt to generate political capital for the home athletes. One of the articles that appeared on the final day ended with a plea for the Taiwanese Government to find regular employment for its deaf athletes. During a review of the Deaflympics, President Ma ordered the Sports Affairs Council to increase the prize money awarded to its athletes to encourage them to 'hone' their skills.

He also hoped to see physically and mentally disabled athletes "get out and enjoy the sunshine and exercise". ('Taiwan Times' 17-9-2009). Another article criticised the Sports Affairs Council for not mentioning any of the deaf athletes it had funded, nor offering them official congratulations. It was reported that the athletes would have preferred to have been given sustainable employment or had their part-time contracts renewed as the prize funds would not be sufficient to maintain a living whilst training. ('Taiwan Times' 17-9-09)

The socially constructed ideal of sport, as devised by Karin DePauw, was illustrated in many of the news articles. These are: Physicality (the socially accepted view of able-bodied, physical ability); Masculinity (aggression, independence, strength, courage); and Sexuality (socially expected and accepted view of sexual behaviour). Some examples of physicality and sexuality references were made to female athletes – the oldest female athlete was a 60 year old Finnish bowler, who was complemented on her good looks; *"I always smile and keep a happy mood,"* she said. Taiwan's 47-year-old tennis veteran, Ho Chiu-Mei, who described tennis as *'my beauty care medication'* followed this. A description of the Ukrainian Women's Beach Volleyball team noted that they *"not only have good looks but have good game skills as well".* The *'Italian Spice Girl'* of tennis, Barbara Odonne was described as having a *'gorgeous body'*. During a press conference, she explained that her focus on tennis meant that she was still single. A journalist asked if she would consider marrying a Taiwanese, to which she replied; *"Does any of you want to marry me?"* A volunteer interpreter responded immediately with *"I do!"*

Naturally, sport celebrates physical skill and prowess. The impairments of disabled athletes are exacerbated in the arena. On the whole, disabled people are ousted to the margins of society and therefore involving them in sport is seen as one of the threshold of inclusion/exclusion of society (Howe 2008:139). Media coverage perpetuates the marginality by measuring ability in light of disability; the ability to overcome, rather than athleticism, becomes the focus of praise and admiration (Howe 2008:139). This is the perception of sport as a benefit to disabled people that is not obvious to people watching high-performance deaf athletes.

How were the ideals of the Deaflympics reflected in the coverage?

During the Deaflympics there were no specific references to the ICSD or the 2009 strap line *'Power In Me'*. Official comments from the ICSD only ever appeared in the reporting of the Closing Ceremony *'Our Games were 'the best ever' ICSD chief says'* ('Taipei Times' 16/9/09). Ammons praised the event organisers for the excellence of the venues, the organisation and efficiency. Her comments reflected the ICSD mission statement:

- More and better athletes with higher standards of excellence; *"high quality of referees", 'meticulous about visual information on big screens and scoreboards', "as a Deaf person I felt like a first class citizen".*
- A significant level of international recognition; *"the media coverage was more than had ever been received".*
- An increased and sound budget; *"an exceptional number of volunteers".*
- An efficient and effective organisation; *"organisers resolved any problems quickly".*

In the same article, a quote from ICSD Executive member David Lanesman reflected the ICSD motto PER LUDOS AEQUALITAS (Equality through Sports), citing that the care put into the event made him *"feel like a human being"*.

Throughout the coverage, photographs were in colour and of high quality, delivering a range of messages: 'action, aggression, drama, emotion, performance, camaraderie, friendship, team-work and skill' – but there was nothing to demonstrate visually the uniqueness of the Deaflympics: sign language, starting lights, use of flags and other equipment. It is interesting to compare this with newspapers covering the 2012 Paralympics, with front page and headline photographs focusing in on prosthetic legs, and so on. The articles promoting the build up to the Deaflympics frequently ended by repeating that the event originated in Paris in 1924 and was sanctioned by the IOC in 1955.

A knowledgeable audience would have been able to subscribe to the ideals and benefits of the Deaflympics when references were made to:

- The altruism of volunteers and their learning of sign language - transport workers being taught sign language.
- 'The Thoughtful Games' - promoting a better understanding of and empathy with those who are deaf. ('The China Post' 6/9/12).
- Improved road safety measures with increased police vigilance.
- Fire and Police hotlines made accessible by text.
- Venues being made accessible for disabled people.
- The President calling for greater employment opportunities for deaf people ('Taiwan Times' 17/9/09).
- The Deaflympic experience enabling Taipei to bid to host more World-Class events. (' The China Post' Dec 2011).
- Increasing the global profile of Taiwan.

In the same way that lower lesion paraplegics and leg amputees benefit from the media promotion of technology, that is the product of the normalising disability industry, and are seen as the most worthy of media and sponsorship attention (Howe 2008:139), the ICSD needs to consider how its media coverage can begin to focus on the aforementioned ideals of benefits that the Deaflympics can bring to the inclusion of deaf people into society.

The ICSD is not experienced at working with or managing the media. With no major backers, it has partnered with small companies that have a specific deaf focus. It needs, however, to engage with mainstream media so that the profile of the Deaflympics can be taken to scale; but, without the level of financial investment commensurate with the IPC and its monopoly with the IOC, the resources available to the ICSD to maintain and sustain heightened profile are limited. However, what we can learn from Taipei 2009 is that by engaging with nations, who benefit socially and politically from hosting the Deaflympics, the ICSD could actually further disseminate the benefits of the Deaflympic experience and obtain the media exposure that it requires.

When asked to comment on Paralympic marketing beyond London 2012 (Burrell 2012), Mike Parker, Director of Sponsorship at media agency Carat, advised that sponsors looking to achieve maximum value should create long-term partnerships with Paralympic associations and individual athletes of note. The IPC have a 'watch' list of athletes' names it promotes to ensure that public dialogue and interest in the Paralympics is maintained between Games. For Deaf sport, it has been the Internet that has become its route to market, to stimulate debate, to inform and to enthuse.

17

IT and Deaf Sport

For the Athens 2004 Olympics, the International Olympic Committee (IOC) granted permission for major broadcasters to stream video coverage over the Internet; though they had to remain within their geographical restrictions, to protect broadcasting contracts elsewhere. The IOC forbade athletes, coaches and all other team personnel from setting up blogs or websites that would enable them to give their own personal perspectives of the Olympics. This included a ban on the broadcast and dissemination of all audio, photo or video material that they may have taken. The only exception was for websites that had not been set up specifically for the Olympics.

Up to that point in time, Internet coverage of the Deaflympics was limited to the uploading of pictures and text, which was aimed at keeping the target market abreast of results. For Melbourne 2005, the International Committee of Sport for the Deaf (ICSD) contracted *Deaf Nation* to provide a video streaming platform, which attracted 1.1 million viewers during the course of the 12-day event. The ICSD saw this as an opportunity to deliver an enhanced exposure to the wider community and to bring young deaf children into contact with Deaf role models (ICSD 1/3/05). At the same time, the British team employed Red Lizard to maintain a website, which hosted short video clips and interviews with athletes. These were streamed back to the UK within hours of being filmed. The coverage was still limited in comparison to the Paralympics, with support from the IOC, over 300 million people watched TV coverage of the 2000 Sydney Paralympics (Right to Play 2008). Since 2005, other companies have entered the video-streaming marketplace. *H3 TV* and *Moxio Ab* are two examples, which have both covered a range of Deaf sports and competitions. The 2013 Deaflympics website had over 200 hours of live streaming; and, less than two weeks after the event closed, the coverage had been viewed over 300,000 times. This does not account for all other streaming from other sources.

The IOC Congress of 2009 in Copenhagen considered contributions made by a *Virtual Olympic Congress* (October 2007- February 2009) enabling stakeholders of the Olympic Movement and the general public to put forward contributions[11] on five themes. In total, the Congress made 66 recommendations for all constituents of the Olympic Movement and especially to the IOC, IFs and the NOCs for their consideration (IOC 2009b). This included information technology under the heading of *The Digital Revolution* and recommendations 59, 62 and 65 stated:

2009 Clause 59 - *'A new strategy should be defined to enable the Olympic Movement to communicate more efficiently with its own membership and stakeholders as well as to allow for effective information dissemination, content diffusion and interactivity with the global population, in particular with the youth of the world. It should be an integrated strategy, which includes the full coverage by all media and in all territories, of the Olympic Games, as well as the recognition of the new*

[11] Contributions were made by post or electronically by email or otherwise

opportunities to communicate the fundamental principles and values of Olympism through all media."

2009 Clause 62- *"The IOC and all other constituents of the Olympic Movement should explore all possibilities offered by the digital revolution; ensuring the broadest coverage of the Olympic Games, including the Youth Olympic Games, as well as of all other games and other major international sport competitions recognised by the IOC or to which the IOC has granted its patronage"*

2009 Clause 65 - *"The IOC and constituents of the Olympic Movement must recognise that despite the emergence of a new digital age, the widely varying rates of adoption of these technologies are at a different pace in different regions and among different populations. As part of its obligation to ensure the widest possible global reach, it is therefore important that this is addressed and that appropriate technologies are used to ensure that all have access to the Olympic Games and Olympism in a legitimate and equitable manner and that the issues presented by the digital divide are addressed."*

ICSD President Crowley and the Executive Board approved the IOC report and recommended: that the ICSD should use it when constructing and implementing *Deaf Sport Reform*; and that it is presented in a way that enables ICSD member countries to use it to influence their own national governments and sports at Olympic level. (ICSD 2011b). So, what are the opportunities and expectations available?

2009 Clause 59 – The Olympic Movement as a whole should be making it easier for deaf people to access digital information in an appropriate format to ensure that *effective information dissemination, content diffusion and interactivity with the global population* reaches deaf people.

2009 Clause 62- The Olympic Movement as a whole should be making it easier for deaf people to access coverage of the *Olympic Games, Youth Olympic Games and all other games and other major competitions recognised by the IOC* - and the IOC/IPC and ICSD should also explore the possibilities to help the ICSD to broaden the coverage of the Deaflympics.

2009 Clause 65 – As well as tackling the issues of global access to technologies in developing countries, the Olympic Movement needs to ensure that access issues are provided in deaf-friendly formats to ensure that it no longer remains an *issue presented by the digital divide.*

The development of video-based technology is a preferred medium for Deaf people, as written language is not always fully accessible. Since 2009, the ICSD website has broadcast video bulletins in International Sign in place of written media. The videos are produced in an ICSD branded video format and are archived at www.deaflympics.com and on the You Tube *Deaf Sports Channel*.

This method of communicating has not been replicated quickly, because of the high costs involved in producing quality-designed presentations to match the standards required by today's websites. In 2012, the ICSD website was upgraded, so that it now has a more comprehensive database that tracks individual athletes and their competition histories. There are also some useful statistics on nation state participation trends.

A cursory sweep of the Internet in April 2013 (Table D) revealed that only 44% of the 105 national deaf sport federations in the ICSD have websites. The number of countries without websites in the ICSD regions are: 11 European (26%); 6 Pan American (50%); 19 African (90%); and 23 Asia Pacific (77%). This represents a distinct challenge for the ICSD as it looks to foster and develop Deaf sport in the developing world. Despite these limitations, there is an evolving social media, blogging and forum network, which allows for discussion on Deaf sport. This network is in its infancy and, ideally, should be harnessed in a way that supports the Deaflympic Movement. Below you can see the number of people connected to social media and networking sites of each ICSD member nation in April 2013. This was prior to the Sofia 2013 Deaflympics.

Table D: Number of Social media followers on NDSF sites (April 2013)

	Facebook	Twitter	You Tube	Other
ICSD	17,858	64	449	
Great Britain	1,707	3,421	19	
USA	1,358	1,301	25	
Ireland	1,789	244	43	
Spain	1,807			
Malaysia	1,447			
Portugal	1,025			
Sweden	991			
Canada	827			
Latvia	714			H3 TV
Finland	530		0	
New Zealand	305	156		
South Africa	365			
Australia	3	299		
Norway	279			H3 TV
Israel	261	5	2	
Netherlands		235		
Germany		148		
Switzerland	54			

Interestingly, coverage of the London 2012 Paralympics indirectly helped to raise the profile of the Deaflympics. Consumers were able to respond and communicate with journalists on-line. Social media forums and other networks enabled the real time recording of results, narrative and commentary. *Forumosa.com* is an illustrative source of the public interest for the 2009 Deaflympics. Threads related to the event covered a range of topics on deafness and sport ; some discussions were serious and others more humorous. Certainly, developing the means to monitor such sites would enable the ICSD to evaluate public opinion better (Forumosa.com 2012).

Whilst the media coverage of disability sport appears to create more positive and accurate perceptions, it can also have the opposite and diverse affect. During the London 2012 Paralympics, on-line discussions started to assess the options for merging the Deaflympics into the Paralympics. A deaf contributor argued that the ICSD was incorrectly promoting that deaf people could not participate in the Paralympics and backed his argument by cited TV evidence that showed a Paralympic runner using sign language. What the contributor did not make clear was that the athlete concerned was not participating under his Deaflympic classification of 55dB, but using his International Paralympic Committee classification (AoHL Forum 2012). It is likely that millions of other viewers arrived at the same incorrect conclusion. So, when they come across information to the contrary, they are confused or choose to disregard it, because they believe what they saw on TV.

The Internet is now a tool for global decision-making; enabling, as it does, individuals and organisations to mobilise and make collective decisions, which influence change. An example of this was the international reaction to the cancellation of the 2011 Winter Deaflympics in Slovakia. The news was initially announced by the ICSD in a press release dated 11th May 2010, published on the ICSD website and e-mailed to all its federations. Months of acrimonious attrition followed as participant countries argued for the Winter Deaflympics to be reinstated and the ICSD Executive succumbed to pressure on 3 December 2010 and reinstated the event. The ICSD's reputation took a further blow, when, in February 2011, three days before the Games were due to begin, they were cancelled again.

The 2013 Summer Deaflympics in Sofia, were a limited affair in terms of what was achievable on a restricted budget, and with only 10 months planning time available from the moment that the Bulgarian government and National Deaf Sports Federation were approved as hosts. The months leading up to the Deaflympics were an anxious time for the visiting athletes and their national federations, because there was very little information provided until the very last moments, owing to the Organising Committee working in a restricted manner. Against this background, the internet and social media came into its own; and in many ways demonstrated its power to provide instantaneous and updated information to enable athletes to prepare as well as possible for their events and for spectators to know what was happening and where. Some of the coverage was the live-streaming of some events, with an increase in the number of nations who paid for the rights to provide their own internet-based media teams to cover the trials and tribulations of their own athletes. At the time of publishing, data had not been collated in order to make comparisons of the impact of IT and how much public coverage has been achieved in comparison with previous Deaflympics.

SECTION 5

Why are the Deaflympics not recognised and supported?

"The deaf need courage, persistency and optimism but because their affliction is not readily apparent to the general public, the help and sympathy, which is so generously given to other afflicted classes, is often thoughtlessly withheld from them."

(Noel Curtis- Bennett, 1935. in Whalley (2010):233)

18

Disability Sport Politics

Paternalism

Howe (2008) describes paternalism as being "rooted in the notion that a lack of physicality requires rehabilitation towards a normative goal" which were also the Guttmann principles in establishing the Stoke Mandeville Games. Medically, understanding impairments has shaped political culture surrounding disability and has impacted on sport in the disabled community. Sports coaches often want to understand deafness in sport in the same way – medically and not socially. Issues of disability have been considered problematic in Western philosophy, and using sports for rehabilitation was seen as a method of dealing with a social problem, and so paternalistic attitudes are prevalent within disabled sport. Since sport is a Western construct, it is not surprising that the provision for disabled sport has its foundations in the West, so the relationship between politics and disability has an impact on how sport for the disabled has developed (Howe 2008:61). Howe suggests that the legacy of the Seoul Paralympics in 1988 was a watershed in the Paralympic movement, because the Koreans wanted to respect Paralympic athletes in the same way as they did for Olympians. The local impact was similar to that of the Deaflympics in Taipei – the Korean taxi drivers at the time were more at ease in dealing with wheelchair users than those in the West, where Howe still found it problematic (Howe 2008:42). This suggests that the Paralympic and the Deaflympics Movements have much to thank Eastern philosophy and its attitude towards disability for.

Paralympic Dominance

In Chapter 12, I discussed the profiles of the leaders of the Olympic, Deaflympic and Paralympic movements. I have attempted in this book to illustrate the complex manner in which the International Olympic and Paralympic Committees now dominate and monopolise the landscape. I am now going to examine this politically in relation to Disability Sports in the United Kingdom, because this is where the Paralympic Movement was established. It is where the current IPC President resides and serves as a member of the Executive Board of the British Olympic Association.

Globally, Professor Guttmann is credited as the pioneer of the Paralympic Movement in Great Britain, through the establishment of the International Stoke Mandeville Games. In 1961, he inaugurated the British Sports Association for the Disabled (BSAD) as an umbrella organisation to lead on political lobbying and national co-ordination of disabled sport, which suited the National Sports Council, who funded the BSAD accordingly. Guttmann has been highly praised by history, but rarely criticised, although he has been described as a difficult person to work with (Howe in Chapter 3). In Chapters 5 and 6 I examined how the balance of power, in the establishment of the

IPC monopoly through their constitutional change of replacing IDSOs with NPC representatives in the IPC board, does very little to embrace Deaf sport.

When interviewed in 2000, Bernard Altha, President of the English Federation of Disability Sport (EFDS) and Bob Price, Chairman of the British Paralympic Association (BPA) both indicated the extent, to which wheelchair sport dominated political influence in the 1980s and 1990s, in their references to Guttmann's highly private and idiosyncratic views. They described his ambitions as exclusively limited to those with spinal injuries and the inclusion of other disabilities was not something he had much concern for (Thomas 2003).

Guttmann's IPC predecessor, Canadian Dr Robert Steadward, was, at the time, committed to his convictions as an able-bodied administrator, whose leadership was inevitably associated with the fundamentals of sports science and high performance sport, albeit, as founder of the Alberta Wheelchair Sports Association. Some could have seen this as maintaining the hegemony of wheelchair sport.

At the same time that the ICC was engineering the establishment of the IPC in Dusseldorf in 1989, the UK government carried out a review of disability sport as a result of earlier criticisms of BSAD by other National Disability Sports organisations (NDSOs) and National Governing Bodies (NGBs). The review criticised the NDSOs for creating confusion and duplication and recommended that the NGBs should take on a greater role of sport provision for the disabled.

Mainstreaming had become government policy for disabled sport, but by 1996 nothing had changed, as neither the NDSOs nor the NGBs had coordinated their efforts. The government convened a conference and a taskforce was charged with the job of providing recommendations for mainstreaming disability sport by 2000. The result was the establishment of the EFDS in 1998.

The slow progress of change was partly due to the NGBs not acknowledging disability sport and, according to Bob Price, it was partly due to the reluctance of the non-disabled administrators of the NDSOs to relinquish their personal crusades. Casey, the CEO of Sport England at the time, and Altha concurred with Price that the attraction of working in elite disability sport meant that NDSOs were not relinquishing roles that could have been better served by different or mainstream organisations (Thomas 2003).

The dominance of able-bodied administrators in the governance and policy development of disability sport in Great Britain during the 1980s – 1990s was a replication of the able-bodied dominance of the International Organisations of Sport for the Disabled, who were dominating the Paralympic Movement.

Nigel Thomas in *'Disability and Sport'* (2003) described how, at the time, there were very few disabled people in positions of authority and influence within organisations that represented them. In the voluntary sector in the UK during the 1980/90s, there were few disabled people holding influential positions; and organisations led by able-bodied people had more resources and staff than organisations led by the disabled, and they were also more likely to receive financial support from the government. Despite the Disability Discrimination Act (1996), disabled people were still in subordinate, powerless positions (Thomas 2003).

Thomas & Smith acknowledged briefly in *Disability, Sport and Society* (2009) that the British Deaf Sports Council (BDSC) was the CISS representative in the UK and, although active in the Deaf community, it remained on the periphery and relatively independent of developments within both mainstream sport and disability sport (Thomas & Smith 2009: 25-26).

In 1991, I had moved to London to teach at Blanche Nevile School for the Deaf and was soon recruited as a volunteer onto the management committee of the BSAD London. It was during my decade in London that I became acutely aware of the BDSC reluctance to engage with the changes going on around them. Along with fellow trustees of the BSAD, I became actively involved in the government review of BSAD in 1996 – 1998 and was concerned at the lack of representation by the BDSC in the process. When I questioned this, I was told that representatives had been invited to meetings but seldom attended. When I had the opportunity to discuss this with the Executive Officer of the BDSC, I was told that the Deaf, who did not want to work with disabled sports organisations, guided his work. I was aware that, on a local/regional basis, there were BDSC representatives on local BSAD committees, but there was no representation where it mattered – strategically and nationally.

Deaf sport was losing ground fast; the government was already looking ahead 20 years into the future, as were sports coaches and administrators like Peter Keen who had just coached Chris Boardman to Olympic gold in 1992 and was laying down plans to gain a slice of Lottery funding, which would eventually result in GB dominating Olympic cycling. The British disability sports organisations were paying attention, but Deaf sport continued to stay away.

Government Policy

UK government policy and practice for disabled sport in the 1990s was about mainstreaming disabled people into sport. Deaf sport, fearing that it had too much to lose, stayed away. It was already suffering from falling rolls in schools for the Deaf; and past experience taught many Deaf leaders at the time to be very wary of letting non-deaf people in, because they might take over and dominate.

Shortly after becoming a school-leaver in 1982, I became involved in the Deaf-led organisation Friends for Young Deaf People and was trained, using sport and other interests, to work in partnership with hearing people in a way that safeguarded the welfare and interests of the Deaf. The FYD concept of integration was equality and, in order to achieve that, people had to examine their own beliefs of what is 'normal' and reconstruct it. It was, inadvertently, working on the principles described in Stewart's *Deaf Sport, the Impact of Sports within the Deaf Community (1991a),* which showed Deaf people how to use sport to obtain a balanced life, how to adjust to working and living effectively in a hearing society, and mainstreaming deaf and hearing people into Deaf sport and the Deaf community.

The IPC / IOC Treaty of 2001 coincided that year with the appointment of Philip Craven as President of IPC and Jacques Rogge as President of the IOC. Craven had previously been Chairman of the British Wheelchair Basketball Association and then President of the International Wheelchair Basketball Federation and was therefore involved in British interests in procuring government support for the Paralympic Movement.

In 2006, the UK government announced a funding package of £300m for UK Sport to prepare GB competitors for the 2012 Olympic Games. As a result of its 'no-compromise' approach, UK Sport cut its £42,000 annual grant to UK Deaf Sport and consequently all other funding available to Deaflympics preparations. Table H below shows funding comparisons.

Table H: UK Sport Funding 2000 -2012

	Sydney 2000	Athens 2004	Beijing 2008	London 2012
Olympic	£58.9 m	£70 m	£235.1 m	£264.1 m
Paralympic	£10 m	£14.8 m	£29.5 m	£49.2 m
Deaflympic*	£0	£0.075 m	£ 0	£ 0

*Deaflympic funding was for 2001 & 2005

UK Deaf Sport appealed against the decision; a second appeal took the decision to arbitration, which found in favour of UK Sport, which claimed that its no-compromise approach was justified and that Deaf sport would need to join the IPC, so that eligible athletes could be assessed under the World Class Funding programme. Having exhausted all options for appeal, because it did not have the funds to take the matter to court, UK Deaf Sport refocused its strategy to compete for recognition, within a landscape that was being monopolised by support for IPC-related organisations, and seek its 'slice of the pie'; and, in doing so, in 2009 was awarded £281,974 by Sport England for a 3 year Inclusive sport programme and then, in 2011, a further £125,000 for an 18 month talent development programme. Both projects have now given UK Deaf Sport the capacity to appoint staff to push ahead with its new strategy for 2013- 2017. The future is still uncertain, because government funding for all other aspects of disability sport Talent pathway development (School Sport, School Games – Youth Sports Trust; LTAD - ParalympicGB; World Class events - Commonwealth Games, Youth Olympics and so on) are based on the Paralympic pathway for the foreseeable future, at least to Rio 2016.

Classification

Howe (2008) argues that the financial benefits of associating with the Paralympics are the direct reason for the IPC's changes in classification, that have been about packaging the most attractive and commercially viable product. This is not a new way of working for the IPC. It has always been this way; and it began with the formation of the ICC, which, in its official correspondence, declared that 'every handicap is ours!'(Peers 2012:295- 316). The IPC wanted to make the IOC feel more comfortable with it, by organising events featuring well-muscled, lower-level paraplegic athletes who 'moved and looked more like able-bodied' athletes. To get closer to achieving integration into the Olympics, the ICC lobbied the IOC to hold demonstration events at the Olympics in the 1980s. To maintain its legacy, the

ICC suggested paraplegic athletes and blind athletes, because they were the nearest representation of being able-bodied. But the IOC was against integration and chose to host wheelchair sports, which reinforced the freak-show phenomenon in order to further differentiate and maintain the gap between disability and Olympic sport (Peers 2012).

I suggest that the Deaflympics can no longer afford to resist change and needs to move away from the politics of culture and linguistics (which were sown by the young competitors of the 1920s, who were led by Rubens-Alcais) and move forwards now with the priority of providing elite sports competition, in order to raise its profile and deal with contemporary issues. In December 2012, the ICSD elected Dean Barton-Smith and Terence Parkin as interim joint chairs of the ICSD athletes' commission. Barton-Smith pledged that they would both work together and ensure athletes were consulted on the ICSD governance review and other key decisions (ICSD 2012b)

UN Convention on the Rights of persons with Disabilities – Article 30.5

Donalda Ammons contributed a short essay in a 2007 publication by the International Disability in Sport Working Group (IDISWG 2007) to demonstrate ICSD's commitment to support the efforts to protect the human rights of individuals with disabilities. In her opinion, Article 30.5 holds significance for deaf and hard of hearing people:

- Promoting ICSD motto 'Per Ludos Aequalitas' (Equal through Sport).
- Providing a legally-binding document, expanding athletes' abilities and protecting their rights to play and compete on an equal playing field.

- Working closely with IPC to address inequalities or discrepancies that may arise at national level between the affiliated organisations.
- Athletes with a disability having a global stage to display their sporting spirit and dedication by participating in the Deaflympics.
- More and better athletes allowed to reach the pinnacle of disability-specific competitions and establish higher benchmarks.
- More significant levels of respect and recognition for deaf and hard of hearing athletes, who want to compete in the Deaflympics.
- Challenge to work with national governments, NGOs, international and national sports organisations in understanding that;
- Deaf and hard of hearing athletes will be treated with the same respect and dignity accorded to athletes with other disabilities.

Article 30.5 has a history at the United Nations going back to 1987 and the formation of the UN Disabled Persons Charter. The UN monitors the implementation and impact of Article 30.5 as often as possible and the Deaflympics has much to learn from others in how it can be utilised.

The most recent review to date was chaired at the UN by Eli Wolff, Director of Inclusive Sports Initiative for the Institute of Human Centred Design, who moderated a side event at the 5th Conference of State parties for the UN Convention on Disability Rights in September 2012. This review session was headed by a panel of four, which included Craig Crowley ICSD, Ann Cody IPC, Kristin Hughes SOI and Eric Dienes UNOSDP. Wolff's (2012) summary of the event makes interesting reading and indicates some of the strategies other international disability sports organisations are using to leverage Article 30.5.

When developing local initiatives, the UNOSDP has taken on what Rubens-Alcais intended, by bringing together young men and women from around the world (on Youth Leadership Camps) to develop their skills in project development and leadership so that they can strengthen their communities.

In the information-age, statistics are power. The Special Olympics infrastructure and membership has enabled it to demonstrate its grassroots reach. There are 4 million Special Olympic athletes around the world, and in 2011 over 50,000 grassroots competitions took place; but they only reached a mere 2% of the world's population of people with Intellectual Disabilities.

Crowley spoke to affirm the need for more acknowledgements of Deaf athletes by the disability community and the greater sporting community. The rest of the panel agreed that there is still much improvement to be made in politics, participation and media coverage if disabled people are to achieve parity with their non-disabled peers in sport. Political resolve, however, appears to be lacking; as one of the five thematic groups of the International Working Group on Sport for Development and Peace that is coordinated by UNOSDP and has the remit for *sport for persons with disabilities* was, as of September 2012, inactive owing to lack of leadership by member states. Dr Ted Fay concluded the session:

> ***"Many of us, personally or in advocacy for others, have witnessed shame and the destruction of life based on a person's identity group. We will no longer accept any excuses. We are coming from a cloak of shame to a future of fame!"***

The lack of political motivation may be symptomatic of the monopolistic profile of the Paralympics that lulls everyone into a false sense of security that all is well. It is now in the hands of National Deaf Sports Federations to engage in national politics and lobby for the equality of the Deaflympics as part of the Olympic family.

19

Deaflympics and Elite Sport

It is purported by some in the Deaf community, the public at large, decision makers and others in sport, that the Deaflympics are not an Elite sporting event. Therefore, it lacks the recognition and support that the ICSD, its members and athletes believe it deserves.

Public Opinion

During the 2010 World Deaf Golf Championships, I had a conversation with Stuart Lloyd from the Championship Committee of the Royal & Ancient (R&A). He had come into the Scoring tent where I was supervising proceedings and asked to have a look at the scores, as he was working as Head Referee. "Where's the Cut?" he asked me. I explained to Lloyd, that although this was our 9th Championship, the event was not yet mature enough to execute a cut in the field.

I reminded him that it was an amateur competition and that, unlike professional golf, those who missed the cut were not compensated for with an appearance fee to help recoup their costs; and that the competition continued with a full field right through, as they were also collectively scoring for a team event. The Deaf Golf World Championship, like all elite sporting spectacles, continues to grow in the number of participants competing and the standard of play. Sport makes progress, one championship at a time.

The deaf public can be very critical of the Deaflympics. A Deaf columnist in the Belfast Telegraph was critical of the event as he belittled the World Record results as 'inferior'. The journalist also criticised the introduction of the 55dB classification, because it allowed the non-culturally deaf to get involved. He suggested that, if things continued, there would no longer be any sign language users and the athletes would all be those who could manage in the 'oral' Paralympic setting. The article accused the competitors of being *Olympic Wannabes* (McCullough 2005). In reply to those who share these views, all I can say is that I respect you as experts on Deaf culture, language and linguistics, but leave the sport to us!

Like many events, unless you have experienced the Deaflympics, it is difficult to appreciate the occasion. In the words of Curtis-Bennett in 1935: 'seeing is believing'. A delegate from the British Olympic Association was able to visit the 2009 Deaflympics in Taiwan at the invitation of UK Deaf Sport. She agreed to meet UKDS officers at the badminton event and as the meeting drew closer, the Deaf representatives were anticipating having to convince the BOA of the Deaflympics merits. There was no need for the concern; her first words were that she had been observing events for a few days and was very impressed with what she had seen and did not need convincing any further. In the same venue a few days later, a stranger came and sat down within our group of spectators and we watched the badminton together. During a break in play, I introduced myself and discovered that he was over from the UK on business and had a few days free and had just wandered in to see what was going on. In summary, by the end of his short encounter with us, he was very impressed with what he saw in terms of standard of performances, atmosphere and quality of event; but he was equally disgusted with his own government for not providing equality of funding for its Deaf athletes.

A member of the Taipei public commented on-line that he had watched the Belarus volleyball 'machine' 'cream' their opponents (Forumosa.com 2009). The Russian Federation Commission on Youth and Tourism Affairs spoke of 'glory, pride, heroism, persistence and purposefulness that victory gives to the most persevering and the most brave". (RCDS 2009).

Elitism

In his discussion of Elitism, Howe (2008) deals with assumptions, such as those like "Comishandy" (2012) who called the Deaflympics 'a bit of a joke', because it is not a large event and the low numbers involved are the reason for its underfunding. An event with a larger number also cannot be considered 'elite'. In Howe's example, a marathon could have 25,000 runners but only 35/40 that are 'elite' (Howe 2008:56-57). Other examples given are the women's pole vault competition or steeplechase, which have a comparatively low number of available competitors, making it difficult to define where the status of high-performance begins. Is it fair to say that, because there is only one team or competitor, that a competition is not elite, high-performance? (Howe 2008:57)

Being an elite athlete is not tantamount to playing high-performance sport. 'High performance' means being very close to standards that have been pre-determined. This is not elite status. Elite status is having an intensive and long-term commitment to training and competition. Therefore, an athlete who may be lacking in physical skills can be 'elite', because they embody elite habits. They make sacrifices both socially and physically. These are the 'cultural capital' of elitism. In the majority of the sporting world, 'elite' and 'high-performance' are one and the same thing (Howe 2008:57).

In the culture of elite sport for the disabled, it is the 'hierarchy' of 'acceptable' impairment, which is directly linked to the classification of athletes (Howe 2008; 72). This is also what constitutes the differences between being 'deaf' or 'Deaf'.

I draw parallels with the Deaf from Howe's discussions on perceptions of high-performance sport for the disabled. Media commentators use terms like 'perfect' and 'faultless' when, in fact, both are unattainable. It can be suggested that the media coverage of the Deaflympics has been limited because it lacks perfection. The Deaflympics also has to compete with the visual impact of the Paralympics, where the disabled body is made hypervisual by showcasing wheelchair and amputee athletes. The Deaflympics are also perceived to be lacking in serious sporting endeavour, because non-deaf people still find it difficult to understand the ICSD discourse in the cultural and linguistic identity of the Deaflympics.

Elite Deaflympic athletes, who are not part of a world-class funding programme, face greater challenges in trying to balance their sporting, employment/academic and personal lives, in comparison with those who have the benefits of professional support to enable them to cope with and focus on attaining peak performance when it most matters. Howe (2008) suggests that the term 'elite' in disability sport works best when it describes the practice and attitude towards making personal, social and economical sacrifices in what, I would suggest, is the pursuit of personal excellence. Therefore, Deaflympic athletes are 'elite', because in their preparations, they sacrifice the social benefits of Deaf sport to train and compete in the less socially beneficial hearing sport, and because they seek a higher standard of training and performance. (Atherton et al 1999:47)

Similarly, some Deaf athletes choose to seek out the expertise of Paralympic performance specialists to help them reach and maintain their standards.

Aspirations need to be realistic; Deaflympic athletes cannot be expected to endure economic sacrifices. According to Action on Hearing Loss and the National Deaf Children's Society, in the UK alone, 71% of deaf children failed to achieve acceptable grades in subjects including English and Maths, which reduced their chances of finding gainful employment. Deaf people are four times more likely to be unemployed than the general population (AoHL 2010). The economic impact on deaf people is significant.

A growing number of nations recognise the elitism of the Deaflympics by the manner in which they reward success financially. In Kenya, Russia, Taiwan and elsewhere, when their Deaflympic athletes win medals, they are recognised as equals to their Olympic and Paralympic contemporaries. Whilst other nations will not present specific sums of prize money per medal won, they do reward their governing body with continuing funds to maintain their sport into the next quadrennial cycle; and the athletes themselves will be given living and training allowances based on their performances against set standards. Either way, the failure to recognise Deaflympic athletes in equal measure and thus maintaining an able-bodied dominated monopoly on disability sport has become detrimental.

Good practice in Deaflympic sport is also about finding the right balance in the governance, leadership and administration of elite sport. It is difficult to determine without proper study; but it would be useful to analyse, over a period of time, how performance of elite deaf athletes changes when under the supervision of deaf or hearing administrators and coaches. The trend is now moving further towards the appointment of non-deaf World–class experienced coaches, with overall sport responsibility for performance, and leading a team of secondary agents, assistant specialist coaches, medical practitioners, officials and interpreters, who are a mixture of deaf and hearing people. This increasing input of specialised support cannot go on being underfunded.

Technology and the Level Playing Field

For the uninitiated, their first competitive encounter in Deaf sport is very challenging, because they have to compete without the use of the assistive technology that enables them to overcome their everyday disability. They have to leave their hearing aids and cochlear implants in the kit bag. I am always met with incredulity from new athletes, their families or significant others and would like to present the reasoning behind this in the context of fair play and the level playing field of sport.

The use of technology in the Paralympics has become a dilemma played out in the scrutiny of the public eye; and it is also bringing to the fore some of the faults within its system, which has always been biased in favour of the less severely disabled, whilst allowing others to take advantage of performance enhancing technology. The dilemma of 'how much technology to allow' (Gilbert & Schantz 2008:117) has been slowly creeping up on the IPC since the Stoke Mandeville Games in 1940s. 60 years of sporting evolution has now come to the point where the IPC is being publicly challenged to create a clear, ethical framework.

The CISS overcame its 'Level playing Field' dilemma in 1983 when, after 59 years of international competitions, it stipulated that, as well as meeting the 55dB eligibility criteria to compete, athletes were also not allowed to wear their hearing aids or cochlear implants during competition.

Being able to hear using assistive technology is seen as performance-enhancing; and so the Deaflympic ruling challenges all competitors to compete unaided using only their mind, body and spirit, and the equipment that is available according to the regulations of each International Sports Federation.

The self-imposed challenge, created by deaf people themselves, is in tune with the definition of sport coined by the sports philosopher Bernard Suit, whose definition of sport suggests that it is a voluntary attempt to overcome 'unnecessary obstacles' (Suit 2005). In the Paralympics, the equivalent measures of creating the level playing field are the blindfolds worn by visually impaired athletes. In the Olympics, it is the WADA code and the notions of fair play by not taking any competitive advantage from doping.

Failure to comply, with either the rules of disability classifications or anti-doping, results in severe penalties for those who try to overcome the unnecessary obstacles that their physical body has limited them to. Able-bodied people know their limitations; they know that Olympians have supreme natural bodies and talent that can be taken to the extreme – unaided. The majority of us accept this and enjoy the process of supporting them to deliver a world-class performance and celebrate their success.

In Paralympic sport, the boundaries have been allowed to become blurred. For example, in swimming, athletes are not allowed any device to improve their functional anatomy but in athletics they are allowed. It is suggested that we have allowed athletics to have an unequivocal disregard for elitism in sport by allowing athletes, who have been classified functionally as amputees for example, to use technology to remake their impaired bodies (Howe 2008:120-121). In other words, they are given the unfair advantage in overcoming unnecessary obstacles. This is the equivalent to Deaflympic athletes passing the eligibility test and then being allowed to wear their hearing aid/cochlear implant for competition, or the Visually Impaired footballers being allowed to take off their blindfolds. For the Olympians, it would be the freedom to take banned stimulants.

But for a very small group of exceptional people, Olympians, by and large, are physiologically limited to specific sports in which they can excel at Olympic level. Consider for now, Cerebral Palsy (CP) athletes running on the track: they have no assistance to improve their performances and they compete using the bodies that they have; and they are performing naturally according to their physical limitations. Compare this with amputee athletes. When choosing which sport to train for, they have the choice to either run on prosthetics or swim without. Their first option could be seen as unnatural and unfair and the second choice as natural and fair. Howe (2008:135) explains that, although mobility technology is unnatural in the context of high-performance sport, it produces super-human results and therefore it has become accepted currency.

Some athletes are multi-disciplined, like Yin Lung-Hung of Taiwan, who gets up at 5am to orienteer every day and practices track and field in the afternoons. She also finds the time to practice basketball. Her coach Hsieh Ching-Liang says she has the genes for sports even though each sport requires different training and body adaptations. She can register at three different sports (Deaflympics09 9/9/09). Decathletes, heptathletes and other multi-disciplinary athletes are in this category of naturally adapting their bodies for multi-disciplined ability to overcome unnecessary obstacles.

My critics could then argue that it is unfair to be forced to drop some sports from the Paralympic programme because of this. But this is what the IPC has been doing! They have been designing the Paralympics in favour of some disabilities, at the expense of others, in order to provide a more 'attractive and palatable' spectacle for the spectator (Preer p310) and so, in turn, serve the needs of corporate sponsors and media executives.

The dominance of higher order classifications has affected disabled women and athletes with more severe disabilities and the Deaflympic Movement. The competitiveness of these three marginalised groups and others has been the legacy of the IPC; as it has continued to change its classification framework, with the aim of reducing the number of events, which, in turn, has a ripple effect on the performance pathways of those who have been marginalised (Howe 2008:140). The IPC has set an unwelcome precedent, which now needs to be challenged before changes become irreversible.

If the goal of sport is partly the pursuit of overcoming *unnecessary obstacles* imposed on us by the limitations of the human body. By introducing prosthetics, hearing aids, wheelchairs and so on, the *unnecessary obstacles* are removed to make life easier and more comfortable. But that is not what sport is about, according to Ivo van Hilvoorde, a Professor of Human Movement studies, who has challenged the IPC to create a clear, ethical framework on the use of new technology, otherwise the Paralympics could lose its credibility (IPC 2013).

The Deaflympics has developed its own use of technology, such as starting lights to start races and control time-outs and breaks in play. If society wants to venture further down the road of inclusion, then it has to introduce this technology and other forms of effective communication as standard in mainstream sport; otherwise we will continue to see the likes of Wendell Gaskin, a high school rival of Maurice Green, lose out on the opportunity to reach their true potential, because they are still having to wait for another runner to move before they can start their sprint (Fussell 2011).

Olympic Pathway

The Deaflympics have always been considered as a pathway event to the Olympic Games and some athletes have achieved this through competition in Deaf sport. It is interesting to see from the list below (Table I) how there has been a continuing increase in the number of Deaf athletes at successive Olympic

Games. The table below includes athletes, who have been described as deaf or have declared their deafness. This is not a complete and definitive list. What would be useful to know is how many of these athletes, and others unknown to us then and in the future, would be eligible to compete in the Deaflympics?

Table I: Deaf people who have competed at the Olympic Games

Olympic Games	Athlete	Event
Paris 1924	Gertrude Ederle (USA)	Swimming – Gold
Amsterdam 1928	Carlo Orlandi (ITA)	Boxing
	Donald Gollan (GBR)	Rowing
Rome 1960	Ildiko Ujlaky-Rejto (HUN)	Fencing
Tokyo1964	Jim Ryun (USA)	Athletics
	Ildiko Ujlaky-Rejto (HUN)	Fencing
Mexico City 1968	Jim Ryun (USA)	Athletics – silver
	Ildiko Ujlaky-Rejto (HUN)	Fencing
Munich 1972	Jim Ryun (USA)	Athletics
	Ildiko Ujlaky-Rejto (HUN)	Fencing
Montreal 1976	Ildiko Ujlaky-Rejto (HUN)	Fencing
Los Angeles1984	Jeff Float (USA)	Swimming – Gold
	Marie Roethlisberger (USA)	Gymnastics
Barcelona 1992	Dean Barton-Smith (AUS)	Decathlon
Sydney 2000	Terence Parkin (RSA)	Swimming – Silver
Athens 2004	Frank Bartolillo (AUS)	Fencing
	Tamika Catchings (USA)	Basketball – Gold
	Tony Ally (GBR)	Diving
	Jueri Jaanson (EST)	Single Sculls- Silver
	Hugo Passos (PORT)	Wrestling
	Terence Parkin (RSA)	Swimming
Beijing 2008	Tamika Catchings (USA)	Basketball - Gold
	Chris Colwill (USA)	Diving
	Maria Belen Dutto (ARG)	BMX Cycling

	Jueri Jaanson (EST)	Double Sculls- Silver
	Norbert Kalucza (HUN)	Boxing
	Fausto Quinde (ECQ)	Race Walking
London 2012	David Smith (USA)	Volleyball
	Tamika Catchings (USA)	Basketball – Gold
	Chris Colwill (USA)	Diving

International Sports Federations

There needs to be an increase in the number of internationally certified IF officials and coaches who are deaf. This would enable ICSD to improve conditions for elite competitors, who are deaf, in creating a clear, continuing professional pathway for officiating and coaching and a register of those who are deaf and hard of hearing, as well as those who are hearing and have experience of or sign language skills. As well as national team coaches and officials, there is usually an influx of IF-registered officials at National, International and Deaflympic events, who could be included in this register as a resource for national organisers. National and International Seminars would be an excellent forum for discussion and sharing of experience and research that could also include deaf and hearing personnel from sports science industries. This register should initially be administered by the ICSD as a central reference point.

20

Fighting for a slice of the Pie

In the 1990s David Stewart predicted that friction between Deaf sport and the wider sports community was emerging, as everyone was competing for *'the use of facilities, federal support, private sponsorships, research funds and spectators.'* (1991a: 2). Although government intervention had created umbrella organisations to bring together Disability sport, and provided Deaf sport with indirect access to funding, he was concerned about the growth in strength of the Special Olympics and Wheelchair sport associations and their demand for *'a larger piece of the pie.'* (Stewart 1991a: 96). When the IPC began forging closer ties with the IOC, commercial sponsors started to emerge (Howe 2008:84).

In this book, I have done as much as I can to highlight the difficulties that the Deaflympics have when competing for spectators and sponsors against the IOC/IPC monopoly. This is compounded by the difficulties of obtaining government support in persuading National Olympic and Paralympic Committees to respect the equal status of the Deaflympics granted by the IOC. In this chapter, I want to examine how far Stewart's predictions have manifested themselves and to help people to understand how funding for Olympic–level events is provided and how the *pie* needs to be accessed.

Low Incidence and Hidden

In Section 2 we examined how the low socio-economic and political profile of Deaf sports leaders, the decline of Deaf sport, the misunderstanding of the Deaflympics and the lack of media coverage and marketing has resulted in the Deaf community and Deaf sport becoming a low incidence and hidden feature in the sports landscape. Throughout the book, I have examined the varying ways in which deafness remains stigmatised and compounds the marginalisation of deaf people in society. As a result, there is no critical mass of people to provide the capacity for fundraising from within the community and, as a result, income generation for Deaf sport is sporadic at the best of times.

Newcomers to the Deaflympics do comment on the vast areas of empty seats in the larger arenas and stadiums, Breivik et al describe this as *abandoned modernity*, where the ICSD (and other less-well resourced organisations) have no 'command over large economic resources' and have to rely on the 'facilities of modern society' being available to 'groups on the margins of society at certain times of the year, and in certain areas of recession' (Breivik et al 2002:37).

In both developed and developing countries, evidence suggests that persons with disabilities are disproportionately represented amongst the world poor and tend to be poorer than non-disabled people (UN 2011). In the United Kingdom, severely and profoundly deaf people are four times more likely to be unemployed than the general population, even during times of low unemployment (AoHL 2010); and we can assume that this alarming statistic is representative of the global Deaf community. Therefore, the economic capacity of the severely and profoundly deaf individual, who would meet the audiological eligibility criteria of the Deaflympics, to make a personal contribution to the Deaflympic Movement, either as a participant or a philanthropist, is limited.

In Finland, the ratio of deaf to hearing is 1:1,000 an extremely small proportion of the community when compared to 1:6 in the UK, where the combined spending power of the disabled community is approximately £80bn per year. Governments have done very little to leverage this spending power and invest in disability sport. Barton-Smith estimated that government investment into Deaf Sport Australia amounted to 0.03 cents per person annually. It is not surprising then that Deaf sports organisations are going to struggle to encourage their community to take up sport as healthy lifestyle choice (Barton-Smith 2009). Elsewhere, developing nations like Kenya give recognition and support to Deaflympic athletes alongside their Olympians/Paralympians. Likewise, so do Russia and other former Soviet states, Taiwan and others, who also provide financial recognition of Deaflympic sport through medal bonuses and other initiatives.

However, there is a potential for political support for Deaf sport within some governments, as indicated by two Early Day Motions presented to the House of Commons in the UK. Deaf sport needs to find ways of engaging more effectively with decision makers (Bruce 2009 & 2012), Evidence of untapped support was manifested when local politicians in Allerdale Council (UK) gave financial support to one Deaflympic athlete, because they were shocked to learn that no government-directed funding was available to Deaflympic athletes. The council found it unfair in the light of financial gains made from the London 2012 events that deaf athletes have to fund their own participation in the Deaflympics (Barwise 2013).

The World Health Organisation and others are predicting an alarming increase in the burden of deafness on the world economy and that we are also going to experience an epidemic of deafness in the future. I suggest that the Deaflympics can be a vehicle to help highlight this inevitable strain on world resources; but before we discuss that, we need to examine who is currently *'eating the pie'* and whether or not the Deaflympic Movement is being given a fair share.

How much does it all cost?

The 2005 Deaflympics in Melbourne, Australia, are estimated to have required a AUS$10m government investment. There was a surplus of AUS$400,000 of which AUS$150,000 was given to Deaf Sports Australia and the remainder returned to the State of Victoria. There was also an estimated AUS$16.5 million dollars of direct expenditure in the state of Victoria as a result of the Deaflympics. Despite this economic contribution, the subsequent quadrennial government investment in Deaf Sports Australia was a pitiful AUS$0.3 – 0.4m. A drop in the ocean compared to support for the Australian Paralympic Committee of AUS$20m (Barton-Smith 2009).

The estimated costs for the 2009 Taipei Deaflympics was US$100m with a further US$94.3m rebuild of the athletics stadium and US$18m for a new swimming pool. 10 weeks earlier, the country had also hosted the World Games, roughly the same size in sports and the number of competitors, coaches and officials. The investment there was over NT$900m. Support for the Deaflympics came from the national sports authority Sports Affairs Council, National Olympic Committee and the Taipei city government ('The China Post' 23/1/08 and 6/9/08).

The 2009 Winter Deaflympics in Salt Lake City, was a much smaller event for around 240 competitors and cost in the region of US$1.4m, which was raised by the American Deaf Sports Federation with no government backing.

The Bulgarian advertising and marketing agency KRES,

charged US$170 per photographer and US$3,000 per video crew for the 1993 Sofia World Games for the Deaf. It was also the first time that the CISS allowed athletes to have sponsors logos on kit (within regulations of the IOC). An examination of a report from Melbourne 2005 showed that the ICSD had only made a marginal change in charging for broadcast and media rights of US$2,500 for National TV crews and US$2,000 for private crews. Photographers/Journalist were charged US$700 for teams of two or US$500 per person. The National Deaf Sports Federations were also charged US$250 for bringing their own media representatives (Melbourne 2005).

The number of athletes at the Summer and Winter Deaflympics is limited only by the capacity of National Deaf Sports Organisations to secure sufficient funding to field potential medal winners. The costs of getting athletes and their support staff to the Deaflympics has to include international travel, quality accommodation and sustainability for the duration of the event, fees for competition entry, local transportation, personal kit and equipment, communications support resources, sports science support and logistical support from the Chef de Mission's team. For the last three Summer Deaflympics, 2005, 2009 and 2013, this has cost approximately £3,600 per athlete to travel from the UK to compete at each event. I was frustrated to read in 'The China Post' (8.10.09) that the UK government Overseas Trade Department was looking to combine UK creativity with Taiwanese manufacturing to bring business to London and support the 2012 Olympics on the back of a British company having helped to host the Deaflympics. If this was indeed the case, then potential commercial support opportunities were missed by UK Deaf Sport to contribute to, and obtain mutual benefits from, the economy only owing to the lack of capacity that urgently needs supporting.

Despite its recognition of the Deaflympics as an equal to the Paralympics, we know from earlier chapters that the IOC invests very little into Deaf sport. Public and media commentary has focused on the discrepancies in support given to different national Deaflympics teams suggesting, for example, that Russia and other nations are only dominating the Deaflympic medals table, because their athletes are benefiting from government incentives for medalling. By having an understanding of how the IOC generates and spends its income, and how Olympic and Paralympic sport is funded from this and other sources, I hope that you, the reader, will be in a better position to put the needs of the Deaflympics into a proper context.

Where does the money come from? The International Olympic Committee

According to its own website, the IOC sources its income from the following: Broadcasting rights (47%), Sponsorship (45%), Ticketing (5%) and Licensing (3%); and according to Lubin and Delevingne (2012) the 2005-08 IOC quadrennial revenues were almost US$6 billion. The IOC distributes 90% of its revenues to member organisations throughout the Olympic Movement to support the staging of Olympic Games and the worldwide development of sport (Table J).

Table J: IOC Income and Expenditures 2005-2008	
Income	
Broadcasting	$2.57b
Global Sponsorship	$870m
OGOC Domestic sponsors	$1.55b
Licensing	$190m
Tickets	$270m
Expenditure	
National Olympic Committees	$370m

International Federations	$0.42b
Olympic Games Organising Committees	$700m
Figures taken from Lubin & Delevingne (2010)	

When the IOC was asked to create a funding agreement for the Deaflympics that was similar to its pact with the IPC, the ICSD was told that this would be unfair, as it had no such agreements with fifty other similar organisations. Today, the ICSD is competing with sixty other IOC Recognised organisations for a fair slice of the pie. (Table K with full list in Appendix 1)

Table K: IOC Recognised Organisations	Number of Orgs.
IF Associations	4
NOC Associations	8
Multi- Sports Organisations and Events/Sport for All	15
Disabled Sport	3*
Education/Dissemination of the Olympic Ideal/Fair Play	7
Sports Medicine and Sciences	4
Sports Equipment and Facilities	2
Media- Information	6
Other Recognised Organisations (incl. CAS and WADA)	12
* IPC, ICSD and Special Olympics.	

Correspondence and notes of meetings between the CISS/ICSD and the IOC give an indication of the ways in which the IOC tries to support the Deaflympics. In 2002, the CISS and IOC discussed an impending approach by the Victorian Government Minister to the IOC President to seek a financial contribution towards the running of the 2005 Deaflympics, which the State of Victoria was considering supporting. The IOC suggested to CISS that, if the Games Organising Committee went through CISS to make a request for special funding from the IOC to support athletes from 'developing' nations, it would receive a favourable response; as it had already supported a grant for Rome Deaflympics 2001. Felli suggested that this grant would also stand a better chance if it were match-funded by host governments (Lovett 2002b).

The IOC continues to support the ICSD with an annual operations grant, support for the organisation of seminars and workshops, and support towards each Deaflympics Games. The amounts are negotiated on an ongoing basis and pale into insignificance when set against support to the IPC. For example, for the marketing of the 2008 Paralympics, the IPC were granted approx US$8m, whilst the ICS received a mere 150,000 in Swiss francs for the whole of 2005-2009.

In 2003, the IOC explained to the CISS that it was reluctant to allow derivative use of the word Deaflympics as it *'may take away sponsorships from the IOC'*. Felli suggested that the CISS should approach the subject again *'in a few more years'* after *'people within the IOC become more accustomed to the term Deaflympics'* (CISS 2003).

National Olympic Committees

The IOC recognises sports nationalities rather than political nationalities; therefore, on the whole, National Olympic Committees do not receive government funding, and instead they rely on subsidies from the IOC and their own methods of income generation. How this is demarcated at national level is quite interesting: for example, the athletes of Trinidad and Tobago (T&T) are recognised legally as US citizens but compete under the T&T NOC as its nationals. The British Olympic Association (BOA) is the NOC for the United Kingdom, the Isle of Man, the Channel Islands and the UK Overseas Territories, which do not have their own NOCs.

The United States Olympic Committee (USOC) and the BOA raise funds from private enterprise and philanthropy, and rely on the work of volunteers to deliver operations. Funds are raised through private and corporate donations and sponsorship, licensing fees, licensed apparel and items in catalogues and online stores. They also bid to host the Olympics and Paralympics and establish Olympic Organising Committees to manage the events and benefit from any revenues.

The Olympic Partner (TOP) programme provides corporate multinationals with exclusive worldwide marketing rights and, in addition to supporting the IOC and Organising Committees, they also support NOCs and their Olympic teams.

The US Olympic Foundation was established after the 1984 Los Angeles Olympics to support Olympic and Amateur sport in the US. It began with a founding capital of US$155m raised from the sale of commemorative coins and surplus from the 1984 Olympics. The Foundation reinvests 50% of its annual income, whilst the other 50% is disseminated through grants to member organisations to develop sport.

The NOCs are the national voices of the Olympic Movement and lead and prepare athletes for the Summer and Winter Olympics. Their roles include talent identification, training, selection, entering and funding national teams and the trips to the Olympics and Paralympics. They work with National Governing Bodies of sport to provide the selection and training of athletes. The funding for NGBs comes through their own membership fees, competition fees, clothing accessories/ equipment, promotional items, donations and philanthropy from Alumni (Hunter 2008). USOC has provided US$1.2m to Rowing, with each Olympic athlete getting approximately US$400-$800 per month to help pay bills (Grossman 2012).

The USOC and the BOA provide no support to Deaflympic athletes.

Government support – World Class Funding

In 1978, the Ted Stevens Olympic and Amateur Sport Act chartered the USOC, which, in 1998, was expanded to cover the US Paralympians.

Even though the NOCs remain independent from government funding, governments do provide indirect support for athletes to prepare for international competitions via state-funded mechanisms. Most governments provide athletes with financial bonuses and incentives for winning medals, but the UK is a rare exception to this rule.

To enable Great Britain to compete successfully at the Olympics, the UK government established UK Sport as its distributor of National Lottery funds and established the *World Class Performance programme* in 1997. Starting with sports that were best placed to deliver medalling success; UK Sport provided 'development' funding to enable others to catch up. Funding is awarded to sports on the 1st April in the year immediately following an Olympics for a period of four years. The money is provided to individual athletes through two channels. Firstly, to their respective National Governing Bodies, who receive on average £55,000 annually per athlete at the Podium level and £30,000 to those on the Development stage. This funding is used to co-ordinate athlete back up for:

- World Class Coaches
- Sports science and medicine support
- Warm weather training and acclimatisation
- International competition schedules
- Athlete development programmes
- Access to appropriate training facilities.

The second channel of funding available to athletes is the Athlete Personal Award (APA) paid directly to athletes to contribute towards ordinary living costs and personal sporting costs. There are different levels of awards based on set criteria (table L)

Table L: UK Sport Athlete Personal Awards (sourced Nov 2013)

APA Bands	Criteria	Maximum annual award levels (2013)
Band A	Medallist at Olympic or World Championship level	£ 27,737
Band B	Top 8 finish at Olympic or World competition	£ 20,804
Band C	Likely to be major championship performers, but flexibility given to individual sports to set their own criteria	£ 13,869

The actual size of the APA is means-tested, with a maximum income threshold of £65,163 (including the APA), above which an individual's APA is deducted pound for pound. This allows any athlete to earn an extra £37,426 from sponsorship, prize money or earned income before it affects the maximum of APA they can achieve. The higher earners benefiting from high levels of commercial sponsorship still benefit from the services provided in the programme support of their NGBs. The average APA payment to athletes on the Podium programme is £18,500; and £7,500 on the Development programme (UK Sport website 2013).

The Indonesian government supports its athletes with funds to cover their training and competition expenses; and China and Korea provide pensions and retirement assistance as well as medalling incentives through lottery programmes (Grossman 2012). We know from Spry (2012) that the Canadian government started the *Own the Podium* programme in 2005, aimed at success for the Vancouver 2012 Winter Olympics. This provided CAN$62m annually: CAN$34m for Summer, CAN$22m for Winter and CAN$6m for team sports.

Government Support - Medalling Bonuses

With the exception of the UK, 43 countries are known to award financial bonuses and incentives to athletes who win medals. The list, compiled by Wallsten (2012), only includes those countries which volunteered or published information. The list shows payouts to gold medallists, ranging from US$11,000 by Kenya and US$1.2m by Georgia. This method of funding has recently attracted public interest (Taylor, Emily, Smith, Wallsten, all 2012). According to Taylor, the US$25k for gold, US$15k for silver and US$10k for bronze awarded to US athletes in the 2005-8 quadrennial cycle had not changed in 10 years, thus losing about US$5k in real term values.

According to Wallsten (2012), in addition to medalling bonuses, Belarus offers its athletes free meat for life, and North Korea supposedly provides an incentive of two extremes – for medallists, they earn bonuses, cars, apartments, refrigerators and TVs and so on; while poor performing athletes are apparently sent to labour camps.

Funding for the Majority

Olympic cycling gold medallist Chris Hoy, who earned around £24k annually from UK Lottery funding and small sponsorships before medalling in Beijing and making his living from more lucrative commercial deals (Hubbard 2012), is amongst a minority of his peers. The majority of World Class Athletes worldwide have to rely on alternative sources of income to maintain their performances. In the USA, the Track and Field Foundation confirmed that only 50% of the athletes ranked in the US top ten make more than US$15k annually from athletics. Athletes in other sports may get nothing (Taylor 2012). Generous individuals who want their national athletes to succeed have made personal pledges; a Malaysian gold mine owner offered US$600k to badminton players (Smith 2012).

Writers and commentators have all listed examples of how National Governing Bodies have provided their own gold medalling incentives drawn from their own funds;

From Taylor (2012), incentives were:

- *Living The Dream* by USA Wrestlers with US$250k for medalling gold, in an Olympics or World championships.
- Swimming Australia offered AUS$36k for gold with relay teams taking a share of AUS$63k.

From Grossman (2012):

- Host families are offered US$400 a month to accommodate individual members of sports squads when they are at training camps in their locality.
- The IAAF has offered competition awards since 1997.
- USA Swimming pays out US$3k monthly from its membership fees to team members ranked above 16th.

There are critics of the different methods used to fund elite class sport. Spry (2012) calculated that the *Own The Podium* initiative from the Canadian government was worth CAN$7m for medals and felt that this was a waste of taxpayers' money. He argues that the money should be targeted at grassroots sport and the Olympians should get employment and commercial sponsorship to make ends meet. But, even with government subsidies, many athletes already take on part-time employment, such as working as a website/graphic designer for their NGB, or, as with a swimmer, taking modelling and speaking engagements. Others are working for sports clothes manufacturers. I am reminded of an earlier mention in Chapter 16 where Deaflympic Taiwanese athletes, who had been awarded medalling bonuses, said that they would have preferred to have been given employment contracts, as these would have been a better method of sustenance during quadrennial training than were their bonuses.

Whatever sovereign incentive is available to elite athletes, there is no justification for excluding Deaflympic and other World Class Deaf sport athletes. Isidore (2004) suggested an idea that the IOC should drop its amateur eligibility rules and offer prize money as well as medals, so that athletes from the poorer nations or less commercially attractive sports would have some financial compensation for their efforts. Based on the number of Olympic medals (in 2004), Isidore calculated that if the IOC offered prize money for the following: Gold US$25k, Silver US$15k and Bronze US$10k, this would have only cost the IOC US$49m; and it would ensure that funds went directly to the athletes, who were the real deserving beneficiaries of the Games. Similarly, as a hypothetical illustration, if the IOC had adopted this strategy with the 2009 Deaflympics it would only have to contribute $9.4m (Table M)

Table M: Isidore's theory applied to the 2009 Deaflympics

	Gold	Silver	Bronze
Number of Medals Awarded	178	176	205
Suggested IOC Payouts per medal $	25 K	15 K	10 K
Estimated Cost to IOC US$	4.45m	2.64m	2.05m

The Bank of Mum and Dad

The demands of elite sports performance now requires Long Term Athlete Development. Young people, who are not economically self-sufficient, have relied on parental and family support to help them through the formative years. Funding has to be found to hire sports coaches, purchase equipment, clothing and travel and accommodation for training and competitions. Many parents give up careers and take up part-time jobs so that they can fit their lives around their children's schedules. Roberts-Grey (2012) mentions a survey of 254 USA Olympic athletes, which found that the physical and emotional discipline needed to prepare for the Olympics often transcended their financial habits and attitudes, with many believing that the discipline helped them to be better budget managers.

Whilst some young deaf athletes have support from their parents, this number will be proportionately lower than the norm, because over 90% of deaf people are born to hearing families with little interest or knowledge of the Deaflympic Movement and its potential value to their children.

Deaf Sport is not immune to Scandals or Difficulties of finance

Like the IOC, the ICSD has learnt the hard way how to be more vigilant concerning corrupt dealings within sport. In her report to the IOC in 2008, ICSD President Ammons stated that Deaflympic Organising Committees collaborated with governments and national sports organisations but only in 'some instances' (Ammons & Eickman 2011). This suggests that until the time Crowley risk-assessed the 2011 Winter Deaflympics, the CISS and ICSD did not always comply with stringent guidelines with regards to bidding and hosting of the Summer and Winter Deaflympics and that the ICSD Congress had been appointing host cities without sufficient due diligence.

Soon after taking up the ICSD Presidency in October 2009, one of Crowley's first actions was to ensure that preparations for the 2011 Winter Deaflympics were on track. He was not satisfied with what he saw and so, after repeat visits to Slovakia and failures of the organisers to provide evidence of developing and organising adequate funding, detailed planning, final preparation of venues, comprehensive quarterly progress reports and high standards of marketing efforts, the ICSD announced the cancellation of the event (ICSD 2010b).

Within six months, the Winter Deaflympics were reinstated, despite some outstanding financial issues, because 'great strides' had been made to reassure the ICSD. Ultimately, the event was cancelled again, only a few days before the Opening Ceremony; and the President of the Slovakian Deaflympics Committee was arrested for embezzlement of funds.

Collaborative Leadership

Regardless of campaigns in the USA by the Deaf and Hard of hearing Alliance in 2003, the US Olympic Committee still fail to recognise Deaflympic athletes. The campaign was arguing that the IOC recognised the Paralympics and Deaflympics as equal events (NAD 2003)[12]. The question to ask is: Will these problems continue as long as the administrators of Deaf sport insist on wanting full control of their organisations and events? The world has moved on since 1924 and 1995, with some improvements in the quality of life for disabled people, but they are by no means complete and, perhaps, never will be. I believe the next step in the process towards equal opportunities for the Deaflympics is to work more collaboratively.

Governments always seek the easier options, as they have to justify public expenditure. Deaf sport continues to try and effect change from the periphery and this is not working. There is no one model to fit all nations, because there will always be differences; but those of us in Deaf sport should support the ICSD in its continuing dialogue with the IPC to find a way through. It is time to reconsider the options of bringing some sports events for the Deaf into the Paralympics. The

[12] NAD – National Association of the Deaf, USA

options have to be examined: nothing will be taken lightly. The long-term interests of Deaf sport can be taken into serious consideration.

In *Awakenings* (1994), Stewart and Ammons accepted that changes are unstoppable. Western nations cannot reverse the impact of educational mainstreaming. The critical mass of schools for the Deaf cannot be revived; sport has to work with mainstream education. It is feasible that the richer, western representatives of the ICSD, who can afford to continue the resistance of joining the IPC, are doing so at the cost of other nations, whose organisations cannot afford to do so.

In Russia, there is the legacy of a Party-sponsored constitutional congress, The All-Russian Organisation for the Deaf (VOG), established in 1922 under the Welfare Department of the Party. The Russian mind-set of the Deaf community was tolerant of the need for Oralism in education, as it aided employment; but they still held on to their sign language to preserve their Deaf community, without trying to impose it on Russian society (Burch 2000). Whether directly or indirectly as a result of this, the Russian government continues to give considerable equitable support to its Deaflympic athletes by providing state- sponsored sports events, organisations and rewarding medal winners with financial compensations.

Some Deaf sports administrators who continue to insist that they are not disabled, as a reason for not considering merging some events into the Paralympics, still apply for and benefit from disability-based legal protections and government funding and welfare. The problem of the ICSD Constitution insisting that national membership can only be given to Deaf sports organisations whose Presidents are Deaf can be dealt with without having to make constitutional changes. Why not have national organisations that have joint Presidents or Chairpersons, who are deaf and hearing? In France, the deadlock between the ICSD and the French Federation Handisports (FFH) was resolved the situation by having a Deaf representative on the Board of the FFH.

Deaf sport has already shown that it can work collaboratively with non-deaf people, as previous CEOs and Chairs of the World Games for the Deaf and Deaflympics have been hearing. Deaf administrators know how to utilise the skills of hearing people in roles that aid communications for business; and Deaf sport should be no different. Stewart & Ojalas (1995) suggested that collaborating with other disability sports organisations could reduce financial burdens on Deaf sport. In the late 1990s, Roland Haythornthwaite of the British Deaf Sports Council believed that the best chance of obtaining government funding was for Deaf sport to come under 'umbrella' organisations (Atherton et al 1999). There is, however, one issue around the practicalities of providing high level spoken/sign language interpreters for meetings between Deaf and hearing organisations (Ammons & Eikman 2011:1153) - who funds the costs of this?

If some Deaf sports were entered into the Paralympics would it be damaging to the sports that are left out? One possibility in this situation would be to continue with the Deaflympics, because the event would then serve as a pathway feeder to both the Paralympics and the Olympics, making it more attractive to NOCs and NPCs. Things cannot change overnight; evolution takes time. But, for as long as NDSFs remain on the periphery, it will be harder for them to create long-term strategies; so engaging in collaborative leadership should create more possibilities.

Would it be fair to suggest that the IPC appears not to have wholly engaged with the spirit of its MoU with the ICSD, and that this is partly constrained by the IOC attitude in not considering that it has the right to interfere with national politics? The IOC has also advised the ICSD to do the same. But the ICSD leadership needs to support its national members, by showing the options available in using the UN Convention and the IOC

Clause 39 to engage with their respective National Olympic and Paralympic Committees.

Politics plays an important part in the work of the IOC family and, to this end, the ICSD Executive led by Crowley has further consolidated its engagement, with the expertise of its political partner the World Federation of the Deaf, by signing a new MoU at the Sofia Congress 2013 (see pages 189-190). What the ICSD should learn from this is that the WFD has succeeded in building a high profile in UN politics by remaining active within the politics of deafness as a disability. As a consequence, it is represented on the Board of the International Disability Alliance.

Deaf sport organisations need to do all they can to network with as many commercial and political bodies as possible during Deaflympic quadrennials, by establishing relationships with organisations such as the BTCO (The Taipei-based British Trade and Cultural Office) whose Director, David Campbell, noted that GB was participating in the 2009 Deaflympics (chinapost.com 6/11/09).

National Deaf community organisations could do more work with national deaf sports organisations (Barton-Smith 2009). Indeed, more could be done to work collaboratively to use sport to tackle obesity, health and mental health in the Deaf community. Such activity would raise the profile of Deaflympic athletes and teams. There are also other issues that the Deaflympics has in common with the wider community that can be used as a force for good.

Managing the Epidemic

According to the American Speech-Language-Hearing Association (Oyler) and Action on Hearing Loss (AoHL), governments and health authorities should be concerned about the oncoming epidemic of hearing loss and its burden on the economy. Mathers et al highlighted the WHO Global Burden on

Disease Study 2000, that calculated adult-onset hearing loss as the world's 2nd leading cause of YLDs (Years Lost to Disability).

Currently 17% of the adult population in the US, 30% of 60-70 year olds and 50% of those over 75, have a significant hearing loss. Between 9% and 22% of this group also have a dual sensory impairment of severe sight and hearing loss. It is the world's third most prevalent chronic health condition facing older adults (Collins in Oyler) and, in the UK, it is expected be in the top ten disease burdens, above cataracts and diabetes, by 2031. Western nations are facing an ageing population in 2010-2030 as the baby boomers reach the age of 65. Currently only 20% of Americans with a hearing loss and 1 in 3 in the UK seek help, leaving a total of 32.8m with no support to manage life with their hearing loss.

In the UK, 45% of people who report a hearing problem to their doctor are not referred for a hearing test. The onset of age-related hearing loss is related to age, genetics, noise exposure or head injury and is also associated with chronic disease such as diabetes, acute kidney disease and chronic heart disease. There is a strong correlation between hearing loss and dementia, as people with a mild, moderate or severe hearing loss are twice, three times and five times more likely to develop dementia than the general population.

Schein and Delk's census in 1972 recorded that just over 66% of respondents who were unable to hear or understand speech had an onset age of 19 years. For those who had a Bilateral hearing loss (deaf in both ears), age of onset was from their mid-twenties and upwards. Another study by Ries in 1992 found that 73.4 % reported age of onset as 19 years (in Howe 1993). There is an impending public health crisis on the way, because, not only does deafness inflict a high personal social cost, it is also expensive to treat and will drain economies if left unattended. Howe (1993) argues for research and funds to be directed at training and rehabilitation programmes to meet the needs of the late-deafened population instead of chasing a cure.

Untreated hearing loss places the individual at significant risk of developing depression, anxiety, frustration, social isolation and fatigue. There are higher rates of depression, anxiety and other psychological disorders with decreased social/emotional communication and cognitive functions. For the 9%-22% of older people, who have a loss of both their visual and hearing senses, there will be a more negative impact on health, social participation and daily activities as they will experience the greatest difficulties when both sensory systems are impaired, because they are less able to compensate for it.

Action on Hearing Loss is concerned that the response by policy makers to this significant economic costs is inadequate; and this is just one area where collaborative leadership with Deaf sports organisations could help to raise the public profile of this problem. The Deaflympic Movement could associate itself with organisations like the ASHA and AoHL to help them to ask:

- Governments to take urgent action and bring research spending into line with projected impact of hearing loss.
- Governments to recognise hearing loss as a public health issue and embed it with national strategies and plans.
- For the introduction of screening programmes for Age Related Deafness (that would save £2b in the UK).
- Research councils to collaborate on related conditions such as neurodegenerative diseases and neurological conditions.
- Doctors and health professionals to recognise the importance of early intervention, with timely referrals to audiology and hearing services.

- Pharmaceutical and Biotech industries to recognise the commercial value of, and to invest in, medical treatment for hearing loss.
- The music and entertainment sector to protect staff from harmful effects of loud music and inform audiences when their hearing is at risk.
- Individuals and families to take action to protect and regularly check their hearing and ensure that people are wearing hearing aids (Hearing People 2020).

The Deaflympic Movement could be associated with Deaf Awareness programmes to promote inclusion and participation by asking governments and inspectorates to:

- Set standards and monitoring to ensure that deaf people are never excluded because of communication problems.
- Invest in training of communication support professionals to meet growing demand.
- Ask public and private providers always to consider inclusive design to make services more accessible.
- Ask employers to plan the delivery of supporting an ageing workforce and the increasing number of people with age-related hearing loss.
- Increase the awareness and uptake of employment initiatives such as Access to Work (UK).
- Ask schools to provide proactive, timely and appropriate communication support to deaf children.
- Ask media and broadcasters to respond to public demands to reduce background noise.

- Ask individuals to improve community awareness about why communication counts.

Sports authorities often focus on the fact that the higher prevalence of deafness is in the elderly population and therefore of little relevance to the development of Deaf sport and the Deaflympics. This attitude is really missing the opportunity available to sport to have a greater impact on public health than with all other types of disability, which will have less of a combined economic impact than deafness alone. The media campaign of the London 2012 Olympics played on public fears and concerns about becoming disabled through traumatic incidents and I can only imagine how people aged 20-40 years old would react if they were told that they had a definite 50% likelihood of losing up to 7 years of their life span (Mathers et al 2001) and were at risk of developing depression, anxiety, social isolation, chronic health conditions and mental health unless they took action to look after their hearing.

Raising the Game

It is mentioned earlier in this chapter that ICSD and its members need to become more politically engaged if they want their slice of the pie. Deaf Sports Australia[13] and other groups have attempted to engage politically with on-line government petitions to improve funding for deaf sport. However, there is evidence to show that Deaf people suffer from the lack of access and understanding of how to engage effectively with political processes.

Research by the Deafness Advocacy Association of Nova Scotia revealed that none of the Deaf people surveyed had

[13] *Deaf Sports Australia on-line petition* http://www.change.org/en-GB/petitions/australian-government-sports-minister-we-need-improved-funding-for-deaf-hard-of-hearing-sports-programs

ever voted in political elections. Issues were not clear, written information was too difficult to read and there was no provision of interpreters at public meetings (DAANS 2003). Indeed, it would be reasonable to assume that the respondents in the DAANS study would not be able to digest this book (in its current format) and take action politically.

The ICSD and the World Federation of the Deaf have agreed to cooperate internationally and nationally through their respective constituents (national deaf sports associations and national associations of the deaf.). The ICSD/WFD MoU (ICSD/WFD (2013b)) confirms agreement on:

Article 1: General provision:

- Work within a formal co-operation framework to reduce duplication of resources to achieve common objectives.

Article 2: Areas of Cooperation:

- Encourage collaborative agreements between national deaf sports associations and their national associations of the deaf.
- Promote Human Rights regarding deaf people within the framework of the UN Human Rights convention.
- Promote and support the recognition of national sign languages.

Article 3: Consultation and exchange of information:

- Keep each other informed on a regular basis and through meetings, consulting on matters of common interest that are likely to require mutual collaboration.
- Mutual promotion via each others' websites.

- Invite each other as observers to their own meetings, assemblies and so on.

Article 4: Representation:

- When representing the Deaf community at international meetings there is a clear delineation of roles.
- Both parties recognise the primacy of the WFD to advance political, cultural, educational and sign language rights of deaf people throughout the world.
- Both parties recognise the primacy of the ICSD to advance all matters related to sports and Deaf sports.
- Where attendance at meetings is unavailable they may delegate mandates to each other at the following forums:
- The WFD shall represent the deaf community, participate in the work of and/or cooperate with the following institutions/ organisations:
  - United Nations Treaty based Bodies, such as the Committee on the Rights of Persons with Disabilities (CRPD Committee).
  - United Nations Economic and Social Council (ECOSOC), its functional and regional commissions as well as specialised agencies, such as; UNESCO, ILO, WHO, GPDD and the ITU.
  - United Nations Secretariat and its offices and departments, such as; OHCHR, DESA and DPI.
  - United Nations programmes and funds, such as UNICEF.
  - and the UNHRC, UPR, CoE, WASLI, ICED, ICSD and IDA.

  (See Appendix 2 for full list of organisations names).

The ICSD shall represent the deaf community to participate in the work of and/or cooperate with the following institutions/organisations at the international level in relation to sports

- International Olympic Committee (IOC).
- International Paralympic Committee (IPC).
- All other international sports governing bodies, including the International Sports Federations (IAAF for athletics, and so on), the World Anti-Doping Agency, etc.

The ICSD needs to collaborate with its political partners and learn how to use Clause 39 and Article 30 in the UN Convention on the Rights of Persons with Disabilities to seek the same level of provisions granted to athletes with other disabilities.[14] I propose that the emerging relationship between the ICSD and WFD should include workshops for Deaf sports administrators at Deaflympic events and other International competitions to enable them to become more politically literate.

In the first instance, the biggest difference that all sovereign systems could make for their Deaflympic athletes would be to provide sufficient funding to meet participation costs to compete at the Deaflympics. Collaborative leadership with National Olympic Committees would also enable leaders in Deaf sports organisations to understand how to become more financially sustainable and, in return, society would benefit from *Deaf Gain*. With a compelling campaign that benefits society beyond Deaf sport and the Deaflympics, there is an increased likelihood that the stakeholders, supporters, significant others and Alumni of the Deaflympics may be more motivated and confident about philanthropic actions to create Deaflympic legacies.

---

[14] UN Article 30 *Participation in cultural life, recreation, leisure and sport*. Found at http://www.un.org/disabilities/default.asp?id=290 located on Feb 2013

SECTION 6

A Conclusion

"It is natural for us, as human beings, to look forward. Our eyes naturally look ahead. In this sense, we are made for moving toward a goal."

(Daisaku Ikeda)

21

Summary

In this penultimate chapter, before I suggest where we all go from here, we need to sum up our situation. How did we get to this point and what is the current situation?

What are the Deaflympics?

Starting in 1924 by Eugene Rubens-Alcais and Antoine Dresse, the Summer Deaflympics have become the world's largest multi-sports events for one single class of disability after the Olympics. Beginning in Paris, France, with 7 sports and with 148 athletes from 9 nations in 1924, the event has been held every four years except for the enforced break during the Second World War. The event has continued to grow and, at the last count, the 21st Summer Deaflympics in Taipei hosted 3,894 athletes and their officials, 21 sports and 77 nations. Altogether, there are now 101 nations in the Deaflympic Movement. The Winter Deaflympics held their first event in 1949 and it has been run every four years. They are much smaller in size than the Summer Deaflympics, but nevertheless are an event for elite deaf athletes; the best the world has to offer. The Deaflympics have been recognised by the IOC as an International Federation of Olympic standing since 1955.

Unfortunately, numbers at local grassroots level do not match this growth. The increase in numbers is related to the increase in the number of nations now joining the ICSD and the emergence of the former Soviet states. There has been an overall decline in the number of deaf people playing sport and the main causes are found in the answers to the next question.

Why are the Deaf not in the Paralympics?

Difficulties in establishing relationships with the other able-bodied, non-deaf members of the IPC and the difficulty of persuading the IPC to share the funds from the IOC proportionally, and to incorporate all 17 Deaf sports into the IPC programme and provide interpreters, culminated in the CISS withdrawing from the IPC and continuing alone. This withdrawal had the respect and support of the IOC. Deaf athletes have always been able to compete in the Paralympics, but they have only done so under the classification of their 'other' disability. This duality of eligibility to compete in both the Deaflympics and Paralympics was formally recognised in the 2004 ICSD/IPC Memorandum of Understanding.

Part of the reason why the Deaflympics is characterised as a contrary member of the Olympic family is because of the term 'disabled'. Like other disabled people, the deaf, in general, are uneasy with the term 'disabled', because of its stigmatising connotations with the notions of inferiority, subordination and incapacity. By championing the empowerment of disabled people, rather than prospering, the CISS has found itself a victim of its own success. The dominant hearing and speaking society views deafness in simple terms as another sub-group of the larger collective and therefore treats it this way in terms of politics and legislation.

How does Deafness affect sports performance?

'Deafness is a communication disability in a hearing society' (Ammons 1990) and every deaf or hard of hearing person is affected by it in their own unique way. Deafness can affect the human body's ability to perform in sport, to a greater or lesser degree, in each athlete. Deafness does, over time, affect balance, the ability to hear, the ability to speak and the ability to understand what is going in a world that is predominantly a hearing and speaking culture.

There are an extremely small number of deaf and other disabled athletes who have competed in the Olympics and other world-class events. Most of these deaf athletes have reached the pinnacle in sports primarily for individual athletes (in contrast to team sports, which have more complex dynamics impacting on deaf persons' ability to achieve and maintain their performance at elite levels). There are different reasons for this, and one of these is the ability of the individual to thrive in any given environment. Baron Coe, who is now Chairman of the British Olympic Association and was the Chairman of LOCOG 2012 Olympics and Paralympics, understands the impact of the environment on athlete performances better than most, because his 'template' for providing any type of sports system is to put the athletes at the 'centre' of everything and then 'it all falls into place'.

Talent alone is not enough to enable any athlete to develop and maintain his or her high-performance level for a sustainable amount of time. Athletes rely heavily on the support of secondary agents – primarily the sports clubs, fellow athletes, coaches and a spectrum of sports science professionals. Although there are no adaptations to the Rules of sport for deaf people, there are adaptations to the environment and the resources that are used in order to provide the optimal performance. These adaptations are: the use of signals to control the start and stopping of contests; and communication systems to enable deaf athletes to know as much as possible about what is going on around them; so that they are competing on a 'level playing field'. The number of sports that are developing these adaptations is increasing, but they have not yet been used in mainstream sport to make it accessible for both the recreational and elite athlete.

Once recreational and elite deaf athletes begin to accept themselves as disabled athletes with a communication disability, the situation has a greater potential to change and bring them the support they need. Once we begin to do this, we can start to understand the impact that stigmatisation of deafness is having on the development of sports opportunities for deaf and hard of hearing people and, in turn, this should improve the profile, access and understanding of sports pathways, which, for the recreational and elite athlete, will culminate in a more effective Long Term Athlete Development programme across as many sports as possible.

Why have I not heard of the Deaflympics?

It is suggested that the leadership profiles of those who have been leaders of the Deaflympic Movement have not been as well connected socially and politically as those leading the Paralympics. The Deaflympic Movement is Deaf-led, which in general terms, like other types of disabled-led organisations, gets less recognition, support and resources than disabled organisations that are led by non-disabled people for the disabled. In Western nations, the closing down of schools for the Deaf and mainstreaming deaf children into their local schools has broken up the profile of the Deaf sports pathway and its wider connections to society. Worldwide, young deaf people and their families often do not hear about the Deaflympics until their children leave school or leave home. Society prefers to homogenise groups of people and, by not remaining a member of the IPC, the

Deaflympics has not benefitted from the IOC/IPC Treaty of 2001, which provided millions of dollars worth of funding for marketing and media, as well as access to sponsorship resources that have gone into creating the Olympics/Paralympics.

In 2001, the IOC sanctioned the name 'Deaflympics' but severely restricted its usage under the Olympic Charter, unlike the Paralympic name that has been allowed to proliferate under the IOC/IPC Treaty. This monopolising of the Olympic brand has inevitably taken its toll on the CISS/ICSD, creating confusion about its status, and has ostracised the Deaflympic Movement at national and international levels. But the ICSD visited the IOC in July 2013 and, during the Deaflympic Flame Relay, IOC President Rogge, who was coming to the end of his tenure, declared its continuing support.

> ***"IOC is pledged to continue supporting Deaflympics now and for the future"***
> (Rogge July 2013)

This was a pivotal moment as Rogge used the word 'Deaflympics' publicly for the first time, given the fact that he was reluctant for the ICSD to use it during his time in office.

Why are the Deaflympics not supported and recognised?

The Paralympic Movement has come to monopolise and dominate disability sports politics. International and national policies and fiscal systems for disabled sport have assumed Paralympism as the all-encompassing solution. Society itself believes (rightly or wrongly) that the Paralympic movement now empowers all disabled people and contribute towards a better, more inclusive society worldwide.

The Deaflympic Movement has now existed for almost a Century, and throughout this time has maintained that the empowerment of deaf people in sport is fundamental for the greater good of the Deaf community within the wider world. Politics, decision making and all other factors of change have not been accessible to deaf people, because they are based on speaking and listening, reading and writing – the four most inaccessible systems of empowerment.

Over time, Deaf sport has allowed the politics of Sign Language and Deaf culture to dominate its manifesto. By making contradictory statements and decisions in relation to disability and deafness in the context of sport, it has failed to be taken seriously, because 'hearing' people have not easily understood the Deaflympic Movement. Unlike the Deaf community in Russia, Western Deaf communities were unable to accept the benefits of Oralism as a 'solution' (Burch 2000). Taiwanese society has embraced the Deaflympics, Deaf Culture and Sign Language and its potential as a form of empowerment for everyone.

Because the ICSD has historically based the Deaflympics on Deaf culture, it has failed to promote it as an elite high-performance event and has therefore not attracted the attention it deserves. I hope that with the help of examples from around the world, from the stories of some of our Deaflympic athletes, their coaches and the people that support them, you can now appreciate the untapped potential that now deserves your attention and, whether you are deaf or hearing, you are now inspired to get behind the Deaflympic Movement.

After reading this book, it is up to you to decide whether or not you believe that the Deaflympic Movement now deserves a greater slice of the Olympic pie in terms of fiscal and human resources. However, I suggest that, if the Deaflympic Movement is willing change and manage that change in a way that does not become disempowering to deaf and other disabled people, the Deaflympics has a better chance of raising its profile and status, with the support and recognition that it deserves, for as long as there are deaf people in this world who want to play sport.

22

A Way Forward

As we come to the conclusion of this book, I take myself back to the time when I first read David A. Stewart's *Deaf Sport: The Impact of Sport Within the Deaf Community* when I was studying for my Physical Education degree. His concluding recommendations have remained with me throughout my professional life and the journey of creating this book has been, in part, the opportunity to discover for myself if his suggestions still have any meaning for us today. David was encouraging us all to take up a series of actions to ensure the sustainability of Deaf sport. My conclusion is that the actions are still implementable, but the recommendations need rephrasing. I hope David would have approved of my updated approach to his *Future Directions*.

Crossroads

In her closing President's message in May 2009, Ammons impressed upon the ICSD Executive and its members to make one of three choices:

1. To continue working vigorously in retaining the privileges of the name 'Deaflympics' by fulfilling the IOC requirements, or;
2. Return to the name 'World Deaf Games' with fewer restrictions and requirements, or;
3. Consider full integration with other disabled sport groups in the Paralympics.

She had guaranteed that the process for creating a new Memorandum of Understanding between the ICSD and IOC had been set in motion with *Deaf Sport Reform* (ICSD 2008) as the central document in this process.

Deaf Sport Reform

The main goal of the Reform is to create a new *International Deaflympic Committee* to be recognised as an equal to the IOC and IPC. The Deaflympic Movement will be a representation of the Olympic Movement in the Deaf sports community and mirror the Olympic Movement with three main constituents: *The International Deaflympic Committee; The International Committee of Sports for the Deaf* and *The National Deaflympic Committees.* The IDC will create three main documents: T*he Deaflympic Charter, The IDC Organisations Regulations* and *The IDC Competition Rules*.

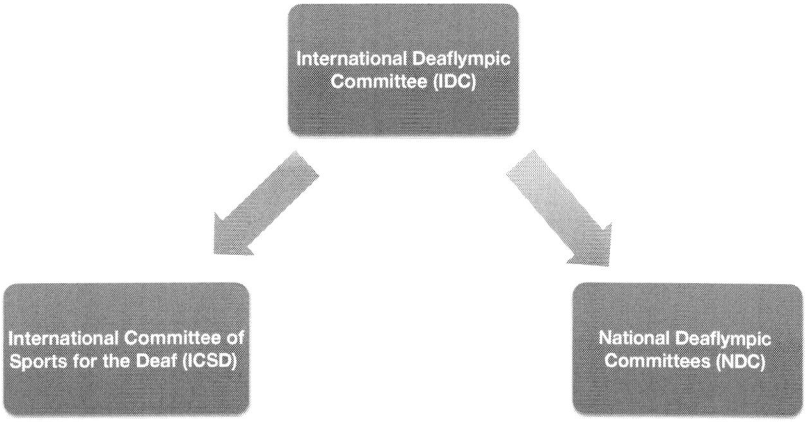

Table N – Illustration of the proposed International Deaflympic Committee governance.

Crowley stated in his inaugural President's Message in November 2010, that the *Deaf Sport Reform* resolves that there is no turning back, and Deaf sport must start by looking ahead with a higher sense of purpose. This expects ICSD having to change. He quoted Barrack Obama:

> *'The greatest risk we can take is to try the same old politics with the same old players and expect a different result.'*

The imminent Memorandum of Understanding with the IOC is to be designed to protect the name 'Deaflympics' under the rights of the Olympic partners, and ICSD is confident that this will open more doors of opportunity for marketing, media and sponsorship. It will end the perception of ICSD and IOC 'taking sides', with the two organisations no longer working in isolation but working in conjunction with the IOC Charter, competition rules of the International Federations and WADA.

In the aftermath of the doomed 2011 Winter Deaflympics, the ICSD hinted at changes of faces around the ICSD Executive Board and ICSD Office, with a new approach to the management of the Deaflympics and Deaf sports structure. The ICSD recognised that it had taken itself to an unsustainable point with the Taipei Deaflympics requiring a US$72m budget of 100% government funding. It had been continuing to accept bids for future events without ensuring that they had guarantees of government support. The Vancouver 2017 bid also folded, because it was arranged on the basis that it did not require the approval of a host National Deaf Sports Organisation. Towards the end of 2012, ICSD and the Council of Bulgarian Ministers signed contractual agreements and set out logistical plans to deliver the 22nd Deaflympics Sofia, 2013. For now, the Summer Deaflympics 2013 have been delivered and assurances for 2017 are in place.

National sovereignty has to be respected so we have to recognise that NDSFs exist under different models, either with complete independence or as self-organising entities within NOCs, National Disabled Sports Organisations or NPCs (IOC 2009a). ICSD expects *Deaf Sport Reform* to take approximately 10 years to implement. Meanwhile, what can be done to help speed up the process? Progress has been made; Crowley and Rogge met in September 2012 with the IOC suggesting four challenges to move things forward:

- Make the Deaflympics more visible to the outside world and raise awareness.
- Athletes and their experience are IOC first priority.
- Need for best practice examples to showcase and educate less developed counties.
- Continue negotiations towards a stronger relationship with the IOC through a new MOU, which would result in greater resources for ICSD.

The five sections of this book were written to help you, the reader, to provide the information and support that the IOC and ICSD need to develop Deaf sport. Whether you are a senior administrator of an IF, NOC, NPC, government official, or you are a parent, teacher, coach, or sports volunteer, you can help. You can contribute to the actions I am about to suggest.

1. We must define who we are in sport.

In Section 1, I wanted to contribute one of Stewart's actions to *preserve the legacy of Deaf sport for future generations.* If you have not been to a Deaf sports event yet, I hope that Section 1 has given you a sense of 'seeing is believing' and of what the Deaflympics are and who they are for. At your earliest opportunity, get on the internet and find out when the next local Deaf sports event nearest to you will take place; go along, watch, and then offer to help in whatever way you can to keep things going. Your 'offer' does not have to be sports related, as there are many other ways to get involved.

The campaign for protecting Sign Language and the Deaf community has hijacked the Deaflympics. Culture politics has gradually crept into Deaf sport. Of course, it is important to preserve these assets, but we need to put sport first with the very best elite athletes that we can produce. One of the by-products of hosting the Deaflympics is the promotion, sustainability and preservation of sign language and Deaf culture. Those who want to preserve sign language and culture need to consider that by bringing in 'oral/mainstream' athletes we are exposing them to the values of what is it to be D/deaf and how to live effectively in a speaking and listening world. There are many examples of how exposure and involvement in Deaf sport has brought in deaf and hearing 'outsiders' to sustain the Deaf community.

Gerald Jordan said that deaf people are disabled in the hearing world, which is why we have the Deaflympics. We have a 'communication' disability. The Deaf community and the organisations and economy that surround it need to embrace Deaflympics. To those of you who work daily to preserve Sign Language and Deaf culture, I ask you: please respect the expertise of Deaf Sport to deliver sport. You can work with them to make the Deaflympics accessible to the world. You can develop more opportunities for the cause of Sign Language by working with the Deaflympics, but you must allow Deaf sport to put sport first.

To Deaf Sport, I suggest that, if we are to put our very best athletes on playing fields, arenas and the podiums of the Deaflympics, Paralympics and Olympics, we have to put sport first. To do this, you have to work with mainstream sport; the expertise is out there waiting to be married up with your expertise of how to work effectively with tomorrow's medal winners. This means you have to be prepared to share or allow others to take the lead. They are going to need your help, and you can work with them as equals to develop yourself too. Bryan Whalley has done this. In 1989, in spite of getting enough money to send a tennis team to Christchurch, he decided that the money was better invested in building for the future. The progress of Deaf tennis for Great Britain has not looked back and continues to look forward. In early 2013, the Tennis Foundation appointed Deaflympic medal winner Cathy Fletcher as their head coach for Deaf tennis. Have confidence; give it time; think of others before yourself.

Baines, Crowley, Kaufman, Ammons and others recognise the inevitability of change for the Deaflympics, as without this, things are unsustainable. This book has highlighted some changes needed to the Paralympics to accommodate Deaflympic competitors. Unfortunately, the matter is complex and requires patience to work through all options. Only then will we really know the possibilities.

2. IOC: Make the Deaflympics and the ICSD more visible to the outside world to raise awareness.

David Stewart (1991a) recommended that Deaf sport must promote itself beyond the boundaries of the Deaf Community and must be committed to the development of grassroots connections. This requires an increase in the visibility of both elite and grassroots sport to demonstrate to funders and sponsors that there is a market base for them. We should work with International Federations of sport and their national organisations to stage Deaf sports events as part of their programmes. Some sports may find it easier than others, so let's start there and see where we get.

The Deaflympics needs regular, high profile, media exposure or it could become unsustainable to maintain; and harder to recruit athletes and build a wide talent base. What Taipei 2009 proves is that by engaging with nations, who would benefit socially, politically and economically from hosting the Deaflympics, countries gain the experience to bid (maybe successfully) to host the Olympics and spread the experience further around the globe; and this would increase ICSD chances of persuading the IOC to provide the support it needs for sustainable media and marketing. ICSD should create its own "Ones to watch List", in an attempt to provide the world media with a range of international athletes, who can be covered during non-Deaflympic years.

3. We must make Athletes and their experience our first priority.

Our responsibility for athletes should be from the moment they are introduced to sport right up until the time they decide to stop. ICSD needs to find, through research, the best models for implementing the following: the components of optimal training and competition environments for team and individual sports; when, and when not, to use sign language interpreters;

what training they need to give their best. National federations should also replicate the athlete's commission of the ICSD; and then sports reform must also be replicated as far as our sovereignty allows. We can safeguard our interests and rights using the UN Article 30.

Before we can consider taking Deaflympic athletes into the Paralympics we should ensure that the organisers are able to meet their needs as elite athletes, using Sebastian Coe's template for organising any sports event with athletes at its centre. There are many opportunities for this to be worked on at other events within the Olympic Movement, (Clauses 2, 4 and 9 in IOC 2009b). Things can be tried out on a smaller scale and then built up from there. It requires both the ICSD and IPC working together pooling their expertise. Only through this process will we find our answers one way or another.

We need to begin working earlier with our future athletes. Stewart (2001a) recommended that Deaf sport needed to do more to engage with deaf children in schools. We need to give them opportunities to meet with all types of Deaf sport role models in sport, to reflect the true representation of deafness in a way that encourages greater cohesion between those who see themselves as culturally Deaf and those who do not. The IOC Congress recommendations (2009) on Olympism and Youth, should impel national organisations, sports clubs and schools to ensure that their cooperation, to develop sporting events and competitions for young people at all levels (Clauses 50 and 57, in IOC 2009b), is proactively meeting the needs of deaf youth in partnership with national deaf sports federations. Children and young people need to be consulted to find out what they want and who is committed to sport or wants to try sport. We start by helping those who are ready to benefit from sport provision or mentoring. Others can follow on.

Deaf sport should engage more with parents and families of deaf children by working in partnership with other organisations that specialise in family support. Information on the Internet needs to capture parents' imaginations about the potential for their children through sport and compel them to encourage participation. Deaf sport needs to demonstrate how self-governance and Deaf-led sport is the best way to ensure a more optimal and effective model of inclusion. We know that Deaflympic athletes have used the events to focus their ambitions to compete in the Olympic and Commonwealth Games. Investment into LTAD funding for Deaf sport could have positive long-term impacts beyond the culmination at the Deaflympics. It is worthwhile investment. Deaf leaders need to accept external LTAD expertise and work at it. Depending on sovereignty, there are different models of LTAD to adopt. There needs to be a modification of the delivery and communication environment in which LTAD is provided, in order that we can more economically serve larger groups of athletes simultaneously.

The Deaflympics are life-changing for the athletes and others who take part. For the host, they are a means to an end, whether it is to achieve international recognition, gain experience to host bigger events or create an impact to make changes closer to home for both the deaf and hearing members of society. It may be that hosting the Deaflympics is beyond your reach both economically and practically, but what you can do is: find a variety of ways in which you can use your time to introduce deaf children and young people to sport and Deaf sport.

4. We need to provide ICSD with best practice examples to showcase and educate less developed counties.

We need to collate good practice examples of where deaf people have used sport to obtain a balanced life, adjusting to working and living effectively in a hearing society; and examples of mainstreaming deaf and hearing people into Deaf sport and the Deaf community. There are no reasons why we could not have national federations and sports organisations that have joint Presidents or Chairpersons, who are deaf and hearing. We need examples of deaf athletes, who have succeeded by staying completely within the Deaf-specific sports pathway, and those who have succeeded by choosing to seek out the expertise of Paralympic performance specialists to help them reach and maintain their standards. Although it has not been made a topic of discussion in this book, the Deaflympics should continue in its work to create more opportunities for deaf women as per Clause 18, IOC (2009b);

> ***"High priority should be given to the advancement of women in both sport and through sport. The Olympic Movement should at times seek to promote equal opportunities for women, both in their participation in sports competition and in administration and coaching.'***

Good practice in Deaflympic sport is also about finding the right balance in the governance, leadership and administration of elite sport. It is difficult to determine without proper study, but it would be useful to analyse, over a period of time, how performance of elite deaf athletes changes when under the supervision of deaf or hearing administrators and coaches.

There needs to be an increase in the number of internationally certified IF officials and coaches, who are deaf. We need the creation of a clear, continuing, professional pathway for officiating and coaching and a register of those, who are deaf and hard of hearing, as well as those, who are hearing and have experience of sign language skills.

National and International Seminars would be an excellent forum for discussion and sharing of experience and research that could also include deaf and hearing personnel from sports science industries. This register should initially be administered by the ICSD as a central reference point.

Send ICSD Technical Directors around the world to advise and train both deaf and hearing. They should become the first port of call when planning for Deaf sports in the Paralympics, because they have the experience and expertise required, with the foresight to prevent problems occurring. Likewise, with overall event planning and co-ordination, there should be an influx of deaf and hearing volunteers with the skills to help optimise the Paralympic environment.

I hope this book has inspired politicians and those who work with them to use the evidence provided to continue the lobbying that they have already begun. ICSD leadership should be supporting its national members by showing them how to use the UN Convention and the IOC recommendations for *The Structure of the Olympic Movement* and Clause 39 (IOC 2009b) to engage with their respective NOCs and NPCs. Politics plays an important part in the work of the IOC family, and therefore the ICSD and its members should consider engaging the expertise of political advisors. Indeed, it is making inroads at this current time to establish closer working relationships with the World Federation of the Deaf.

Stewart (1991a) recommended that the institution of Deaf sport must always be committed to the development of grassroots connections. Increased media profile by having some of our Deaf Sports in the Paralympics may also see an increase in new participants joining national Deaf sports organisations. Falling school rolls, fewer children being born, communities getting older – what is the fan base for Deaflympic sport? How many of us want to support a well- recognised and supported system and come back as fundraisers, supporters, coaches, administrators and event volunteers?

Everyone should not be asking: how much does it all cost to put in place systems for deaf people to participate in sport or host world-class events? We should ask: what are the wider cost implications of NOT doing this?

5. We must support the ICSD, IOC and the IPC in their continuing negotiations to towards a stronger relationship.

I hope that the IOC can agree on a new MoU with the ICSD that will enable everyone to move forwards. When that is completed, it must be communicated effectively to National Federations in order that they too can be proactive locally. Previously, the ICSD has tried to engage directly with NOCs and NPCs to reinforce its MoUs with IPC and the IOC, but this appears to come into conflict, owing to sovereignty. The ICSD needs to train its National Federations to help them maintain frequent dialogues with their respective NOCs and NPCs, demonstrating the intentions of the new MoU and the Deaf Sports Reform, seeking their opinions and insights.

In their deliberations over the potential inclusion of Deaflympic athletes into the Paralympics, the ICSD, IPC and IOC should take heed of Clause 22 (IOC 2009b):

> ***"Members of the Olympic Movement should regularly review the qualification systems for each sport and discipline in order to achieve a fair balance between the imperative of securing the participation of the world's best athletes at the Olympic games and the highest levels of fairness required to respect the principle of universality."***

The basis for national strategies is dependent on local models and infrastructures, but Deaf sport strategic plans should ensure that deaf people's rights under Article 30.5 are addressed, for participation in cultural life, recreation and sport. Most nations will have to challenge national sports policies that are unfairly biased towards Paralympism and, until that situation is resolved either way, national governments should recognise and respect the status of the Deaflympics and recognise its athletes accordingly. Clause 15 (IOC 2009b) recommends high priority from NOCs, NPCs and IF national representatives to ensure that deaf athletes are not being denied the right to be representatives at the Deaflympics – the IOC recommends:

> ***'...open access to sports for all peoples and all cultures, from grassroots to Olympic level and to all benefits and opportunities which sport provides.'***
>
> (Clause 15, IOC 2009b)

The Last Word

I interviewed Crowley after Rukhledev had succeeded him as ICSD President. It is Crowley's view that, after gaining worldwide acceptance and prominence following London 2012, the IPC has not considered the ICSD to be at the top of their agenda; and that either the timing is not right or they do not need to bring in another new disability or classification. Maybe they still see the Deaflympic Movement as a potential threat to their own strategic aspirations. This was one of Crowley's main motivations for ensuring that the 2013 ICSD Congress adopted the new governance reform and strategy, in order to fulfil one of the main IOC and IPC expectations, which wished to see the ICSD moving forward, becoming more apt, modern and fit for purpose, by welcoming partnerships with the rest of the international sports community.

Crowley suggests there are potentially three main political scenarios coming ahead:

- IPC wanting to see if the ICSD has really changed its ways before commencing talks – and now that Crowley has been outvoted and replaced, the IPC's suspicions may have been confirmed and they will still not believe that the ICSD will change its ways.

- The IPC know that if they rebuff ICSD's approach for advanced talks about proposed agreements, they will face the wrath of the IOC. It is in the interests of the IPC to try and accommodate the ICSD in one way or another.
- Crowley has not seen any evidence that Rukhledev intends to steer the ICSD Board to take the IOC recommendations forward. He hopes that things will not go 'backwards', because of ICSD wanting to continue going 'alone'.

Ideally, Crowley would like the scenario to be:

1. The ICSD re-join the IPC as an associate member and still retain its independent international federation status as per the 1955 recognition from the IOC;
2. The ICSD still retains its Deaflympic Movement and ethos;
3. ICSD continues to hold its own Congress; and
4. Still organises the Deaflympics; whilst
5. Considering ways forward for including Deaflympic and World Championship events within the IPC programme (in a way that the Deaflympic Marathon worked in favour of raising the profile of Deaflympics); and
6. That deaf athletes have their visibility and recognition via both Deaflympics and Paralympic events.

This is based on the fact that the IPC would not be interested in another disability within the Paralympics, as it means shuffling the cards around too much; and ICSD membership within the IPC is more of a door opener to government support. There would also be companies and organisations that cannot afford to sponsor the Paralympics, but would be able to support the Deaflympics if it were part of the IPC programme; because ideally the IPC could consider this on the back of IOC clause 39.

Crowley's last words are that the ICSD must follow the IOC advice to work with the IPC. It is still a *door closer* if the ICSD continues to negotiate with the IOC alone, rather than become an associate member of the IPC.

APPENDIX

Appendix 1

Organisations recognised by the International Olympic Committee (IOC) taken from http://www.olympic.org/content/the-ioc/governance/affiliate-organisations/all-recognised-organisations/ on 16 November 2013

IF Associations	
ASOIF	Association of Summer Olympic International Federations
AIOWF	Association of International Olympic Winter Sports Federations
ARISF	Association of IOC Recognised International Sports Federations
	Sport Accord
NOC Associations	
ANCO/ANOC	Association of National Olympic Committees
ACNOA/ANOCA	Association of National Olympic Committees of Africa
OCA	Olympic Council of Asia
COE/EOC	The European Olympic Committees
ODEPA/PASO	Pan-American Sports Organisation
ODESUR	Organizacion Deportiva Suramericana

ONOC	Oceania National Olympic Committees
ODECABE/CACSO	Central American and Caribbean Sports Organisation
Multi-Sports Organisations and Events/ Sport for All	
FISU	International University Sports Federation
ISF	International School Sport Federation
FISEC	International Catholic Schoolsport Federation
CSIT	International Workers and Amateurs in Sports Confederation
CISM	International Military Sports Council
USIP	Union Sportive Internationale des Polices
IWGA	International World Games Association
CIJM	International Committee of Mediterranean Games
FIEP	International Federation of Physical Education
FISPT	International Sport for All Federation
TAFISA	The Association for International Sport for All
CJIE/CICG	Committee of the International Children's Games
CGF	Commonwealth Games Federation
IMGA	International Masters Games Association
WTGF	World Transplant Games Federation
Disabled Sport	
IPC	International Paralympic Committee
CISS/ICSD	International Committee of Sports for the Deaf
SOI	Special Olympics Inc.
Education/ Dissemination of the Olympic Ideal/ Fair Play	
AIO/IOA	International Olympic Academy
CIPC	International Pierre de Coubertin Committee
IPC	Pierre de Coubertin Institute
PI	Panathlon International
CIFP	International Committee for Fair Play
ICHPER-SD	International Council for Health, Physical Education, recreation, Sport and Dance
APAO	Pan-Iberic Association of Olympic Academies

Sports Medicine and Sciences	
ECSS	European College of Sport Science
AICVS	International Association for Non Violent Sport
CIEPSS/ICSSPE	International Council of Sport Science and Physical Education
FIMS	International federation of Sports Medicine
Sports Equipment and Facilities	
IAKS	International Association for Sports and Leisure Facilities
WFSGI	World Federation of the Sporting Goods Industry
Media- Information	
AFP	Agence France Presse
	Reuters Limited
AIPS	International Sports Press Association
FICTS	Federation Internationale du Cinema et Television Sportifs
AP	The Associated Press
IASI	International Association for Sports Information
Other Recognised Organisations	
AMO/WOA	World Olympians Association
CITO/IOTC	International Olympic Truce Centre
	Fondation Internationale OLYMPAFRICA
FIC	International Federation of Timekeepers
ENGSO	European Non-Governmental Sports Organisation
FITO/IOTF	International Olympic Truce Foundation
ISOH	International Society of Olympic Historians
RTP	Right to Play
	Generations for Peace
	Office of the Permanent Observer for the International Olympic Committee to the United Nations
Useful Addresses	
CAS	Court of Arbitration for Sport
WADA	World Anti-Doping Agency

Appendix 2

Agencies listed in the ICSD/WFD Memorandum of Understanding	
CoE	Council of Europe
DESA	Department of Economic and Social Affairs
DPI	Department of Public Information
GPDD	World Bank (Global partnership for Disability and Development)
ICED	International Congress on the Education of the Deaf
IDA	International Disability Alliance
ILO	International Labour Organisation
ITU	International Telecommunications Union
OHCHR	Office of the United Nations High Commissioner for Human Rights
UNEASCO	United Nations Educational, Scientific and Cultural Organisation
UNHRC	United Nations Human Rights Council
UNICEF	United Nations Children's Fund
UPR	Universal Periodic Review (UPR)
WASLD	World Association of Sign Language Interpreters
WHO	World health Organisation

References

AoHL (2010) *Hearing Matters – Taking Action on Hearing Loss in the 21st Century*. Action on Hearing Loss UK. 2010

AoHL (2012) *Deaf Sports. (online)* in Deafness and Hearing Loss, Action on Hearing Loss Community Forum

http://www.actiononhearingloss.org.uk/community/forums/deafness-and-hearing-loss.aspx?g=posts&t=8293 (Oct 2012)

Ammons, K,D. (1990) *'Unique Identity of the World Games for the Deaf'.* In Palaestra, Winter/Spring, Vol6 No2, p 40-43

Ammons, K,D. (2008) *Deaf Sports & Deaflympics*. Paper presented to the International Olympics Committee. ICSD 2008

Ammons, K,D. (2009) *President's Message January 2009.* http://www.deaflympics.com/news.asp?1400

Ammons, K,D. and Eickman, J. (2011) *Deaflympics and the Paralympics: Eradicating misconceptions*, in Sport in Society: Cultures, Commerce, Media, Politics, 14:9, 1149-1164

Atherton, M.,Russell, D., Turner, G. (1999) *'Playing to the Flag: A history of Deaf football and Deaf footballers in Britain'.* University of Central Lancashire. In The Sports Historian No.19,1 (May 1999) British Society of Sports History.

Bailey, S. (2008) *Athletes First: A History of the Paralympic Movement*. John Wiley & Sons.

Baines, J. (2010) *'Should Deaf athletes take part in the Paralympic Games ? – A Critical Discussion',* in Whalley, B. (2010) *History of Deaf Tennis*, Bryan Whalley 2010 p421-427

Baines, J. (ed.) (2012) *'Accessibility review for deaf and deafblind people'*. Part of the *Learning Legacy: lessons learned from planning and staging the London 2012 Games.* Published by LOCOG 2012

Bart (2012) *The Deaflympics failed by the IOC*, Bart, 7 Sept 2012 sourced at The Translation Blog (no longer trading) Sept 2012 http://www.quicklingo.com/en/blog/entry/translating-success-the-deaflympics-failed-by-the-ioc

Barton-Smith (2009) *Fragile State of Deaf Sport in Australia*. Posted in Sept 1 2009 in *The Rebuttal*, sourced at : http://therebuttal2.com/2009/09/01/the-fragile-state-of-deaf-sports-in-australia-by-dean-barton-smith-ex-olympian-commonwealth-games-athlete-and-deaflympian/ (11 Feb 2013)

Barwise, J. (2013) Sponsorship Joy for Cumbrian Deaflympics Hopeful. Sourced at: http://www.newsandstar.co.uk/news/sponsorship-joy-for-cumbrian-deaflympics-hopeful-1.1022177?referrerPath=home (14 Feb 2013)

Bauman, H-D. and Murray M,J. (2009) *Reframing: From Hearing Loss to Deaf Gain* in Deaf Studies Journal Gallaudet University, issue 1 Fall 2009.

Bernd (2012) *Why not Deaflympics and Deaf in the Paralympics?* Forum discussion sourced at: http://www.gehoerlose.de/viewtopic.php?f=7&t=3809

Bowell, T. (2013) *Sekou Kanneh is lighting the way for future starts of athletics after breaking a 21-year record*. Sourced at http://m.couriermail.com.au/questnews/east/sekou-kanneh-is-lighting-the-way-for-future-stars-of-athletics-after-breaking-a-21year-record/story-fni9r0lo-1226748383492 (29 October 2013)

Breivik, J,K., Haualand, H. and Solvang, P. (2002) *Rome- A temporary Deaf City!* in *Transnational Connections in Deaf Worlds*, Stein Rokkan Centre for Social Studies, Bergen University Research Foundations June 2002

Brisebois, J (2009) *Deaflympics delivers glittering benefits*. Sourced at Taipei City Government website (18/9/2009) http://english.taipei.gov.tw/ct.asp?xitem=993128&CtNode=8472&mp=100002 (February 2013)

Bruce, M (2009) *Early Day Motion 934* http://www.parliament.uk/edm/2008-09/934

Bruce, M (2012) *Early Day Motion 480* http://www.parliament.uk/edm/2012-13/480

Burch, S. (2000) *Transcending Revolutions: The Tsars, the Soviets and Deaf Culture*. in Journal of Social History Dec 2000.

Burrell, I. (2012) *Paralympic coverage beyond 'wildest dreams' says governing body as they appeal for continued coverage of sports*. The Independent (online) 10/9/12

http://www.independent.co.uk/sport/olympics/paralympics/paralympic-coverage-beyond-wildest-dreams-says-governing-body-as-they-appeal-for-continued-coverage-of-sports-8120602.html (10 September 2012)

Carpe Diem (2012) commenting in the *Action on Hearing Loss Community Forum* at http://www.actiononhearingloss.org.uk/community/forums/deafness-and-hearing-loss.aspx?g=posts&t=8293 (September 2012)

CISS (1995) *CISS Meeting with President Samaranch of IOC 26th June 1995, Lausanne Switzerland*. CISS Meeting Notes.

CISS (2003) *IOC and CISS Meeting, 16 December 2003*. Meeting notes

Clydebank Post (2012) *Aiming for the Top* 'Clydebank Post' (online) 18 December 2012

http://www.clydebankpost.co.uk/sport/roundup/articles/2012/12/18/441548-aiming-for-the-top/

Coe, S. (2012) *Running My Life, The Autobiography*. Hodder and Stoughton

'Comishandy' (2012) commenting on the *Action on Hearing Loss Community Forum on 29/8/2012* http://www.actiononhearingloss.org.uk/community/forums/deafness-and-hearing-loss.aspx?g=posts&t=8293 (11th February 2013)

Craven, P. (2002) *'Actions arising from CISS- IPC Meeting'*. By Email to J Lovett CISS. 15th October 2002

Cusing, S,L., Papsin, B,C., Rutka, JA., James, A,L. and Gordon, K,A. (2008) *"Evidence of vestibular and balance dysfunction in children with profound sensori-neural hearing loss using cochlear implants'* in Laryngoscope October 2008 found at http://www.ncbi.nlm.nih.gov/pubmed/18758383

DAANS (2003) *'Access to election campaigns won by deaf and hard of hearing Nova Scotians'* by Deafness Advocacy Association of Nova Scotia. in *Community Action*, April 14, 2003.

'Daily Pilot' (2012) *Thornton, Smith named to the US Olympic Men's volleyball team roster.* 'Daily Pilot', July 5th 2012. http://www.dailypilot.com/sports/tn-dpt-0706-spucivbolympics-20120705,0,6833045.story

Degun, T. (2011) *Deaf Sport sets sights on building bridges with Paralympic Movement.* http://www.insidethegames.biz/insideparasport/109364-exclusive-deaf-sport-sets-sights-on-building-bridges-with-paralympic-movement

Dodson, C. (2011) *Deaf Sports Australia and School Sports Australia Reach Positive Resolution on Discrimination Claim.* sourced at http://www.deafsports.org.au/rotating-banner/deaf-sports-australia-and-school-sport-australia-reach-positive-resolution-on-discrimination-claim?A=SearchResult&SearchID=6759599&ObjectID=90661-7&ObjectType=35

Dummer, G. and Stewart D,A. (1991) *Summary of 1st and 2nd Deaf Canadian Sports Conference*. In Paelestra March 22 1991.

Enerstvedt, R, Th. (1996) *Chapter 2 The development of Education for Deaf People.* pages 1-18 (pdf document) in *Legacy of the Past*. Forlaget Nord Press. www.folk.uio.no/regie/pdfd/Deaf.pdf (April 2013)

Espagnac, S. (1986) *Sport, An Essential Element of Rehabilitation*. in Sport and the Disabled. sourced at the LA84 Foundation.

http://library.la84.org/OlympicInformationCenter/OlympicReview/1986/ore220/ore220zg.pdf (Feb 18, 2013)

Felli, G. (2002) *Re: meeting-Lausanne, 23 July 2002*. A letter to CISS President. 26 August 2002.

Forumosa.com (2009) *Re: Deaflympics*. On-line forum discussion sourced at http://www.forumosa.com/taiwan/viewtopic.php?f=63&t=80826&start=50

Fosshaug, S. (2004) *Deaf Sports: An Empowerment Perspective*. in World Federation of the Deaf News, Vol 17 No.2 . sourced at http://www.deaflympics.com/news/publishedarticles.asp?ID=1135

Fussell, A.J. (2011) *Athletes recall their records and their places in history*. 'The Kansas City Star' posted on 5 Aug 2011 in https://www.deaflympics.com/news.asp?1570/

Gilbert, K. and Schantz, O,J. (eds.) (2008) *The Paralympic Games, Empowerment or Side Show?* Meyer & Meyer (UK) Ltd.

Gold, R, J. and Gold, M, M. (2007) *The Paralympic Games*. in Gold & Gold (eds.) (2001 edition) *Olympic Cities; City Agendas, Planning and the Worlds Games 1896-2016*. Routeledge.

Gorrell, M. (2007) *The Olympic Spirit Returns – 16th Winter Deaflympics welcome global athletes*. 'The Salt Lake City Tribune' 2007

Gorrell, M. (2007) *The Olympic Spirit Returns*. 'The Salt Lake City Tribune'. sourced at http://www.sorenson.com/news_trib_dl

Grossman, A. (2012) *How Do Olympic Athletes Fund their Dream*

http://blog.chron.com/frugalconfessions/2012/08/how-olympic-athletes-fund-their-dream/

Guzman, A. (2006) *Baseball program to help Deaf players*. In 'Daily News' LA California. Oct 19, 2006

Harrison, S. (1995) *An Examination of the Needs and Issues in Establishing a Youth Club for Deaf Adolescents in an Ordinary Secondary School*. M.Ed dissertation. University of Birmingham, Faculty of Education and Continuing Studies. 1995.

Hansard (2009) *UK Deaf Sport*. Parliamentary debate raised by Iain Duncan-Smith MP, House of Commons UK. Hansard 16 June 2009 : Column 47-52 WH

Her, K. (2009) *'The Power of Silence'* 9/1/2009 The Taiwan Review. http://taiwanreview.nat.gov.tw/ct.asp?xItem=59733&CtNode=1360

Holland, K. (2004) *Swimming to Success*. 29 Dec 2004 http://news.bbc.co.uk/sport1/hi/other_sports/disability_sport/4121387.stm (May 2013)

Howe, M. (1993) *Meeting the needs of late-deafened adults*. In American Rehabilitation Dec 22 1993. US Rehabilitation Services Administration.

Howe, P, D. (2008) *The Cultural Politics of the Paralympic Movement*. Routledge

Hubbard, A. (2012) *How Much is a British Gold Medal Worth?*

http://www.independent.co.uk/sport/olympics/how-much-is-a-british-gold-medal-worth-2m-6283727.html (Nov 2013)

Hung, T-M. (n.d) *The Current Development and Impact of Deaflympics on Taiwan.* (powerpoint presentation) by Prof Tsung-Min Hung, National Taiwan Normal University.

Hunter, B. (2008) *Olympic Sports Administration in the United States* in *e-Journal USA,* US Department of State, April 2008, Vol 13 No 4

Hussain, R (2012) *What is the future for Deaf Sports?* http://blogs.bujournalism.info/2011-2012/mammj-rebeccahussain/what-future-deaf-sports/ (June 2012)

ICSD (2004a) *CISS* e-newsletter, August 2004. No 221

ICSD (2004b) *Pact brings together to disabled Sports organisations*. ICSD press release, 30 November 2004 located at: http://www.deaflympics.com/news/pressreleases.asp?ID=522 (May 2013)

ICSD (1/3/05) *DeaflympicsTV Bring in a staggering 1.1 million viewers within 12 days during the Games*. CISS/ICSD Press Release 1/3/2005.

ICSD (2006) *Visit with Japanese Deaf Sports Federation in Tokyo*. ICSD newsletter issue 227, July 2006.

ICSD (2008) *Deaf Sport Reform, Final Draft, 41st Extraordinary Congress, Bratislava SVK 12-13.9.2008* available at www.deaflympics.com

ICSD (2010a) *ICSD remains committed to find solution for French Deaf Athletes*. ICSD Press Release 5 March 2010 – www.deaflympics.com

ICSD (2010b) *ICSD Secretariat Cancellation of the 17th Winter Deaflympics in Slovakia.* 11 May 2010, ICSD press Release http://www.deaflympics.com/news/pressreleases.asp?ID=1487

ICSD (Sept 2011a) *Minutes of 43rd Congress, Rome 2011*. http://www.deaflympics.com/icsd.asp?1637

ICSD (2011b) *Brief ICSD Report of IOC Congress, Copenhagen, Denmark October 2009.* Compiled by Craig A Crowley, ICSD President, on behalf of the ICSD Board.

ICSD (2012a) *Minutes of the ICSD Board meeting, 1-3 September 2012, London.* http://ukdeafsport.org.uk/uploads/ICSD%20Board%20London%202012%20Summary%20Minutes.pdf (Jan 2013)

ICSD (2012b) *ICSD appoints new Joint Chairs of the ICSD Athletes Commission*. posted 13 Dec 2012. http://www.deaflympics.com/news.asp?1631 (Jan 2013)

ICSD (2013a) *Sofia 2013 Deaflympics Flame Relay*. Press release from http://www.deaflympics.com (8 February 2013)

ICSD/WFD (2013b) *Cooperation Agreement between The World Federation of the Deaf and the International Committee of Sports for the Deaf*. July 2013.

Isidore, C. (2004) *Time to Pay Olympic Winners.* http://money.cnn.com/2004/08/19/commentary/column_sportsbiz/sportsbiz/

IDISWG (2007) *Sport in The United Nations Convention on the Rights of Persons with Disabilities.* International Disability in Sport Working Group. IDISWG Secretariat. 2007.

Ikelberg, J., Lechner, I., Ziegler, S. and Zollner, M. (n.d) *Fun Inclusive! Sports and Games as means of rehabilitation, interaction and integration for children and young people with disabilities.* Handicap International

IOC (1966) *'The Olympic Cup presented to the International Committee of the Silent Sports'.* IOC Newsletter 1966 p 121-123.

IOC (1981) *CISS Report*. in News from International Federations an IOC bulletin 1981.

IOC (2009a) Meeting *Report of the IOC/ Sports Department Meeting with CISS/ JLB/22 January 2009.* IOC 2009

IOC (2009b) The *Olympic Movement in Society*. Report from IOC Congress, Copenhagen, October 5, 2009.

IPC (2004) *Disability Rights Toolkit*. International Paralympic Committee 2004

IPC (2013) *Paralympic Movement approaching a crossroads regarding technology.* sourced at http://www.paralympic.org/news/paralympic-movement-approaching-crossroads-regarding-technology

JFD (2010) *Enjoying Deaflympic Sports with the Medallists; Deaflympic Mini Festival.* In Japanese Deaf News February 2010 issue.

Jordan, G. (1996) *The World Games for the Deaf and the Paralympic Games*. December 1996, www.deaflympics.com

Kadar, A. (2010) *Deaflympics medal winners enforce equal treatment*. in *European network of legal experts in the non-discrimination field.*

http://www.non-discrimination.net/content/media/HU-18-HU_ETA_decision_on_gratuity_for_deaflympics_medalists.pdf

Kaftan, C. (2011) *Snowboarding team brings mixture of youth and experience*. 5th February 2011 in USADSF website http://www.usdeaflympics.org/articles/article/2011/feb/05/snowboarding-team-brings-mixture-youth-and-experie/ (14 May 2013)

Kilgallon, C. (Ed) (2012) *London 2012 Paralympic Games. The Official Book.* (2012) Carlton Books Limited

Kinsey, A, A., Buxton, D., Thompson, E, S., Ackers, B,St J. and Ackers, M,J,L. (1880) *Report of the*

Proceedings of the International Congress of the Education of the Deaf held at Milan, September 6-11 1880. (PDF)W.H. Allen & Co, London sourced at: https://ia601208.us.archive.org/18/items/gu_reportproce1880iced/gu_reportproce1880iced.pdf (November 2013)

Kurtz, R.P. *Elite Deaf Athletes have their own Olympics.* April 5th 2009. http://ezinearticles.com/?Elite-Deaf-Athletes-Have-Their-Own-Olympics&id=2252441

Lauff, J. (2007) *Developing Country Participation in International Disability Sport Competition: A historical perspective*. Master Thesis at Norwegian School of Sports Sciences.

Ladd, P. (2003) *Understanding Deaf Culture: In Search of Deafhood*. In Multilingual matters Ltd p 166-167

Legg, D. Wolff, E. A. and Hums, M. (2003) '*Relationships between international sports federations and international disability sport*' (2003) CSSS Research Articles and Reports. Paper 8 http://hdl.handle.net/2047/d10009772

Legg, D., Emes, C., Stewart, D. and Steadward, R. (2004) *Historical Overview of Paralympics, Special Olympics and Deaflympics.* in Paelestra, Jan 1 2004 p 30-36

Lockhart. G. (2003) *Deaflympics 'Silence is Golden…and Silver… and Bronze'*. in Ability magazine , vol 2003 John McGinley, pages 16-19

Lovett, M, J. (2002a) *Meeting Report, IOC and CISS – Tuesday 5th March 2002*. John M. Lovett, 14th March 2002

Lovett, M. J. (2002b) *Meeting with Gilbert Felli, IOC – 23 July 2002*. An email to CISS Board. 25th July 2002.

Lovett, M.J., Eickman, J. and Giansanti, T. (2001) *CISS 2001 A Review*. Red Lizard Ltd

Lubin, G. and Delevingne, L. (2010) *Olympics, Inc: Inside The Secretive, $6 Billion World Of The International Olympic Committee.* Feb 17th 2010. http://www.businessinsider.com/olympics-inc-inside-the-business-of-the-ioc

Mackay, D. (2012) Olympians appointed as joint chairs of ICSD Athletes Commission. Mackay D. 26 December 2012 www.insidethegames.biz (March 2013)

Mackay (2013) *US Hockey confirm Sauer to led Paralympic title defence at Sochi 2014*. Mackay, D. 19 February 2013. http://www.insidethegames.biz/paralympics/winter-sports/ice-sledge-hockey/1012978-us-hockey-confirm-sauer-to-led-paralympic-title-defence-at-sochi-2014 (March 2013)

Markazi, A. (2010) *Deaf Players teammates see inspiration*. sourced at http://sports.espn.go.com/los-angeles/ncb/columns/story?id=4970355 (Nov 2013)

Mason, F. (2002) *Creating Image and Gaining Control: the Development of the Cooperation Agreements between the International Olympic Committee and the International Paralympic Committee*. In The Global News Engaged, Sixth International Symposium for Olympic Research pp.113-122.

Mathers, C., Smith, A. and Concha, A. (2000) *Global burden of hearing loss in the year 2000.* in Global burden of disease 2000. http://www.who.int/healthinfo/statistics/bod_hearingloss.pdf (Nov 2013)

McCullough, B. (2005) *Deaflympics: why it's time to make a change*. 'Belfast Telegraph'. 4 March 2005 http://www.belfasttelegraph.co.uk/imported/deaflympics-why-its-time-to-make-a-change-28231084.html

Melbourne (2005) *Deaflympic Games Media Information Paper, updated*

September 24 2004. Melbourne Deaflympics 2005.

NANHM (2012) *I'm Deaf so can I take part in the Paralympics mummy?,* at Not a Notting Hill Mum Blog sourced at : http://www.notanottinghillmum.co.uk/2012/08/im-deaf-so-can-i-take-part-in-the-paralympics-mummy/

NAD (2003) *Letter from the deaf and Hard of hearing Alliance to the USA Olympic Committee*. sourced at http://www.nad.org/news/2003/4/usoc-deaflympics-dhha-ccpo-letter (Nov 2012)

NDCS (2009) *Education Survey 2009- Briefing Paper 2: Number of deaf children belonging to local authorities and education settings in England.* National Deaf Childrens Society. sourced at:

http://www.ndcs.org.uk/applications/site_search/search.rm?term=number+of+deaf+educated+in+mainstream&searchreferer_id=0&searchreferer_url=%2Fapplications%2Fsite_search%2Fsearch.rm&submit.x=10&submit.y=9

NIDCD (2006) *National Institute on Deafness and Other Communication Disorders (NIDCD), Strategic Plan (FY 2006-2008).* sourced at http://www.nidcd.nih.gov/StaticResources/about/plans/strategic/strategic06-08.pdf

Niyogy, K. & Bhalla, S. (2012) *Levelling the field*. in Time Out Delhi, July 20 2012. http://www.timeoutdelhi.net/around-town/features/levelling-field

Olympic Review (1988) *Innsbruck Once Again Site of World Winter games for Disabled.* Olympic Review No243/244 January 1988

Orelove, F. and Moon, M. (1984) *The Special Olympics program: Effects on retarded persons and society.* Arena Review, 8, 41 45.

Orelove, F. and Wood, J. (1982). *An evaluative review of Special Olympics: Implications for community integration*. Education and Training of Mentally Retarded, 17, 325-329.

Oyler, A.L. (n.d.) *Untreated Hearing Loss in Adults – A Growing National Epidemic.* Sourced at http://www.asha.org/Aud/Articles/Untreated-Hearing-Loss-in-Adults/

Paxinos, S. (2005a) *Two of us.* January 2 2005. Sourced at: http://www.theage.com.au/news/Sport/Two-of-us/2005/01/01/1104345033382.html (October 2013)

Paxinos, S. (2005b) *Italian champions sign in to defend gold crown*. 5 January 2005. Sourced at: http://www.theage.com.au/news/Sport/Italian-champions-sign-in-to-defend-gold-crown/2005/01/04/1104832108554.html (October 2012)

Paxinos, S. (2005c) *Throwing His Hat in the Ring*. 7 January 2005 http://www.theage.com.au/news/Sport/Throwing-his-hat-in-the-ring/2005/01/06/114832243473.html (October 2012)

Peers, D. (2012) *Patients, Athletes, Freaks: Paralympism and the Reproduction of Disability.* In Journal of Sport and Social issues 36(3) p295-316 Sage Publications.

Peterson, A. (2012) *US Volleyball Smith competes with hearing loss*. Associated press http://summergames.ap.org/article/us-volleyballs-smith-competes-hearing-loss

Polk, A. (2008) *Lights down on deaf athletes Paralympic debut*. Sourced at deafeacho.com http://www.deafecho.com/2008/09/lights-down-on-deaf-athletes-paralympic-debut/

Popham, P (2012) *Paralympics sold like a 'freak show', says coach*. Accessed at http://www.independent.co.uk/sport/olympics/paralympics/paralympics-sold-like-a-freak-show-says-coach-8100743.html

RCDS (2009) *Congratulations to the Victory*. Russian government telegrams, source, Russian Committee of Deaf Sports online at: http://www.deafsport.ru/en/news.44.html

Right to Play (2008) *Harnessing the Power of Sport for Development and Peace: Recommendations to Governments*. Right to Play 2008.

Roberts-Grey, G. (2012) *All That Glitters Isn't Gold for Some Olympian Parents*. Sourced at: http://www.foxbusiness.com/personal-finance/2012/08/10/all-that-glitters-isnt-gold-for-some-olympian-parents/

SADSF (2012) *Message from the President*. South African Deaf Sport Federation website, Oct/Nov 2012 http://www.sadeafsport.com/message-from-the-president-nov.html (Feb 2013)

SDSF (2013) *Importance of the deaf sport – why an independent sports organisation?*. sourced at Swiss Deaf Sports website http://www.sgsv-fsss.ch/en/about-us/account/ (Feb 2013)

Sengupta, R. (2012) *'No words needed'*. sourced from

http://www.livemint.com/Leisure/555x3m6xqarT37ML0vz48H/Tough-enough.html?facet=print

Smith, C. (2012) *London Olympics' Unpaid Athletes Fight For Rich Medal Bonuses. Sourced at:*

http://www.forbes.com/sites/chrissmith/2012/07/31/london-olympics-unpaid-athletes-fight-for-rich-medal-bonuses/scUK (2013) *Effective Communication: Coaching Deaf people in sport*. Sports coach UK sourced at: http://www.sportscoachuk.org/site-tools/workshops/about-our-workshops/effective-communication-coaching-deaf-people-sport

SDS (2013) *Lucy Targets 2013 Deaflympics*. Scottish Disability Sports website. Sourced at: http://www.scottishdisabilitysport.com/sds/index.cfm/news/international-sport/lucy-targets-2013-deaflympics/

Spry, M. (2012) *A Message to Olympians: Get a Job*. Sourced at: http://thebarnstormer.com/a-message-to-olympians-get-a-job/#

Stafford, I. (2005) *Coaching for Long term Athlete Development: To improve participation and performance in sport*. The National Coaching Foundation

Stewart, A,D. (1991a) *Deaf Sport, The Impact of Sports Within the Deaf Community.* Gallaudet University Press

Stewart, A,D. (1991b) *Reflections on the 1991 World Winter Games for the Deaf*. in Paelestra Sep 22 1991.

Stewart, A,D. (2001) *The Power of IDEA: Kling v Mentor School District*. in Palaestra Sept 22, 2001

Stewart, A,D.. and Bressler, H.B. (1997) *The VXIII WGD: a musical paradox*. in Palaestra Sept 22 1997.

Stewart, A,D. and Ammons, K,D. (1994) *Awakenings: The 1993 World Games for the Deaf.* In Palaestra 10, 26-31

Stewart, A,D & Ammons, K,D. (2001) *Future Directions of the Deaflympics*. in Palaestra, Summer 2001, Vol 17,No.3

Stewart D.A. & Nulf.R. (1996) *A Hearing Man's Journey into the world of Deaf Softball*. in Paelestra September 22 1996

Stewart, D.A. & Ojalas, R. (1995) *Storm and Ice : the XIII World Winter Games for the Deaf*. in Paelestra June 22 1995

Sushkevych, V. (2013) *NSC 'Olympiskiy' must be accessible for all categories of people.* 13, April 2011. Sourced at: http://nscolimpiyskiy.com.ua/en/stadium/guestsNSC/24726/ (9 May 2013)

Suit, B. (2005) *The Grasshopper: Games, Life and Utopia*. Broadview Press

Swinbourne, C. (2012a) *Craig Crowley says inclusion in the Paralympics is vital for future of Deaf Sport .* In Limping Chicken May 29, 2012 http://limpingchicken.com/2012/05/29/deaf-news-craig-crowley-says-inclusion-in-the-paralympics-vital-for-future-of-deaf-sport/

Swinbourne, C. (2012b) Deaf performers and artists shine at London Paralympics opening ceremony. 30th August 2012 sourced at limping chicken: http://limpingchicken.com/2012/08/30/deaf-performers-and-artists-shine-at-london-paralympics-2012-opening-ceremony/ (September 2012)

Taipei Times Editorial (2009) *Are the Deaflympics being sold short?.* 1st August 2009. sourced at: http://www.taipeitimes.com/News/editorials/archives/2009/08/01/2003450101 (11/2/2013)

Tamil Deaf Sports (2013) https://sites.google.com/site/tnscdeaf/deaf-sports

Taylor, A. (2012) *Here's How much Olympic Athletes Really get Paid.* http://www.businessinsider.com/heres-how-much-olympic-athletes-really-get-paid-2012-7 (19 July 2012)

The Australian (1992) *Smith aims for National first*. from The Australian, reporting on the 1992 Olympics found at: http://www.klac23.org.au/PastAthletes/DeanSmith.htm (11 May 2013)

'The China Post' (6/11/09) *BTCO hold reception to celebrate Queen's birthday*. http://www.chinapost.com.tw/taiwan/intl-community/2009/06/11/211728/BTCO-holds.htm

Thomas, N. (2003) *Sport and Disability*. In Sport and Society, A student Introduction. Houlihan, B. London, Sage

Thomas, N. and Smith, A. (2009) *Disability, Sport and Society*. Routledge, London. pp25-26

UKDS (2006a), *How I Achieved: Tony Ally*. in *Achieve* Sept 2006, UK Deaf Sport.

UKDS (2006b) *How I Achieved: Rebecca Macree*. in *Achieve*, November 2006,UK Deaf Sport

UN (2011) *Panel Discussion on Sports for Inclusive Development: Sports, Disability and Development: Key to empowerment of persons with disabilities and their communities*. 27 June 2011, http://www.un.org/disabilities/default.asp?id=1574

USADSF (2001) *USADSF Joins America's Athletes with Disabilities*, sourced from Paelestra March 22, 2001.

Watson, J, N., Weir, S. and Friend, S. (2005) *The Development of Muscular Christianity in Victorian Britain and Beyond*. Journal of Religion & Society Vol 7 2005.

Wallsten, S. (2012) *Does Paying Olympians for Winning Medals make them More Likely to Win?.* Sourced at: http://www.techpolicyinstitute.org/blog/2012/08/does-paying-olympians-for-winning-medals-make-them-more-likely-to-win/

Whalley (2010) *The History of British Deaf Tennis*. Bryan Whalley

White, J. (2013) Bath flanker Matt Gilbert: I may be deaf but I know how to survive on the rugby field. Sourced at 'The Telegraph': http://www.telegraph.co.uk/sport/rugbyunion/club/9900808/Bath-flanker-Mat-Gilbert-I-may-be-deaf-but-I-know-how-to-survive-on-the-rugby-field.html (2 March 2013)

Wolff. E (2012) *Implementing Article 30.5: The Right to Sport for All Persons with Disabilities.* Sport and Development Project September 2012. Sourced at: http://www.globalconversation.org/2012/09/29/implementing-article-305-right-sport-all-persons-disabilities

Yan-chi Mo. (2009) *Deaflympics may be too much for Taipei to handle*. sourced at: http://www.taipeitimes.com/News/taiwan/archives/2009/05/04/2003442726

Young, C. (2002) *Sound Judgment: Does curing deafness mean cultural genocide?*. in Reason April 1st 2002

Young, S. (2012) *There is no need to integrate the Paralympics into the Olympics*. Sourced at: http://www.abc.net.au/news/2012-09-03/young-paralympics-no-need-for-integration/4239168

Newspapers

(Chapter 16 How the media Portrays the Deaflympics)

The China Post

20/12/07 Cabinet sets aside NT$1bil for tourism
23/01/08 'Sports lotto, Industry boost top priorities for SAC in '08"
26/02/08 Mayor taps heavy hitters to prepare for the Deaflympics
17/05/08 Groups to host underprivileged during Mays Millet Exhibition
29/05/08 Taipei Open cancelled due to venue shortage
31/05/08 EasyCard to be introduced to Taipei section of railway
06/09/08 Ambitious plans for Taipei outlined
06/09/08 Deaflympics to put us on the World Stage Ma
17/12/08 Deaflympics to draw 3965 athletes from 81 countries
17/12/08 ISL volunteers, 50 foreign who speak English and higher level SL.
02/01/09 Taipei mayor Inaugurates 2009 Deaflympics Year
02/01/09 Taipei Lantern Festival open Feb 6
02/01/09 Taiwan to host 2017 Universiade
05/02/09 Deaflympics expected to draw 10,000 foreign visitors
13/02/09 Campaign to name Deaflympics Mascot
18/02/09 Chi Cheng send Birthday card to former President
21/04/09 Jackie Chan under fire for remarks
22/04/09 Jackie Chan remarks, defend right to air them
22/04/09 Jackie Chan unfit to be Deaflympics spokesman
03/03/09 Deaflympics rooms to have special alarms
19/09/09 Deaflympics Taipei to cost about NT$4b
08/10/09 Taiwan, UK should boost partnership; British Official

The Taipei Times

16/09/09 *Our Games were the best ever, ICSD Chief Says.*

Taiwan Times

17/09/09 *Ma asks SAC to look into increasing prize money*

Deaflympics09 (DeaflympicsTaipei 2009 newsletter)

07/09/09 Huang's High Points
08/09/09a Friend from Ukraine
08/09/09b Difficult Road for Lin
09/09/09a Winning without a fight
09/09/09b Bowling Bounty for Chang
09/09/09c More Golf for Taiwan Kuo Sprints to Win
10/09/09 Italian Hot Spice
11/09/09a Confident Coach
11/09/09b Local Rifles Lost Out
12/09/09a Young Gun Take Bronze
12/09/09b Gold Rush Boon for Taiwan Bowlers
15/09/09 US Men Take 14th Title in a Row

21st Deaflympics (21st Taipei Summer Deaflympics 2009 newsletter)

04/09/09a Silence is Golden for Terence Parkin
04/09/09b Four time Deaflympian Darren Dunne, Captain of Ireland
04/09/09c Past and Future Accomplishments of Terence Parkin
06/09/09 Swiss Marksman Thomas Moesching Dedicates Gold Medal to Grandfather
07/09/09 German handball Team Consisting of All Walks of Life.
12/09/09 Hearing and Sight Impairment No Obstacles to Cyril Jonard.

Acknowledgements

This is my first attempt to write a book and I have been blessed in so many ways by fortunate circumstances and timings, which have contributed to its creation.

I am indebted to many individuals and organisations from the past and the present with whom I have been privileged to share professional and voluntary toil in the betterment of joint interests.

We are beholden to the founding fathers of the Olympic, Deaflympic and Paralympic movements, for inspiring us all to find ways of creating a better world through the power of sport, and to the past leaders of the CISS for your pioneering spirit and going through the unknown towards the distant horizon, with an unwavering belief that sport can be empowering for the disabled person.

I express my gratitude to the countless numbers of you at home and abroad for your contributions to deaf sport and those of you who, unbeknown to you, have enriched my thinking through our encounters and shaped the final edition.

Thank you to David Stewart and Donalda Ammons for being the two most productive recorders of Deaf sport and to Bryan

Whalley for your support in allowing me to draw heavily from *The History of Deaf Tennis* for Chapters 1 and 2 as well as access to photographs. The staff at ICSD have also been helpful in providing access to documents and pictures. Thanks also to the following: Sam Perkins for your photography; Derek Simmons for your assistance with initial feedback; and to everyone at AD Books for the inspiration and advice and excellent support in getting this project completed.

To you, the reader, I hope we have all inspired you too.

Finally, I am forever indebted to my wife, Joanne, for steadfastly believing in me and giving me the time and support needed to complete this book through the endless periods of writing.

I dedicate this book to the memory of my grandmother, Mabel Higham, and my mother, Ruth, for instilling a love of books and reading – how right you both were.

actionDEAFNESSBooks

Are you interested in deaf issues? Want to learn sign language? If so, check out our fabulous online store! Action Deafness Books is one of the UK's leading online retailers of deaf-related resources including books and dvds. We pride ourselves on competitive prices and excellent customer service and are constantly sourcing fresh literary talent and exciting new products.

We are delighted to have published works by accomplished deaf authors such as Nick Sturley *(Innocents of Oppression)* and Stuart R Harrison *(Same Spirit Different Team: The Politicisation of the Deaflympics)*, thus empowering deaf authors and enabling them to showcase their talents. Other works we have published include the fascinating *Unravelling the Signs: My Life with a Deaf Schizophrenic Brother* by Sylvia Kenneth and the moving *Meanwhile I Keep Dancing* by Tamsin Coates.

Books like these, together with our popular sign language resources, promote deaf awareness throughout the wider community, allowing our customers to expand their knowledge and experience the rich and beautiful culture of deaf people. Our aim is to spread the word - literally!

We are proud to have worked with renowned authors such as Jacqueline Wilson *(Tracy Beaker novels)*, Julia Donaldson *(The Gruffalo)* and Joyce Dunbar *(the Mouse & Mole series)* and have championed their works at various literary events and via our social media channels.
